Essential Grammar in Use
WITH ANSWERS

Essential Grammar in Use

A self-study reference and practice book for elementary students of English

WITH ANSWERS

Raymond Murphy

CAMBRIDGE
UNIVERSITY PRESS

Published by the Press Syndicate of the University of Cambridge
The Pitt Building, Trumpington Street, Cambridge CB2 1RP
40 West 20th Street, New York, NY 10011–4211, USA
10 Stamford Road, Oakleigh, Melbourne 3166, Australia

© Cambridge University Press 1990

First published 1990
Thirteenth printing 1996

Printed in Great Britain
at the University Press, Cambridge

British Library cataloguing in publication data

Murphy, Raymond *1946–*
Essential grammar in use: a self-study reference and
practice book for elementary students of English: with answers
1. English language. Grammar
1. Title
428.2

ISBN 0 521 35770 5 (with answers)
ISBN 0 521 35771 3 (without answers)

CE

Contents

To the student   (working without a teacher)

This is a grammar book for elementary students of English. There are 107 units in the book and each unit is about a different point of English grammar. There is a list of units at the beginning of the book (*Contents*).

Do not study all the units in order from beginning to end. It is better to choose the units that you *need* to do. For example, if you have a problem with the present perfect ('have done' / 'have been' etc.), use the *Index* (at the back of the book) to find the unit(s) you need to study (Units 15–19).

Each unit is two pages. The explanation is on the left-hand page and the exercises on the right.

Explanation

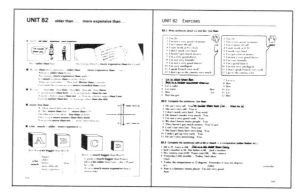

Exercises

Use the book in this way:

1 Look in the *Contents* and/or *Index* to find the unit(s) you need.
2 Study the left-hand page (explanation and information).
3 Do the exercises on the right-hand page (if you want to do them).
4 Use the *Key* to check your answers.
5 Study the left-hand page again if necessary.

Don't forget the six *Appendices* at the back of the book (pages 216–223). These will give you information about irregular verbs, short forms, spelling and phrasal verbs.

To the teacher

The most important features of this book are:
- It is a grammar book. It deals only with grammar and is therefore not intended to be a general course book.
- It is a book for elementary learners. It does not cover areas of grammar which are not normally taught at elementary level.
- It combines reference and exercises in one volume.
- It can be used either for self-study or as supplementary course material.

Organisation of the book

There are 107 units in the book, each one focusing on a particular area of grammar. The material is organised in grammatical categories, such as tenses, modal verbs, questions, pronouns, articles, adjectives and prepositions. Units are *not* ordered according to difficulty, and should therefore be selected and used in the order appropriate for the learner(s). The book should *not* be worked through from beginning to end. The units are listed in the *Contents* and there is a comprehensive *Index* at the end of the book.

Each unit has the same format consisting of two facing pages. The point is explained on the left-hand page and the corresponding exercises are on the right. There are six *Appendices* (pages 216–223) dealing with irregular verbs, short forms (contractions), spelling and phrasal verbs. It might be useful for teachers to draw students' attention to these.

Finally, there is a *Key* at the back of the book (pages 224–253) for students to check their answers. An edition without the *Key* is also available for teachers who might prefer their students to use this.

Level

The book is intended for elementary learners, i.e. learners with very little English, but I would not expect it to be used from the first day of a course for complete beginners. It is intended mainly for elementary students who are beyond the very earliest stages of a beginners' course. It could also be used by lower-intermediate students whose grammar is weaker than other aspects of their English or who have problems with particular areas of 'elementary' grammar.

The explanations are addressed to the elementary student and are therefore as simple and as short as possible. The vocabulary used in the examples and exercises has also been restricted so that the book can be used at this level.

Using the book

The book can be used by students working alone (see '*To the student,*' page viii) or as supplementary course material. In either case the book can serve as an elementary grammar reference book.

When used as course material, the book can be used for immediate consolidation or for later revision or remedial work. It might be used by the whole class or by individual students needing extra help.

In some cases it may be desirable to use the left-hand pages (explanation) in class, but it should be noted that these have been written more for private study and reference. In most cases, it is probably better for the teacher to present the grammar point in his/her preferred way with the exercises being done for homework. The left-hand page is then available for later reference by the student.

A teacher might prefer to keep the book for revision and remedial work. In this case, individual students or groups of students can be directed to the appropriate units for self-study.

Thanks

I would like to thank all the students and teachers at the schools and institutes named below who used the pilot edition of this book. Their comments and suggestions were very helpful. I would also like to express my thanks to Alison Baxter and Angela Wilde of Cambridge University Press for all their help and advice.

Pilot centres:

The British Institute, Florence, Italy; The British School, Bologna, Italy; FAO, Rome, Italy; International House, Arezzo, Italy; International House, La Spezia, Italy; ITC Maggiolini, Parabiago, Italy; IHLS, Budapest, Hungary; International House, Budapest, Hungary; International Language Institute, Cairo, Egypt; LS Kieliopisto, Tampere, Finland; Klubschule Migros, Berne, Switzerland; Klubschule Migros, Lichtensteig, Switzerland; Ecole d'Ingénieurs, Geneva, Switzerland; Capital Institute, Ruwi, Oman; British Institute, Valencia, Spain; International House, Madrid, Spain; International House, Barcelona, Spain; International House, Coimbra, Portugal; Instituto de Idiomas, Lima, Peru; AMES, Hobart, Tasmania; CUCES-Universités, Nancy, France; INFOP, Longvic, France; The British Council Cambridge English School, Tokyo, Japan; Cambridge English School, Ikebukuro, Japan; Cambridge English School, Tokyo, Japan; Stanton School of English, Tokyo, Japan; Katoh Gakuen Gyoshu High School, Japan; The Studio School of English, Cambridge; The Cambridge Centre for Languages, Sawston; University of Glasgow EFL Unit; The Bell School of Languages, Cambridge; The Swan School of English, Oxford; Institute for Applied Language Studies, University of Edinburgh.

Acknowledgements

Drawings by Chris Evans, Leslie Marshall, Ed McHenry, David McKee, Annie McManus and Shaun Williams.
Design and art direction by Peter Ducker MSTD

UNIT 1   am/is/are

She**'s** a doctor.
She **isn't** a nurse.

It**'s** hot.
It **isn't** cold.

They**'re** rich.
They **aren't** poor.

positive

I	**am**	(**I'm**)
he		(he**'s**)
she }	**is**	(she**'s**)
it		(it**'s**)
we		(we**'re**)
you }	**are**	(you**'re**)
they		(they**'re**)

negative

I	**am not**	(**I'm not**)		
he		(he**'s not**	*or*	he **isn't**)
she }	**is not**	(she**'s not**	*or*	she **isn't**)
it		(it**'s not**	*or*	it **isn't**)
we		(we**'re not**	*or*	we **aren't**)
you }	**are not**	(you**'re not**	*or*	you **aren't**)
they		(they**'re not**	*or*	they **aren't**)

- Can you close the window, please? **I'm** cold.
- **I'm** 32 years old. My sister **is** 29.
- My brother **is** a policeman. He**'s** very tall.
- John **is** afraid of dogs.
- It**'s** 10 o'clock. You**'re** late again.
- Ann and I **are** very good friends.
- My shoes **are** very dirty. I must clean them.

- **I'm** tired but **I'm not** hungry.
- Tom **isn't** interested in politics.
- Jane **isn't** at home at the moment. She**'s** at work.
- Those people **aren't** English. They**'re** Australian.

that**'s** = that **is**   there**'s** = there **is**   here**'s** = here **is**:
- Thank you. **That's** very kind of you.
- Look! **There's** George.

▶ Unit 2 **am**/**is**/**are** *(questions)*

UNIT 1   Exercises

1.1 Write the short form (she**'s** / we **aren't** etc.).

1 he is .... *he's* ....
2 they are ....
3 she is not ....
4 it is ....
5 I am not ....
6 you are not ....

Write the full form (she **is** / we **are not** etc.).

7 we aren't .. *we are not* ......
8 I'm ....
9 you're ....
10 they aren't ....
11 it isn't ....
12 she's ....

1.2 Put in **am**, **is** or **are**.

1 The weather ... *is* ..... very nice today.
2 I .... not tired.
3 This case .... very heavy.
4 These cases .... very heavy.
5 The dog .... asleep.
6 Look! There .... Carol.
7 I .... hot. Can you open the window, please?

8 This castle .... one thousand years old.
9 My brother and I .... good tennis players.
10 Ann .... at home but her children .... at school.
11 I .... a student. My sister .... an architect.

1.3 Write full sentences. Use **am/is/are** each time.

1 (my shoes very dirty) .... *My shoes are very dirty.* ....
2 (my bed very comfortable) My ....
3 (your cigarettes in your bag) ....
4 (I not very happy today) ....
5 (this restaurant very expensive) ....
6 (the shops not open today) ....
7 (Mr Kelly's daughter six years old) ....
8 (the houses in this street very old) ....
9 (the examination not difficult) ....
10 (those flowers very beautiful) ....

1.4 Write positive or negative sentences. Use **am / am not / is / isn't / are / aren't**.

1 (Paris / the capital of France) ... *Paris is the capital of France.* .....
2 (I / interested in football) *I'm not interested in football.* ....
3 (I / hungry) I ....
4 (it / warm today) It .... today.
5 (Rome / in Spain) Rome ....
6 (I / afraid of dogs) I ....
7 (my hands / cold) My ....
8 (Canada / a very big country) ....
9 (the Amazon / in Africa) ....
10 (diamonds / cheap) ....
11 (motor-racing / a dangerous sport) ....
12 (cats / big animals) ....

UNIT 2 am/is/are *(questions)*

► Unit 1 **am/is/are**

positive

I	**am**
he she } it	**is**
we you } they	**are**

question

am	I?
is {	he? she? it?
are {	we? you? they?

Am I right?

No, you're wrong.

$\begin{array}{r} 14 \\ +11 \\ \hline 26 \end{array}$

- 'Is your mother at home?' 'No, she's out.'
- 'Is it cold in your room?' 'Yes, a little.'
- Those shoes are nice. Are they new?
- Are books expensive in your country?

- 'How old is Joe?' 'He's 24.'
- 'What colour is your car?' 'It's blue.'
- 'Where are you from?' 'Canada.'
- 'How much are these postcards?' 'They're 40 pence each.'

what's = what is   who's = who is   how's = how is   where's = where is:
- What's the time?   – Who's that man?
- Where's Jill?   – How's your father?

short answers

Yes, I **am.**
Yes, { he she it } **is.**
Yes, { we you they } **are.**

No, I**'m not.**
No, { he's she's it's } **not.** *or* No, { he she it } **isn't.**
No, { we're you're they're } **not.** *or* No, { we you they } **aren't.**

- 'Are you tired?' 'Yes, I am.'
- 'Are you hungry?' 'No, I'm not but I'm thirsty.'
- 'Is he English?' 'Yes, he is.'
- 'Is Ann at work today?' 'No, she isn't.'
- 'Is this seat free?' 'Yes, it is.'
- 'Are these your shoes?' 'Yes, they are.'
- 'Am I late?' 'No, you aren't.'

That's my seat.

No, it isn't.

UNIT 2 Exercises

2.1 Write questions from these words. Use **am/is/are**.

1 (your mother at home?) ...Is your mother at home... ?
2 (your parents at home?) .... at home ?
3 (this hotel expensive?) .... ?
4 (you interested in art?) .... ?
5 (the shops open today?) .... ?
6 (the park open today?) .... ?

2.2 Write questions with **What/Who/How/Where/Why ... ?** Use **am/is/are**.

1 (what colour your car?) ...What colour is your car.............................. ?
2 (where my key?) Where .... ?
3 (where my socks?) .... ?
4 (how old your father?) How .... ?
5 (what colour his eyes?) .... ?
6 (why John angry with me?) .... ?
7 (how much these shoes?) .... ?
8 (who your favourite actor?) .... ?
9 (why you always late?) .... ?

2.3 Ask the questions. (Read the answers to the questions first.)

YOU / PAUL

1 (your name?) ...What's your name...................... ? Paul.
2 (married or single?) ...Are you married or single............... ? I'm married.
3 (British?) .... ? No, I'm not.
4 (where / from?) .... ? From Australia.
5 (how old?) .... ? I'm 25.
6 (a student?) .... ? No, I'm a teacher.
7 (your wife a teacher?) .... ? No, she's a lawyer.
8 (where / from?) .... ? She's Italian.
9 (her name?) .... ? Anna.
10 (how old?) .... ? She's 25 too.

2.4 Write positive or negative short answers (**Yes, I am / No, he isn't** etc.).

1 Are you married? ..No, I'm not.................. 6 Is it dark now? ....
2 Are you tall? ......Yes, I am................... 7 Are your hands cold? ....
3 Is it cold today? .... 8 Are you hungry? ....
4 Are you a teacher? .... 9 Is your father tall? ....
5 Are you tired? .... 10 Is it sunny? ....

UNIT 3   I am doing (present continuous)

She's **eating**.
She **isn't reading**.

It's **raining**.
The sun **isn't shining**.

They're **running**.
They **aren't walking**.

■ The present continuous tense is:
am/is/are –ing (do**ing**/eat**ing**/rain**ing**/runn**ing**/writ**ing** etc.)

I	**am**	(not)	**–ing**	**I'm** work**ing**.
he she it }	**is**	(not)	**–ing**	Tom **is** writ**ing** a letter. She **isn't** eat**ing**. The telephone **is** ring**ing**.
we you they }	**are**	(not)	**–ing**	We're hav**ing** dinner. You're **not** listen**ing** to me. The children **are** do**ing** their homework.

► Unit 1 for the short forms '**m/'s/'re/isn't/aren't**

■ **am/is/are –ing** = something
is happening *now*:

> **I'm** work**ing**
> she's wear**ing** a hat
> they're play**ing** football
> **I'm not** watch**ing** television

past ◄——————————NOW——————————► future

 – Please be quiet. **I'm** work**ing**. (= I'm working now)
 – Look! Joy **is** wear**ing** her new hat. (= she's wearing it now)
 – Don't go out now. It's rain**ing**.
 – 'Where are the children?'   'They're play**ing** in the garden.'
 – *(on the telephone)* We're hav**ing** dinner now. Can you phone later?
 – You can turn the television off. **I'm not** watch**ing** it.

Spelling   ► Appendix 4 (4.3 and 4.4):
come → com**ing**   run → runn**ing**   lie → ly**ing**
smoke → smok**ing**   sit → sitt**ing**   die → dy**ing**
write → writ**ing**   swim → swimm**ing**

► Unit 4   **Are you -ing?** *(present continuous questions)*
► Unit 8   **I am doing** *(present continuous)* and **I do** *(present simple)*
► Unit 21   **What are you doing tomorrow?** *(present for the future)*

6

UNIT 3   Exercises

3.1 Complete the sentences. Use **am/is/are** + one of these verbs:

building   coming   having   ~~playing~~   cooking   standing   swimming

1 Listen! Pat ....*is playing*........ the piano.
2 They .... a new hotel in the city centre at the moment.
3 Look! Somebody .... in the river.
4 'You .... on my foot.'   'Oh, I'm sorry.'
5 Hurry up! The bus ....
6 'Where are you, George?'   'In the kitchen. I .... a meal.'
7 *(on the telephone)*   'Hello. Can I speak to Ann, please?'   'She .... a shower at the moment. Can you phone again later?'

3.2 What's happening at the moment? Write *true* sentences.

1 (I / wash / my hair)   *I'm not washing my hair.*...................................
2 (it / snow)   ....*It is snowing.*..................................
3 (I / sit / on a chair)   ....
4 (I / eat)   ....
5 (it / rain)   ....
6 (I / learn / English)   ....
7 (I / listen / to the radio)   ....
8 (the sun / shine)   ....
9 (I / wear / shoes)   ....
10 (I / smoke / a cigarette)   ....
11 (I / read / a newspaper)   ....

3.3 What is the difference between picture A and picture B? Write two sentences each time. Use **is/are (not) -ing**.

1 ..*In A the man is smoking a cigarette. In B he is eating an apple.*..................
2 In A the man ....   In B he ....
3 In A ....   In B ....
4 ....
5 ....
6 ....

UNIT 4   Are you -ing? *(present continuous questions)*

▶ Unit 3 **I am doing** *(present continuous)*

positive

I	**am**	**-ing**
he she it }	**is**	**-ing**
we you they }	**are -ing**	

question

am	I	**-ing?**
is	{ he she it	**-ing?**
are	{ we you they	**-ing?**

what are you doing?

— '**Are you** feel**ing** okay?' 'Yes, I'm feeling fine.'
— '**Is it** rain**ing**?' 'Yes, take an umbrella.'
— Why **are you** wear**ing** a coat? It's not cold today.
— 'What**'s Roy** do**ing**?' 'He's cooking the dinner.'
— 'What **are the children** do**ing**?' 'They're playing in the garden.'
— Look! There's Jan. Where**'s she** go**ing**?

The word order in these questions is:

	is/are	+	*subject*	+	**-ing**
	Is		he		working today?
	Is		Mr Smith		working today?
Where	are		they		going?
Where	are		those people		going? *(not* 'Where are going those people?'*)*

short answers

Yes, I **am**.		
Yes,	{ he she it	**is**.
Yes,	{ we you they	**are**.

No, I**'m not**.					
No,	{ he**'s** she**'s** it**'s**	**not**.	*or* No,	{ he she it	**isn't**.
No,	{ we**'re** you**'re** they**'re**	**not**.	*or* No,	{ we you they	**aren't**.

— '**Are you** listen**ing** to the radio?' '**Yes, I am**.'
— '**Is Tom** work**ing** today?' '**Yes, he is**.'
— '**Is it** rain**ing**?' '**No, it isn't**.'
— '**Are your friends** stay**ing** at a hotel?' '**No, they aren't**.'

UNIT 4   Exercises

4.1 Look at the pictures and ask a question. Choose one of these verbs:

crying   eating   going   laughing   looking at   ~~reading~~

1 What _is she reading_ .... ?   4 What .... ?
2 Where .... ?   5 What .... ?
3 Why .... ?   6 Why .... ?

4.2 Write the question **'What ... doing?'** with different subjects.

1 (he) _What is he doing_ .... ?   3 (I) .... ?
2 (they) What .... doing?   4 (your wife) .... ?

Now write the question **'Where ... going?'** with these subjects.

5 (we) _Where are we going_ .... ?
6 (those children) .... ?
7 (the girl with long hair) .... ?
8 (the man on the bicycle) .... ?

4.3 Ask the questions. (Read the answers to the questions first.)

1	(you / watch / TV?)	_Are you watching TV_ .... ?	No, you can turn it off.
2	(the children / play?)	.... ?	No, they're asleep.
3	(what / you / do?)	.... ?	I'm cooking my dinner.
4	(what / Rod / do?)	.... ?	He's having a bath.
5	(it / rain?)	.... ?	No, not at the moment.
6	(that clock / work?)	.... ?	No, it's broken.
7	(you / write / a letter?)	.... ?	Yes, to my sister.
8	(why / you / run?)	.... ?	Because I'm late.

4.4 Write positive or negative short answers (**Yes, I am / No, it isn't** etc.).

1 Are you watching TV? _No, I'm not._   5 Are you eating something? ....
2 Are you wearing shoes? ....   6 Are you feeling well? ....
3 Are you wearing a hat? ....   7 Is the sun shining? ....
4 Is it raining? ....   8 Is your mother watching you? ....

9

UNIT 5 I do/work/like etc. *(present simple)*

They have a lot of books.
They **read** a lot.

He's eating an ice-cream.
He **likes** ice-cream.

■ **They read** / **I like** / **he likes** etc. = the *present simple*:

I/we/you/they	**do**	**read**	**like**	**work**	**play**	**watch**
he/she/it	do**es**	read**s**	like**s**	work**s**	play**s**	watch**es**

■ Remember:
he/she/it –s: **he** likes (*not* 'he like') **my sister** plays **it** rains
  – **I live** in London but **my brother lives** in Scotland.

have → has: I have → he/she/it **has**

Spelling ▶ Appendix 4 (4.1 and 4.2):
-es after **-s/-ch/sh**: pass → pass**es** wat**ch** → wat**ches** finish → fini**shes**
    also: do → do**es** go → go**es**
        stud**y** → stud**ies** carr**y** → carr**ies**

■ We use the present simple for things that are true in general, or for things that happen sometimes or all the time:
    – **I like** big cities.
    – The shops **open** at 9 o'clock and **close** at 5.30.
    – He **works** very hard. He **starts** at 7.30 and **finishes** at 8 o'clock in the evening.
    – The Earth **goes** round the Sun.
    – We **do** a lot of different things in our free time.
    – She's very clever. She **speaks** four languages.
    – It **costs** a lot of money to stay at luxury hotels.

■ We use the present simple with **always/never/often/sometimes/usually**:
    – He **always gets** up at 7 o'clock.
    – I **usually go** to work by car but I **sometimes walk**.
    – Jack **eats** very little. He **never has** breakfast in the morning.
    – The weather here is not very good. It **often rains**.

▶ Unit 6 **I don't ...** *(present simple negative)*   ▶ Unit 7 **Do you ... ?** *(present simple questions)*
▶ Unit 8 **I am doing** *(present continuous)* and **I do** *(present simple)*   ▶ Unit 88 *Word order* (**always/never/often** etc.)

UNIT 5 Exercises

5.1 Write the **he/she/it** form of these verbs.

1 read ...*reads*.......   4 listen ....   7 push ....   10 kiss ....
2 repair ....   5 love ....   8 do ....   11 buy ....
3 watch ....   6 have ....   9 think ....   12 go ....

5.2 Complete the sentences. Use the correct form of these verbs:

boil   close   cost   cost   go   have   like   meet   open   smoke
~~speak~~   teach   wash

1 She's very clever. She ......*speaks*........... four languages.
2 Steve .... ten cigarettes a day.
3 We usually .... dinner at 7 o'clock.
4 I .... films. I often .... to the cinema.
5 Water .... at 100 degrees Celsius.
6 In Britain the banks .... at 9.30 in the morning.
7 The City Museum .... at 5 o'clock every evening.
8 Food is expensive. It .... a lot of money.
9 Shoes are expensive. They .... a lot of money.
10 Tina is a teacher. She .... mathematics to young children.
11 Your job is very interesting. You .... a lot of people.
12 Peter .... his hair twice a week.

5.3 Study this information:

How often do you...?	Bob and Ann	George	you
1 drink coffee in the morning?	never	usually	?
2 read newspapers?	often	never	?
3 get up before 7 o'clock?	sometimes	always	?

Now write sentences about Bob and Ann, George and yourself. Use **always/usually/often/sometimes/never**.

1 .....*Bob and Ann never drink coffee in the morning*..
  George .... in the morning.
  I ....
2 Bob and Ann .... newspapers.
  George ....
  I ....
3 ....
  ....
  ....

11

UNIT 6   I don't... *(present simple negative)*

▶ Unit 5 I **do**/**work**/**like** etc. *(present simple)*

■ The present simple negative is **don't**/**doesn't** + *verb*:

She doesn't smoke.

He doesn't work.

positive		*negative*		
I we you they	**work** **play** **do** **like**	I we you they	**do not** **(don't)**	work play do like
he she it	work**s** play**s** does like**s**	he she it	**does not** **(doesn't)**	

– I **drink** coffee but I **don't drink** tea.
– Sue **drinks** tea but she **doesn't drink** coffee.
– You **don't speak** English very well.
– They **don't watch** television very often.
– Rice **doesn't grow** in cold countries.
– We **don't know** many people in this town.

■ We use **don't**/**doesn't** + *infinitive* (**like/do/speak/work** etc.):
– I don't **like** washing the car. I don't **do** it very often.
– She speaks Spanish but she doesn't **speak** Italian. (*not* 'she doesn't speaks')

■ Remember:

I/we/you/they	**don't**	– **I don't** like football.
he/she/it	**doesn't**	– **He doesn't** like football.

– **I don't** like Fred and **Fred doesn't** like me. (*not* 'Fred don't like')
– **My car doesn't** use much petrol. (*not* 'my car don't use')
– Sometimes he is late but **it doesn't** happen very often.

▶ Unit 7 **Do you...?** *(present simple questions)*

UNIT 6   Exercises

6.1 Write the negative.

1 I play the piano very well.   *I don't play the piano very well.*
2 Jack plays the piano very well.   Jack .... very well.
3 You know the answer.   ....
4 She works very hard.   ....
5 They do the same thing every day.   ....

6.2 Write the opposite (positive or negative).

1 I understand.   *I don't understand.*
2 He doesn't smoke.   *He smokes.*
3 They know. They   ....
4 She loves him.   ....

5 They speak English.   ....
6 I don't want it.   ....
7 She doesn't want them.   ....
8 He lives in Rome.   ....

6.3 Study the information and write sentences with **like**.

Do you like...?	Bill and Rose	Carol	you
1 classical music?	yes	no	?
2 boxing?	no	yes	?
3 horror films?	no	yes	?
4 dogs?	yes	no	?

1 *Bill and Rose like classical music.*
  Carol ....
  I .... classical music.
2 Bill and Rose .... boxing.
  Carol ....
  I ....

3 Bill and Rose ....
  ....
  ....
4 .... dogs.
  ....

6.4 Complete the sentences. All of them are negative. Use **don't/doesn't** + one of these verbs:

cost   drive   go   know   play   see   sell   ~~smoke~~   wash   wear

1 'Have a cigarette.' 'No, thank you. I *don't smoke.*'
2 They .... newspapers in that shop.
3 She has a car but she .... very often.
4 I like films but I .... to the cinema very often.
5 He smells because he .... very often.
6 It's a cheap hotel. It .... much to stay there.
7 He likes football but he .... very often.
8 I .... much about politics.
9 She is married but she .... a ring.
10 He lives near our house but we .... him very often.

UNIT 7   Do you ...? *(present simple questions)*

▶ Unit 5   **I do/work/like** etc. *(present simple)*   ▶ Unit 6   **I don't** ... *(present simple negative)*

■ We use **do/does** in present simple questions:

positive

I we you they	**work** **play** **do** **like**
he she it	work**s** play**s** doe**s** like**s**

question

do	I we you they	**work?** **play?** **do?** **like?**
does	he she it	

Do you play the guitar?

■ The word order in these questions is:

do/does + *subject* + *infinitive*

	Do	**you**		**work**	**on Saturdays?**
Where	**do**	**your parents**		**live?**	
	Do	**they**		**like**	**music?**
How often	**do**	**you**		**wash**	**your hair?**
What	**do**	**you**	usually	**do**	**at weekends?**
	Does	**Chris**	often	**play**	**tennis?**
How much	**does**	**it**		**cost**	**to fly to Rome?**
What	**does**	**this word**		**mean?**	

What **do you do?** = What's your job?
        – 'What **do you do?**'   'I work in a bank.'

■ Remember:

    do I/we/you/they   – **Do they** like music?
    does he/she/it   – **Does he** like music?

■ *short answers*

Yes, {	I/we/you/they	**do.**
	he/she/it	**does.**

No, {	I/we/you/they	**don't.**
	he/she/it	**doesn't.**

    – '**Do you** smoke?'   '**No, I don't.**'
    – '**Do they** speak English?'   '**Yes, they do.**'
    – '**Does he** work hard?'   '**Yes, he does.**'
    – '**Does your sister** live in London?'   '**No, she doesn't.**'

▶ Unit 8   **I am doing** *(present continuous)* and **I do** *(present simple)*

UNIT 7 Exercises

7.1 You are asking somebody questions. Write questions with **Do/Does ... ?**

1 I work hard. And you? Do you work hard ?
2 I play tennis. And you? .... you .... ?
3 I play tennis. And Ann? .... Ann .... ?
4 I know the answer. And you? .... the answer?
5 I like hot weather. And you? .... ?
6 I smoke. And your father? .... ?
7 I do exercises every morning. And you? .... ?
8 I speak English. And your friends? .... ?
9 I want to be famous. And you? .... ?

These questions begin with **Where/What/How ... ?**

10 I wash my hair twice a week. (how often / you?) How often do you wash your hair ?
11 I live in London. (where / you?) Where .... ?
12 I watch TV every day. (how often / you?) How .... ?
13 I have lunch at home. (where / you?) .... ?
14 I get up at 7.30. (what time / you?) .... ?
15 I go to the cinema a lot. (how often / you?) .... ?
16 I go to work by bus. (how / you?) .... ?

7.2 Use the verbs in the list to make questions. Use the word(s) in brackets ( ).

cost   do   do   go   have   like   ~~play~~   rain   smoke   speak

1 (he) Does he .... often play...... volleyball?	Yes, he's a very good player.
2 (you) Excuse me, ... English?	Yes, a little.
3 (you) What .... ?	I'm a secretary.
4 (your sister) What .... ?	She works in a shop.
5 (she) .... ?	Yes, 20 cigarettes a day.
6 (it) How often .... in summer?	Not often. It's usually dry.
7 (you) .... dancing?	Yes, I love it.
8 (they) What time .... usually .... to bed?	10 o'clock.
9 (you) What .... usually .... for breakfast?	Toast and coffee.
10 (it) How much .... to stay at this hotel?	£30 a night.

7.3 Write positive or negative short answers (**Yes, he does / No, I don't** etc.).

1 Do you smoke?   No, I don't. ....
2 Do you live in a big city?   ....
3 Do you drink a lot of coffee?   ....
4 Does your mother speak English?   ....
5 Do you play a musical instrument?   ....
6 Does it rain a lot where you live? ....

UNIT 8   I am doing *(present continuous)* and I do *(present simple)*

▶ Units 3–4   *present continuous*   ▶ Units 5–7   *present simple*

Jim is watching television.
He is *not* playing the guitar.

But Jim has a guitar.
He often plays it and he plays very well.

Jim **plays** the guitar
but he **is not playing** the guitar now.

Is he playing the guitar?   **No, he isn't.**   *(present continuous)*
Does he play the guitar?   **Yes, he does.**   *(present simple)*

■ *Present continuous* (**I am doing**) – now, at the time of speaking:

- Please be quiet. **I'm working**.
- Tom **is having** a shower at the moment.
- Take an umbrella. It**'s raining**.
- You can turn off the television. **I'm not watching** it.
- Why are you under the table? What **are you doing**?

■ *Present simple* (**I do**) – in general, all the time or sometimes:

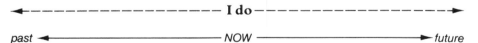

- I **work** every day from 9 o'clock until 5.00.
- Tom **has** a shower every morning.
- It **rains** a lot in winter.
- I **don't watch** television very often.
- What **do you** usually **do** at the weekend?

■ Do *not* use these verbs in the present continuous (**I am –ing**):
**want   like   love   hate   need   prefer   depend   know   mean
understand   believe   remember   forget**

Use the present simple only (**I want/do you like?** etc.):
- I'm tired. I **want** to go home. (*not* 'I'm wanting')
- '**Do you know** that girl?'   'Yes, but I **forget** her name.'
- I **don't understand**. What **do you mean**?

16

UNIT 8 Exercises

8.1 Answer the questions about the pictures.

1 Does he take photographs? _Yes, he does._ Is he taking a photograph? _No, he isn't._
  What is he doing? _He's having a bath._
2 Does she drive a bus? .... Is she driving a bus? ....
  What is she doing? ....
3 Does he clean windows? .... Is he cleaning a window? ....
  What is he doing? ....
4 Do they teach? .... Are they teaching? ....
  What are they doing? ....

8.2 Put in **am/is/are/do/don't/does/doesn't**.

1 Excuse me, ...*do*........ you speak English?
2 'Have a cigarette.' 'No, thank you, I .... smoke.'
3 Why .... you laughing at me?
4 'What .... she do?' 'She's a dentist.'
5 I .... want to go out. It .... raining.
6 'Where .... you come from?' 'From Canada.'
7 How much .... it cost to send a letter to Canada?
8 I can't talk to you at the moment. I .... working.
9 George is a good tennis player but he .... play very often.

8.3 Put the verb in the *present continuous* (**I am doing**) or *present simple* (**I do**).

1 Excuse me, ..*do you speak*.............. (you/speak) English?
2 Tom ..*is having*...................... (have) a shower at the moment.
3 They ..*don't watch*................ (not/watch) television very often.
4 Listen! Somebody .... (sing).
5 She's tired. She .... (want) to go home now.
6 How often .... (you/read) a newspaper?
7 'Excuse me, but you .... (sit) in my place.' 'Oh, I'm sorry.'
8 I'm sorry, I .... (not/understand). Please speak more slowly.
9 'Where are you, Roy?' 'I'm in the sitting-room. I .... (read).'
10 What time .... (she/finish) work every day?
11 You can turn off the radio. I .... (not/listen) to it.
12 He .... (not/usually/drive) to work.
  He usually .... (walk).

UNIT 9   I watched/cleaned/went etc. *(past simple)*

I watch television **every** evening.
(present simple)

I watched television **yesterday** evening.
(past simple)

watched is the *past simple*:

I/we/you/they he/she/it	watch**ed**

■ The past simple is often **-ed**. For example:

work → work**ed**   clean → clean**ed**   start → start**ed**
stay → stay**ed**   live → liv**ed**   dance → danc**ed**

These verbs are *regular* verbs.

- I clean my teeth every morning. This morning I **cleaned** my teeth.
- Terry **worked** in a bank from 1981 to 1986.
- Yesterday it **rained** all morning. It **stopped** at lunchtime.
- We **enjoyed** the party last night. We **danced** a lot and **talked** to a lot of people. The party **finished** at midnight.

Spelling ▶ Appendix 4 (4.2 and 4.4):

stud**y** → stud**ied**   marr**y** → marr**ied**
sto**p** → sto**pp**ed   pla**n** → pla**nn**ed

■ Some verbs are *irregular* (not regular). The past simple is *not* **-ed**. Here are some important irregular verbs (see also Appendix 1–2):

begin	→ **began**	fall	→ **fell**	leave	→ **left**	sell	→ **sold**
break	**broke**	find	**found**	lose	**lost**	sit	**sat**
bring	**brought**	fly	**flew**	make	**made**	sleep	**slept**
build	**built**	forget	**forgot**	meet	**met**	speak	**spoke**
buy	**bought**	get	**got**	pay	**paid**	stand	**stood**
catch	**caught**	give	**gave**	put	**put**	take	**took**
come	**came**	go	**went**	read	**read** (/red/)	tell	**told**
do	**did**	have	**had**	ring	**rang**	think	**thought**
drink	**drank**	hear	**heard**	say	**said**	win	**won**
eat	**ate**	know	**knew**	see	**saw**	write	**wrote**

- I usually get up early but this morning I **got** up at 9.30.
- We **did** a lot of housework yesterday.
- Caroline **went** to the cinema three times last week.
- Mr Todd **came** into the room, **took** off his coat and **sat** down.

▶ Unit 10   **I didn't...   Did you ...?** *(past simple negative* and *questions)*

UNIT 9 Exercises

9.1 Complete these sentences. Use one of these verbs in the past simple:

clean   die   enjoy   finish   happen   live   open   play   rain
smoke   start   stay   want   watch

1 Yesterday evening I **watched** television.
2 I .... my teeth three times yesterday.
3 Bernard .... 20 cigarettes yesterday evening.
4 The concert last night .... at 7.30 and .... at 10 o'clock.
5 The accident .... last Sunday afternoon.
6 When I was a child, I .... to be a doctor.
7 Mozart .... from 1756 to 1791.
8 We .... our holiday last year. We .... at a very good hotel.
9 Today the weather is nice, but yesterday it ....
10 It was hot in the room, so I .... the window.
11 The weather was good yesterday afternoon, so we .... tennis.
12 William Shakespeare .... in 1616.

9.2 Write the past of these verbs.

1 get	....**got**........	6 leave	....	11 buy	....	16 put	....
2 eat	....	7 see	....	12 know	....	17 tell	....
3 pay	....	8 go	....	13 stand	....	18 lose	....
4 make	....	9 hear	....	14 take	....	19 think	....
5 give	....	10 find	....	15 do	....	20 speak	....

9.3 Write sentences about the past (**yesterday / last week** etc.).

1 He always goes to work by car.   Yesterday **he went to work by car.** ....
2 They always get up early.   This morning they ....
3 Bill often loses his keys.   He .... last Saturday.
4 I write a letter to Jane every week.   Last week ....
5 She meets her friends every evening.   She .... yesterday evening.
6 I usually read two newspapers every day. .... yesterday.
7 They come to my house every Friday.   Last Friday ....
8 We usually go to the cinema on Sunday. .... last Sunday.
9 Tom always has a shower in the morning. .... this morning.
10 They buy a new car every year.   Last year ....
11 I eat an orange every day.   Yesterday ....
12 We usually do our shopping on Monday. .... last Monday.
13 Ann often takes photographs.   Last weekend ....
14 We leave home at 8.30 every morning. .... this morning.

9.4 Write sentences about yourself. What did you do yesterday or what happened yesterday?

1 ....
2 ....
3 ....
4 ....
5 ....

UNIT 10   I didn't…   Did you…? *(past simple negative and questions)*

►   Unit 9   **I watched/cleaned/went** etc. *(past simple)*

■   We use **did** in past simple negatives and questions:

infinitive	*positive*		*negative*			*question*		
watch clean play do go have begin	I we you they he she it	watch**ed** clean**ed** play**ed** **did** **went** **had** **began**	I we you they he she it	**did not** (**didn't**)	watch clean play do go have begin	**did**	I we you they he she it	watch? clean? play? do? go? have? begin?

■   **do/does** *(present)* → **did** *(past)*:
  - I **don't** watch television very often.
  - I **didn't** watch television **yesterday**.
  - **Does** she often go out?
  - **Did** she go out **last night**?

■   We use **did/didn't** + *infinitive* (**watch/clean/do** etc.):

   I watch**ed**   *but*   I didn't **watch**   (*not* 'I didn't watched')
   he **went**   *but*   did he **go**?   (*not* 'did he went?')
  - I play**ed** tennis yesterday but I **didn't win**.
  - Don **didn't have** breakfast this morning. (*not* 'Don hadn't breakfast')
  - They **went** to the cinema but they **didn't enjoy** the film.
  - We **didn't do** much work yesterday.

■   Note the word order in questions with **did**:

           did +   *subject*   + *infinitive*

	Did	**Sue**	**give**	you a birthday present?
What	**did**	**you**	**do**	yesterday evening?
How	**did**	**the accident**	**happen**?	
Where	**did**	**your parents**	**go**	for their holidays?

■   *short answers*

Yes, { I/we/you/they
     he/she/it } **did**.
	No, { I/we/you/they
	     he/she/it } **didn't**.

  - '**Did you** see Joe yesterday?'   '**No, I didn't**.'
  - '**Did it** rain on Sunday?'   '**Yes, it did**.'
  - '**Did Helen** come to the party?'   '**No, she didn't**.'
  - '**Did your friends** have a good holiday?'   '**Yes, they did**.'

UNIT 10 Exercises

10.1 Complete these sentences with the verb in the negative.

1 I saw John but I *didn't see* Mary.
2 They worked on Monday but they .... on Tuesday.
3 We went to the shop but we .... to the bank.
4 She had a pen but she .... any paper.
5 Jack did French at school but he .... German.

10.2 You are asking somebody questions. Write questions with **Did ... ?**

1 I watched TV last night. And you? *Did you watch TV last night* .... ?
2 I enjoyed the party. And you? .... you .... ?
3 I had a good holiday. And you? .... ?
4 I got up early this morning. And you? .... ?
5 I slept well last night. And you? .... ?

10.3 What did *you* do yesterday? (Your sentence can be positive or negative.)

1 (watch TV) *I watched TV yesterday.* (*or* *I didn't watch TV yesterday.*)
2 (get up before 7.30) I ....
3 (have a shower) I ....
4 (buy a magazine) ....
5 (speak English) ....
6 (do an examination) ....
7 (eat meat) ....
8 (go to bed before 10.30) ....

10.4 Write questions with **Who/What/How/Why ... ?**

1 I met somebody. Who *did you meet* .... ?
2 Harry arrived. What time .... Harry .... ?
3 I saw somebody. Who .... you .... ?
4 They wanted something. What .... ?
5 The meeting finished. What time .... ?
6 Pat went home early. Why .... ?
7 We had dinner. What .... for dinner?
8 It cost a lot of money. How much .... ?

10.5 Put the verb in the correct form of the past (positive, negative or question).

1 I *played* (play) tennis yesterday but I *didn't win* (not/win).
2 We .... (wait) a long time for the bus but it .... (not/come).
3 That's a nice shirt. Where .... (you/buy) it?
4 She .... (see) me but she .... (not/speak) to me.
5 '........................ (it/rain) yesterday?' 'No, it was a nice day.'
6 That was a stupid thing to do. Why .... (you/do) it?

UNIT 11   was/were

Now Charlie **is** at work.

At midnight last night he **wasn't** at work.

He **was** in bed.
He **was** asleep.

am/is *(present)* → **was** *(past)*:
- I **am** tired (now).
- **Is** she at home (now)?
- The weather **is** nice today.

I **was** tired **last night**.
Was she at home **yesterday morning**?
The weather **was** nice **yesterday**.

are *(present)* → **were** *(past)*:
- You **are** late (now).
- They **aren't** here (now).

You **were** late **yesterday**.
They **weren't** here **last Sunday**.

positive		*negative*		*question*	
I he she it	**was**	I he she it	**was not** (**wasn't**)	**was**	I? he? she? it?
we you they	**were**	we you they	**were not** (**weren't**)	**were**	we? you? they?

- Last year she **was** 22, so she **is** 23 now.
- When I **was** a child, I **was** afraid of dogs.
- We **were** tired after the journey but we **weren't** hungry.
- The hotel **was** very comfortable and it **wasn't** expensive.
- Where **were** you at 3 o'clock yesterday afternoon?
- **Was** the weather good when you **were** on holiday?
- Those shoes are nice. **Were** they expensive?
- Why **was** he angry yesterday?

short answers

Yes, {	I/he/she/it	**was.**
	we/you/they	**were.**

No, {	I/he/she/it	**wasn't.**
	we/you/they	**weren't.**

- 'Were you late?'   'No, I wasn't.'
- 'Was Ted at work yesterday?'   'Yes, he was.'
- 'Were they at the party?'   'No, they weren't.'

UNIT 11   Exercises

11.1 Look at the pictures. Where were these people at 3 o'clock yesterday afternoon?

GEORGE	CAROL AND JACK	SUE	MR AND MRS BAKER	BEN

1 ...*George was in bed*............................
2 Carol and Jack ....
3 Sue ....

4 ....
5 ....
6 And you?   I ....

11.2 Put in **am/is/are/was/were**. Some sentences are present and some are past.

1 Last year she ..*was*... 22, so she ...*is*..... 23 now.
2 Today the weather .... nice, but yesterday it .... cold.
3 I .... hungry. Can I have something to eat?
4 I .... hungry last night, so I had something to eat.
5 Where .... you at 11 o'clock last Friday morning?
6 Don't buy those shoes. They .... too expensive.
7 Why .... you so angry yesterday?
8 We must go now. It .... very late.
9 This time last year I .... in Paris.
10 We .... tired when we arrived home, so we went to bed.
11 Charlie Chaplin died in 1978. He .... a famous film star.
12 'Where .... the children?'   'I don't know. They .... in the garden ten minutes ago.'

11.3 Put in **was/wasn't/were/weren't**.

1 We didn't like our hotel room. It ....*was*..... very small and it ..*wasn't*. very clean.
2 Kate got married when she .... 24 years old.
3 I phoned you yesterday evening but you .... at home. Where .... you?
4 George .... at work last week because he .... ill. He's better now.
5 The shops .... open yesterday because it .... a public holiday.
6 '................ you at home at 9.30?'   'No, I .... I .... at work.'

11.4 Write questions.

1   I saw a film.   (good?) ..*Was it good*..................... ?
2   I met some people.   (friendly?) .... ?
3   I did an examination.   (difficult?) .... ?
4   I bought some boots.   (expensive?) .... ?
5   I went to a museum.   (interesting?) .... ?

23

UNIT 12   I was doing *(past continuous)*

Now it is 6 o'clock.
Sarah **is** at home.
She **is watching** televison.

At 4 o'clock she **wasn't** at home.
She **was** at the sports club.
She **was playing** tennis.
She **wasn't watching** television.

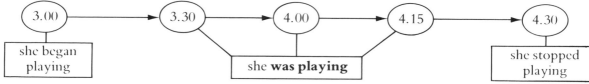

- **was/were -ing** (do**ing**/play**ing**/work**ing** etc.) is the *past continuous* tense:

positive

I he she it	**was -ing**
we you they	**were -ing**

negative

I he she it	**was not** (**wasn't**)	**-ing**
we you they	**were not** (**weren't**)	**-ing**

question

was	I he she it	**-ing**?
were	we you they	**-ing**?

- 'What **were** you do**ing** at 11.30 yesterday?' 'I **was** work**ing**.'
- 'What did he say?' 'I don't know. I **wasn't** listen**ing**.'
- It **was** rain**ing**, so we didn't go out.
- In 1980 they **were** liv**ing** in Canada.
- Today she's wearing a skirt, but yesterday she **was** wear**ing** trousers.
- I woke up early yesterday. It was a beautiful morning. The sun **was** shin**ing** and the birds **were** sing**ing**.

- **am/is/are -ing** *(present)* → **was/were -ing** *(past)*:
  - **I'm** work**ing** (now).   I **was** work**ing** at 10.30 last night.
  - It **isn't** rain**ing** (now).   It **wasn't** rain**ing** when we went out.
  - What **are** you do**ing** (now)?   What **were** you do**ing** at 3 o'clock?

Spelling   (mak**e** → mak**ing**   run → ru**nning**   lie → l**ying** etc.)   ▶ Appendix 4 (4.3 and 4.4)

▶ Unit 13   **I was doing** *(past continuous)* and **I did** *(past simple)*

UNIT 12   Exercises

12.1 Look at the pictures. Where were these people at 3 o'clock yesterday afternoon? And what were they doing? Write *two* sentences for each picture.

1 ANN	2 CAROL AND JACK	3 TOM	4 CATHERINE	5 MR AND MRS MASON
at home/watch TV	at the cinema/watch a film	in his car/drive	at the station/wait for a train	in the park/walk

1 Ann was at home. She was watching TV.
2 Carol and Jack .... They ....
3 Tom ....
4 ....
5 ....
6 And you? I .... I ....

12.2 Sarah did a lot of things yesterday morning. Look at the pictures and then write a sentence for each picture.

8.10 – 8.25	8.30 – 9.10	9.30 – 10.00	10.20 – 11.00	11.30 – 12.00	12.30 – 1.00
have/breakfast	read/a newspaper	wash/her car	listen/to music	swim	cook

1 At 9.45 she was washing her car.   4 At 12.50 ....
2 At 11.45 she ....   5 At 8.15 ....
3 At 9 o'clock ....   6 At 10.30 ....

12.3 Write questions. Use **was/were -ing**.

1 (what / Tim / do / when you saw him?)   What was Tim doing when you saw him ?
2 (what / you / do / at 11 o'clock?)   What .... ?
3 (what / she / wear / yesterday?)   .... ?
4 (it / rain / when you went out?)   .... ?
5 (where / you / live / in 1981?)   .... ?

12.4 Look at the picture. You saw Joe in the street yesterday afternoon. What was he doing? Write positive or negative sentences.

Hi.
I'm going shopping.

1 (he / wear / a jacket)   He wasn't wearing a jacket.
2 (he / smoke / a pipe)   ....
3 (he / carry / a bag)   ....
4 (he / carry / an umbrella)   ....
5 (he / go / to the dentist)   ....
6 (he / wear / a hat)   ....

UNIT 13   I was doing (*past continuous*) and I did (*past simple*)

Jack was reading   The phone rang.   He stopped reading.   He answered the
a book.   phone.

What **happened**? The phone **rang**. (*past simple*)
What **was Jack doing** when the phone rang?
He **was reading** a book. (*past continuous*)
What **did he do** when the phone rang?
He **stopped** reading and **answered** the phone. (*past simple*)

Jack began reading *before* the phone rang. So:
When the phone rang, he **was reading**.

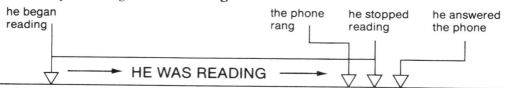

past simple	past continuous
beginning *end* we **played** (complete action) We **played** tennis yesterday. (from 3 o'clock until 4.00)	*beginning* we **were playing** (in the middle of an action) A: What **were** you **doing** at 3.30? B: We **were playing** tennis.

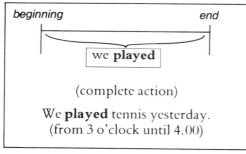
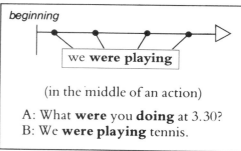

    – Jack **was reading** the newspaper when the phone **rang**.
but Jack **read** the newspaper yesterday.
    – **Were you watching** television when I **phoned** you?
but **Did you watch** the film on television last night?
    – I **started** work at 9.00 and **finished** at 4.30. At 2.30 I **was working**.
    – When we **went** out, it **was raining**. (= it started raining *before* we went out)
    – I **saw** Lucy and Tom this morning. They **were standing** at the bus-stop.
    – Joy **fell** asleep while she **was reading**.   (**while** ▶ Unit 93)

UNIT 13 Exercises

13.1 Look at the pictures and write sentences. Use the past continuous or past simple.

Example (see the pictures opposite): (Jack / read / a book) ..... *Jack was reading a book.* ....
(the phone / ring) .... *The phone rang.* ....
(he / answer / the phone) *He answered the phone.* ....

1
(Tom / walk / down the street)
Tom ....
(he / see / Jack)
....
(he / say / hello)
....

2
(they / sit / in the garden)
....
(it / start / to rain)
....
(they / go / into the house)
....

3
(Carol / paint / the room)
....
(she / fall / off the ladder)
....
(she / break / her arm)
....

13.2 Put the verb into the past continuous (**I was doing**) or past simple (**I did**).

1 When we ..... *went* ..... (go) out, it ..... *was raining* ..... (rain).
2 I wasn't hungry last night. I ..... *didn't eat* ..... (not/eat) anything.
3 *Were you watching* (you/watch) television when I ..... *phoned* ..... (phone) you?
4 Jane wasn't at home when I went to see her. She .... (work).
5 I .... (get) up early this morning. I .... (wash),
.... (dress) and then I .... (have) breakfast.
6 The postman .... (come) while I .... (have) breakfast.
7 We .... (meet) Joan at the party. She .... (wear) a
red dress.
8 The boys .... (break) a window when they .... (play)
football.
9 I was late but my friends .... (wait) for me when I ....
(arrive).
10 I .... (get) up at 7 o'clock. The sun .... (shine), so I
.... (go) for a walk.
11 He .... (not/drive) fast when the accident .... (happen).
12 Margaret .... (not/go) to work yesterday. She was ill.
13 'What .... (you/do) on Saturday evening?' 'I went to the cinema.'
14 'What .... (you/do) at 9.30 on Saturday evening?'
'I .... (watch) a film in the cinema.'

UNIT 14   have/has (got)

■ You can say **have** or **have got**, **has** or **has got**:

I we you they	**have**	=	I we you they	**have got**	(I**'ve got**) (we**'ve got**) (you**'ve got**) (they**'ve got**)
he she it	**has**	=	he she it	**has got**	(he**'s got**) (she**'s got**) (it**'s got**)

I've got a headache.

She**'s got** a headache.
or She **has** a headache.

  – I**'ve got** blue eyes. (*or* I **have** blue eyes.)
  – Tim **has got** two sisters. (*or* Tim **has** two sisters.)
  – They like animals. They**'ve got** a horse, three dogs and six cats.
  – This car **has got** four doors.
  – I don't feel very well. I**'ve got** a headache.

negative

I we you they	**have not** (**haven't**)	**got**
he she it	**has not** (**hasn't**)	

question

have	I we you they	**got**?
has	he she it	

short answers

Yes, No,	I we you they	**have**. **haven't**.
Yes, No,	he she it	**has**. **hasn't**.

  – I**'ve got** a motor-bike but I **haven't got** a car.
  – Mr and Mrs Harrison **haven't got** any children.
  – It's a nice house but it **hasn't got** a garden.
  – '**Have you got** a camera?'   '**Yes, I have**.'
  – 'What **have you got** in your bag?'   'Nothing. It's empty.'
  – '**Has Ann got** a car?'   '**Yes, she has**.'
  – What kind of car **has she got**?

■ In negatives and questions you can also use **do/does + have**:
  – They **don't have** any children. (= They **haven't got** any children.)
  – It's a nice house but it **doesn't have** a garden. (= it **hasn't got** a garden)
  – **Does** Ann **have** a car? (= **Has** Ann **got** a car?)
  – How much money **do you have**? (= How much money **have** you **got**?)

■ The past is **had**. In negatives and questions we use **did + have**   (▶ Units 9–10):

  – I **had** some money.   I **didn't have** any money.   **Did** you **have** any money?

UNIT 14   Exercises

14.1 Write the short form (**we've got/he hasn't got** etc.).

1 we have got ..we've got..
2 he has got ....
3 they have got ....
4 she has not got ....
5 it has got ....
6 I have not got ....

14.2 Write questions.

1 (you / a camera?) .Have you got a camera.. ?
2 (you / a passport?) .... ?
3 (your father / a car?) .... ?
4 (Carol / many friends?) .... ?
5 (Mr and Mrs Lewis / any children?) .... ?
6 (how much money / you?) .... ?
7 (what kind of car / John?) .... ?

14.3 What have Ann and Jim got? What have you got? Look at the information and write sentences about Ann, Jim and yourself.

	Ann (she)	Jim (he)	you?
a camera	no	yes	?
a bicycle	yes	no	?
black hair	no	no	?
brothers/sisters	two brothers	one sister	?

1 (Jim / a camera) Jim has got a camera.
2 (I / black hair) I've got black hair.
    (or I haven't got black hair.   )
3 (Ann / a camera) Ann ....
4 (I / a camera) I ....
5 (I / a bicycle) ....
6 (Jim / a bicycle) ....
7 (Ann / black hair) ....

8 (Ann / two brothers)
    ....
9 (Jim / black hair)
    ....
10 (Ann / a bicycle) ....
11 (Jim / a sister) ....
12 (I / brothers / sisters) ....

14.4 Put in **have got** (**'ve got**), **has got** (**'s got**), **haven't got** or **hasn't got**.

1 They like animals. They 've got............ three dogs and two cats.
2 Sarah hasn't got... a car. She goes everywhere by bicycle.
3 Everybody likes Tom. He .... a lot of friends.
4 Mr and Mrs Johnson .... two children, a boy and a girl.
5 An insect .... six legs.
6 I can't open the door. I .... a key.
7 Quick! Hurry! We .... much time.
8 'What's wrong?' 'I .... something in my eye.'
9 Ben doesn't read much. He .... many books.
10 It's a nice town. It .... a very nice shopping centre.
11 Alice is going to the dentist. She .... toothache.
12 'Where's my newspaper?' 'I don't know. I .... it.'
13 Julia wants to go on holiday but she .... any money.
14 I'm not going to work today. I .... a bad cold.

UNIT 15   I have done (present perfect 1)

His shoes are dirty.

He is cleaning his shoes.

I've cleaned my shoes.

He **has cleaned** his shoes.
(= his shoes are clean *now*)

They are at home.

They are going out.

They **have gone** out.
(= they are not at home *now*)

■ **has cleaned** / **have gone** etc. is the *present perfect* (**have/has** + *past participle*★):

I we you they	**have ('ve)** **have not (haven't)**	cleaned finished **done** **been**
he she it	**has ('s)** **has not (hasn't)**	**bought** **taken** **begun**

have	I we you they	cleaned? finished? **done?** **been?**
has	he she it	**bought?** **taken?** **begun?**

■ We use the present perfect for *an action in the past* with a result *now*:
   – **I've lost** my passport. (= I can't find my passport *now*)
   – She**'s** (= she **has**) **gone** to bed. (= she is in bed *now*)
   – We**'ve bought** a new car. (= we have a new car *now*)
   – It's Kay's birthday tomorrow and I **haven't bought** her a present.
   – 'Bob is on holiday.'   'Oh, where **has he gone**?'
   – 'Are they still having dinner?'   'No, they**'ve finished**.'

★The past participle of *regular* verbs is **–ed**:
   clean → have clean**ed**   finish → have finish**ed**   stop → have stopp**ed**

The past participle of *irregular* verbs is sometimes the same as the past simple and sometimes different. For example:
the same: lose → have **lost**   make → have **made**   have → have **had**
different: do → have **done**   see → have **seen**   write → have **written**

For a list of irregular past participles see Appendix 1–2.

▶ Unit 16   **Have you ever ...?** *(present perfect 2)*   ▶ Unit 17   **How long have you ...?** *(present perfect 3)*
▶ Unit 19   **I have done** *(present perfect)* and **I did** *(past simple)*   ▶ Unit 89   *present perfect* + **yet**

UNIT 15   Exercises

15.1 Look at the pictures. What has happened?

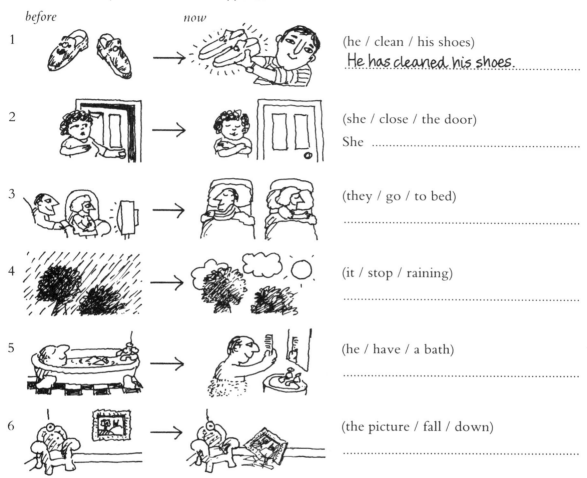

before   *now*

1   (he / clean / his shoes)
     He has cleaned his shoes.

2   (she / close / the door)
     She ....

3   (they / go / to bed)
     ....

4   (it / stop / raining)
     ....

5   (he / have / a bath)
     ....

6   (the picture / fall / down)
     ....

15.2 Complete the sentences with a verb from the list. Use the present perfect (**have/has** + the past participle of the verb).

break   buy   ~~finish~~   do   go   go   lose   paint   read   take

1 'Are they still having dinner?'   'No, they have finished.'
2 I .... some new shoes. Do you want to see them?
3 'Is Tom here?'   'No, he .... to work.'
4 '................... you .... the shopping?'   'No, I'm going to do it later.'
5 'Where's your key?'   'I don't know. I .... it.'
6 Look! Somebody .... that window.
7 Your house looks different.   .... you .... it?
8 I can't find my umbrella. Somebody .... it.
9 I'm looking for Sarah. Where .... she .... ?
10 'Do you want the newspaper?'   'No, thanks. I .... it.'

31

UNIT 16   Have you ever ... ? *(present perfect 2)*

▶ Unit 15   **I have done** *(present perfect 1)*

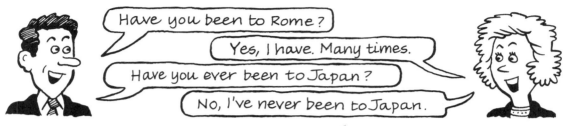

■ We use the *present perfect* (**have been / have played / have done** etc.) when we talk about a time from the past until now – for example, your life:

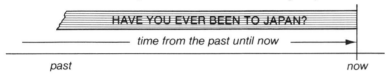

- 'Have you been to France?' *(in your life)* 'No, I haven't.'
- I've been to Canada but I haven't been to the United States.
- She is an interesting person. She has done many different jobs and has visited many countries.
- I've seen that woman before but I can't remember when.
- How many times has Brazil won the World Cup?
- 'Have you read this book?' 'Yes, I've read it twice.' (= two times)

■ You can use the *present perfect* + **ever** *(in questions)* and **never**:
- 'Has Ann ever been to Australia?' 'No, never.'
- 'Have you ever played golf?' 'Yes, once.' (= one time)
- My mother has never travelled by air.
- I've never ridden a horse.

■ **gone** and **been**

He's **gone** to Spain.
(= he is in Spain *now*)

He's **been** to Spain.
(= he went to Spain but *now he is back*)

Compare:
- I can't find Susan. Where **has she gone**? (= Where is she now?)
- Oh, hello, Susan. I was looking for you. Where **have you been**?

▶ Unit 19   **I have done** *(present perfect)* and **I did** *(past simple)*

UNIT 16 Exercises

16.1 You are asking Ann questions beginning **Have you ever ... ?** Write the questions.

```
1  (Paris?)  Have you ever been to Paris ................... ?    No, never.
2  (play / golf?)  Have you ever played golf ................ ?    Yes, many times.
3  (Australia?)  Have ........................................ ?    No, never.
4  (lose / your passport?)  .................................. ?    Yes, once.
5  (sleep / in a park?)  ..................................... ?    No, never.
6  (eat / Chinese food?)  .................................... ?    Yes, a few times.
7  (New York?)  ............................................... ?    Yes, twice.
8  (win / a lot of money?)  .................................. ?    No, never.
9  (break / your leg?)  ...................................... ?    Yes, once.
```

16.2 Look at Ann's answers in Exercise 1. Write sentences about Ann and yourself.

Ann   *You*

1 Ann has never been to Paris ....   I have been to Paris twice ....
2 Ann has played golf many times. ......   I ....
3 She ....   I ....
4 She ....
5 ....
6 ....
7 ....
8 ....
9 ....

16.3 Mary is 65 years old. She has had an interesting life. Write sentences about the things she has done. Use the present perfect.

1 (she / do / many different jobs)   She has done many different jobs. ....
2 (she / travel / to many places) She ....
3 (she / do / a lot of interesting things) ....
4 (she / write / ten books) ....
5 (she / meet / a lot of interesting people) ....
6 (she / be / married five times) ....

16.4 Put in **gone** or **been**.

1 He's on holiday at the moment. He's ...... gone .... to Spain.
2 'Where's Jill?' 'She's not here. I think she's .... to the bank.'
3 'Hello, Pat. Where have you .... ?' 'I've .... to the bank.'
4 'Have you ever .... to Mexico?' 'No, never.'
5 My parents aren't at home this evening. They've .... out.
6 There's a new restaurant in town. Have you .... to it?
7 Paris is a wonderful city. I've .... there many times.
8 Helen was here earlier but I think she's .... now.

33

UNIT 17   How long have you . . . ? *(present perfect 3)*

Jill is on holiday in London.

She arrived in London on Monday.
Today is Friday.

How long **has she been** in London?

She **has been** in London { **since Monday**.
                            for four days.

> She [**is**] in London now. (**is** = *present*)

but   She [**has been**] in London { **since Monday**.
                                        for four days.   (**has been** = *present perfect*)

past

She **has been** in London { **since Monday.**
                             for four days. →

> She **is** in
> London now.

| Monday | | now (Friday) |

Compare:

present simple		*present perfect*
Harry **is** in Canada.	*but*	He **has been** in Canada **since April**. (*not* 'He is in Canada since April.')
Are you married?	*but*	**How long have** you **been** married? (*not* 'How long are you married?')
Do you **know** Sarah?	*but*	**How long have** you **known** her? (*not* 'How long do you know her?') **I've known** her **for a long time**.
Linda **lives** in London.	*but*	**How long has** she **lived** in London? She **has lived** there **all her life**.
We **have** a car.	*but*	**How long have** you **had** your car? We**'ve had** it for **a year**.

present continuous		*present perfect continuous* (**have been –ing**)
I'm learn**ing** German.	*but*	**How long have** you **been** learn**ing** German? **I've been** learn**ing** German **for six weeks**.
It's rain**ing**.	*but*	**It's been** (= it **has been**) rain**ing** **since I got up this morning**.

▶ Unit 18   **for**   **since**   **ago**

UNIT 17 Exercises

17.1 Complete these sentences.

1 Jill is in London. She ...*has been*............... in London since Monday.
2 I know George. I ...*have known*......... him for a long time.
3 They are married. They .... married since 1983.
4 Brian is ill. He .... ill for a week.
5 We live in this house. We .... here for ten years.
6 I know Tom very well. I .... him for a long time.
7 We are waiting for you. We .... waiting since 8 o'clock.
8 Alice works in a bank. She .... in a bank for five years.
9 I'm learning English. I .... learning English for six months.
10 She has a headache. She .... a headache since she got up.

17.2 Make questions with **How long ... ?**

1 Jill is in London. *How long has she been in London* .... ?
2 I know George. *How long have you known him* .... ?
3 Mike and Judy are in Brazil.   How long .... ?
4 Diana is learning Italian.   How long .... ?
5 My brother lives in Germany.   .... ?
6 It is raining.   .... ?
7 Bill is a teacher.   .... ?
8 I know Margaret.   .... ?
9 I have a motor-bike.   .... ?
10 Linda and Frank are married.   .... ?
11 Alan works in London.   .... ?

17.3 Write a sentence for each picture. Use the words below the pictures.

1	2	3	4	5	6
We're married	I'm in hospital	We're watching television	It's raining	I live in Wales	I have a beard
for ten years	since Sunday	for two hours	all day	all her life	for five years

1 ...*They have been married for ten years.*..
2 He .... since Sunday.
3 They .... television ....
4 It .... all day.
5 She ....
6 He ....

35

UNIT 18   for   since   ago

▶ Unit 17   **How long have you ... ?** *(present perfect 3)*

■ **for** and **since**:
We use **for** and **since** to say *how long*:

> – Jill **has been** in London { **for four days**.
> { **since Monday**.

We use **for** + *a period of time* (**four days** / **two years** etc.):

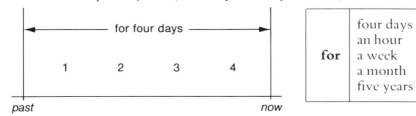

for	four days	ten minutes
	an hour	two hours
	a week	three weeks
	a month	six months
	five years	a long time

We use **since** + *the start of the period* (**Monday** / **9 o'clock** etc.):

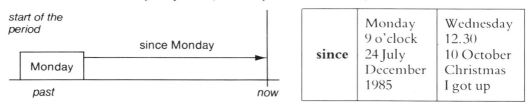

since	Monday	Wednesday
	9 o'clock	12.30
	24 July	10 October
	December	Christmas
	1985	I got up

Compare:
> – Barry has been in Canada **since January**. (= from January to now)
> Barry has been in Canada **for six months**. (*not* 'since six months')
> – I've known her **since 1980**. (= from 1980 to now)
> I've known her **for a long time**. (*not* 'since a long time')

▶ Unit 92   **from ... to   until   since   for**

■ **ago** = *before now*:
> – Susan **started** her new job **two weeks ago**. (= two weeks before now)
> – 'When **did Tom go** out?'   '**Ten minutes ago**.' (= ten minutes before now)
> – I **had** dinner **an hour ago**. (= an hour before now)
> – Life **was** very different **a hundred years ago**.

We use **ago** with the *past simple* (**did/had/started** etc.).

Compare **ago** and **for**:
> – **When did she arrive** in London?
> She **arrived** in London **four days ago**.
>
> – **How long has she been** in London?
> She **has been** in London **for four days**.

UNIT 18 Exercises

18.1 Write **for** or **since**.

1 She's been in London ..*since*.. Monday.
2 She's been in London ...*for*... four days.
3 Mike has been ill .... a long time. He's been in hospital .... October.
4 My aunt has lived in Australia .... 15 years.
5 Nobody lives in those houses. They have been empty .... many years.
6 Mrs Harris is in her office. She's been there .... 7 o'clock.
7 India has been an independent country .... 1947.
8 The bus is late. We've been waiting .... 20 minutes.

18.2 When was ... ? Use **ago** in your answers.

1 your last meal? ....
2 last December? ....
3 1984? ....
4 the last time you were ill? ....
5 the last time you went to the cinema?
....

6 the last time you drank coffee?
....
7 the last time you were in a car?
....
8 the last time you read a newspaper?
....

18.3 Answer the questions. Use the words in brackets ( ) + **for** or **ago**.

1 (four days)   When did she arrive in London? *four days ago*
2 (four days)   How long has she been in London? *for four days*
3 (20 years)   How long have they been married? ....
4 (20 years)   When did they get married? ....
5 (ten minutes)   When did Dan arrive? ....
6 (two months)   When did you buy those shoes? ....
7 (two months)   How long has she been learning English? ....
8 (a long time)   How long have you known Jan? ....
9 (an hour)   What time did you have lunch? ....

18.4 Complete the sentences with **for** ... or **since** ...

1 She is in London now. She arrived there four days ago. *She has been there for four days*.
2 Jack is here. He arrived here on Thursday. He has ....
3 It is raining. It started an hour ago. It's been ....
4 I know Sue. I first met Sue two years ago. I've ....
5 I have a camera. I bought it in 1985. I've ....
6 They are married. They got married six months ago. They've ....
7 Liz is studying medicine at university. She started three years ago.
   She has ....

18.5 Write sentences about yourself. Begin with the words in brackets ( ).

1 (I've lived) ....
2 (I've been) ....
3 (I've been learning) ....
4 (I've had) ....
5 (I've known) ....

UNIT 19   I have done (present perfect) and I did (past simple)

▶ Units 15–17 (present perfect)   ▶ Units 9–10 (past simple)

■ We use the *past simple* (**did/arrived/saw/was** etc.) with a *finished time* (**yesterday/last week/in 1986/six months ago** etc.):

past + finished time

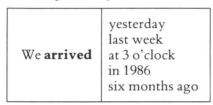

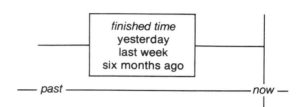

■ We do *not* use the *present perfect* (**have done / have arrived / have been** etc.) with a finished time:

 – I **saw** Jack **yesterday**. (*not* 'I have seen Jack yesterday.')
 – Where **were** you **last night**? (*not* 'Where have you been last night?')
 – We **didn't have** a holiday **last year**. (*not* 'We haven't had')
 – I **got** up **at 7.15**. I **washed**, **dressed** and then I **had** breakfast.
 – William Shakespeare (1564–1616) **was** a writer. He **wrote** many plays and poems.
    (*not* '. . . has been a writer . . . has written many plays')

Use the *past simple* to ask **When?** or **What time?**:
 – **When did** they **arrive**? (*not* 'When have they arrived?')

■ Compare:

present perfect		past simple
I **have lost** my key. (= I can't find it *now*)	*but*	I **lost** my key **yesterday**.
Bill **has gone** home. (= he isn't here *now*)	*but*	Bill **went** home **ten minutes ago**.
Have you **seen** Ann? (= where is she *now*?)	*but*	**When did** you **see** Ann?
time until now (present perfect)		*finished time (past simple)*
Have you **ever been** to Spain? (= in your life, until *now*)	*but*	**Did** you **go** to Spain **last year**?
My friend is a writer. He **has written** many books.	*but*	Shakespeare **wrote** many plays and poems.
We**'ve lived** in Singapore for six years. (we live there *now*)	*but*	We **lived** in Glasgow for six years but now we live in Singapore.

38

UNIT 19   Exercises

19.1 Use the words in brackets (   ) to answer the questions.

1	Have you lost your key?
2	Have you seen Alan?
3	Have you painted the gate?
4	Has Sarah gone to France?
5	Have they had dinner?
6	Has he started his new job?

1 (yesterday) *Yes, I lost it yesterday.*............................
2 (ten minutes ago)   Yes, I .... ten minutes ago.
3 (last week)   Yes, we .... it ....
4 (on Friday)   Yes, she ....
5 (at 7 o'clock) ....
6 (yesterday) ....

19.2 Write questions with **When ... ?** and **What time ... ?**

1	They have arrived.
2	Bill has gone out.
3	I've seen Carol.
4	She's left her job.

1 What time *did they arrive* .... ?
2 What time .... ?
3 When .... you .... ?
4 When .... ?

19.3 In these sentences the verbs are <u>underlined</u>. Are they right or wrong? Correct the verbs that are wrong.

1 Tom <u>arrived</u> last week.   ....RIGHT...
2 <u>Have</u> you <u>seen</u> Pam last week?   ......WRONG.............. *Did you see* ....
3 I <u>have finished</u> my work.   ....
4 I <u>have finished</u> my work at 2 o'clock.   ....
5 When <u>have</u> you <u>finished</u> your work?   ....
6 George <u>has left</u> school three years ago.   ....
7 'Where's Ann?'   'She<u>'s gone</u> to the cinema.' ....
8 Napoleon Bonaparte <u>has died</u> in 1821.   ....
9 Have you ever <u>been</u> to Britain?   ....
10 I <u>haven't seen</u> you at the party on Saturday. ....
11 The weather <u>has been</u> very bad last week.   ....

19.4 Put the verb in the present perfect (**I have done**) or the past simple (**I did**).

1 My friend is a writer. She *has written* .... (write) many books.
2 We *didn't have* .... (not / have) a holiday last year.
3 *Did you see* .... (you / see) Alan last week?
4 I .... (play) tennis yesterday afternoon.
5 What time .... (you / go) to bed last night?
6 .... (you / ever / be) to the United States?
7 My hair is clean. I .... (wash) it.
8 I .... (wash) my hair before breakfast this morning.
9 When I was a child, I .... (not / like) sport.
10 Kathy loves travelling. She .... (visit) many countries.
11 John works in a bookshop. He .... (work) there for three years.
12 Last year we .... (go) to Finland for a holiday. We .... (stay) there for three weeks.

UNIT 20   it is done / it was done *(passive)*

The room **is cleaned** every day.

The room **was cleaned** yesterday.

Compare: Somebody **cleans** │ the room │ every day.   *(active)*

     │ The room │ **is cleaned** every day.   *(passive)*

     Somebody **cleaned** │ the room │ yesterday.   *(active)*

     │ The room │ **was cleaned** yesterday.   *(passive)*

■ The passive is:

			past participle	
present	**am/is/are**		cleaned	**done**
		(not) +	exported	**made**
past	**was/were**		damaged	**broken**

The past participle of *regular* verbs is **-ed** (clean**ed**/damag**ed** etc.). For a list of *irregular* past participles (**made/seen** etc.), see Appendix 1–2.

- Butter **is made** from milk.
- Oranges **are imported** into Britain.
- How often **are** these rooms **cleaned**?
- I **am** never **invited** to parties.

- This house **was built** 100 years ago.
- These houses **were built** 100 years ago.
- When **was** the telephone **invented**?
- I **wasn't invited** to the party last week.
- Six people **were injured** in the accident yesterday.

Two trees **were blown** down in the storm last night.

■ We say **was/were born**:
- 'I **was born** in London in 1958. *(not* 'I am born')
- Where **were you born**?

■ *passive* + **by . . .**:
- We were woken up **by the noise**. (= The noise woke us up.)
- The telephone was invented **by Alexander Bell** in 1876.
- My brother was bitten **by a dog** last week.

UNIT 20   Exercises

20.1 Write sentences from the words in brackets (   ). All the sentences are present.

1 (this room / clean / every day) *This room is cleaned every day.* ....
2 (how often / the room / clean?) *How often is the room cleaned* .... ?
3 (glass / make / from sand) Glass ....
4 (stamps / sell / in a post office) ....
5 (football / play / in most countries) ....
6 (this machine / not / use / very often) ....
7 (what language / speak / in Ethiopia?)   What .... ?
8 (what / this machine / use / for?) .... ?

20.2 Write sentences from the words in brackets (   ). All the sentences are past.

1 (the room / clean / yesterday) *The room was cleaned yesterday.* ....
2 (when / the room / clean?) *When was the room cleaned* .... ?
3 (this room / paint / last month)   This room ....
4 (these houses / build / about 50 years ago) ....
5 (Ann's bicycle / steal / last week) ....
6 (three people / injure / in the accident) ....
7 (when / this church / build?)   When .... ?
8 (when / television / invent?) .... ?
9 (how / the window / break?) .... ?
10 (anybody / injure / in the accident?) .... ?
11 (why / the letter / send / to the wrong address?) .... ?

20.3 Complete the sentences. Use the passive (present or past) of these verbs:

~~blow~~   **build**   ~~clean~~   **damage**   **find**   **invent**   **make**   **make**   **pay**
show   **speak**   **steal**

1 The room ....*is cleaned*........ every day.
2 Two trees ...*were blown*...... down in the storm last night.
3 Paper .... from wood.
4 There was a fire at the hotel last week. Two rooms ....
5 Many different languages .... in India.
6 These houses are very old. They .... about 500 years ago.
7 Many American programmes .... on British television.
8 'Is this a very old film?' 'Yes, it .... in 1949.'
9 My car .... last week. The next day it .... by the police.
10 The transistor .... in 1948.
11 She has a very good job.   She .... £3000 a month.

20.4 Where were they born?

1 (Ian / Edinburgh)   *Ian was born in Edinburgh.* ....
2 (Sally / Birmingham)   Sally ....
3 (her parents / Ireland) Her ....
4 (you / ???)   I ....
5 (your mother / ???)   My ....

41

UNIT 21 What are you doing tomorrow?
(present for the future)

They **are playing** tennis **now**.

She **is playing** tennis **tomorrow**.

■ We use **am/is/are –ing** (*present continuous*) for something happening now (▶ Units 3–4):
  – 'Where are George and Sue?' 'They**'re playing** tennis in the park.'
  – Please be quiet. I**'m working**.

We also use **am/is/are –ing** for the *future* (tomorrow / next week etc.):
  – Carol **is playing** tennis **tomorrow**.
  – I**'m not working next week**.

I am doing something tomorrow = I have *arranged* to do something, I have a plan to do something:

  – Alice **is going** to the dentist on Friday.
    (= she has an appointment with the dentist)
  – They **are going** to a concert tomorrow evening.
    (they have tickets for the concert)
  – **Are you meeting** Bill this evening?
    (= have you and Bill arranged to meet?)
  – What **are you doing** at the weekend?
  – I**'m not going** out tonight. I**'m staying** at home.
You can also say '**I'm going to do** something' (▶ Unit 22).

■ Do *not* use the present simple (**I go/do you go**? etc.) for arrangements:
  – I**'m going** out this evening. (*not* 'I go')
  – **Are you going** out tonight? (*not* 'do you go')
  – Ann **isn't coming** to the party next week. (*not* 'Ann doesn't come')

But we use the present simple for timetables, programmes, trains etc.:
  – The concert **starts** at 7.30.
  – What time **does the train leave**?

Study the difference:
  – I**'m going** to a concert this evening.
    The concert **starts** at 7.30.
    I'm going – *present continuous*: usually for people
    The concert starts – *present simple*: for programmes, trains etc.

UNIT 21 Exercises

21.1 Look at the pictures. What are these people doing next Friday?

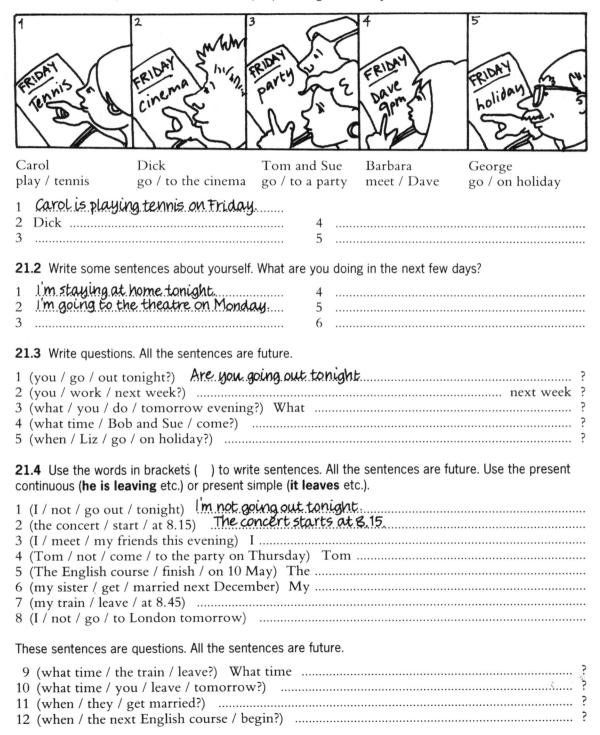

Carol	Dick	Tom and Sue	Barbara	George
play / tennis	go / to the cinema	go / to a party	meet / Dave	go / on holiday

1 *Carol is playing tennis on Friday.*
2 Dick .... 4 ....
3 .... 5 ....

21.2 Write some sentences about yourself. What are you doing in the next few days?

1 *I'm staying at home tonight.* 4 ....
2 *I'm going to the theatre on Monday.* 5 ....
3 .... 6 ....

21.3 Write questions. All the sentences are future.

1 (you / go / out tonight?) *Are you going out tonight* .... ?
2 (you / work / next week?) .... next week ?
3 (what / you / do / tomorrow evening?) What .... ?
4 (what time / Bob and Sue / come?) .... ?
5 (when / Liz / go / on holiday?) .... ?

21.4 Use the words in brackets ( ) to write sentences. All the sentences are future. Use the present continuous (**he is leaving** etc.) or present simple (**it leaves** etc.).

1 (I / not / go out / tonight) *I'm not going out tonight.*
2 (the concert / start / at 8.15) *The concert starts at 8.15*
3 (I / meet / my friends this evening) I ....
4 (Tom / not / come / to the party on Thursday) Tom ....
5 (The English course / finish / on 10 May) The ....
6 (my sister / get / married next December) My ....
7 (my train / leave / at 8.45) ....
8 (I / not / go / to London tomorrow) ....

These sentences are questions. All the sentences are future.

 9 (what time / the train / leave?) What time .... ?
10 (what time / you / leave / tomorrow?) .... ?
11 (when / they / get married?) .... ?
12 (when / the next English course / begin?) .... ?

43

UNIT 22   I'm going to . . .

morning . . .

I'm going to
watch TV
this evening.

this evening...

She **is going to watch** TV this evening.

■ We use **am/is/are going to . . .** for the *future:*

I	**am**			do . . .
he/she/it	**is**	(not)	**going to**	drink . . .
we/you/they	**are**			watch .

am	I		buy . . . ?
is	he/she/it	**going to**	eat . . . ?
are	we/you/they		wear . . . ?

I am going to do something = I have decided to do something, my intention is to do something:

I decided to do it ⟶ | **I'm going to** do it | ─ ─ ─ →

past   *present*   *future*

- **I'm going to buy** some books tomorrow.
- Sarah **is going to sell** her car.
- **I'm not going to have** breakfast this morning. I'm not hungry.
- What **are you going to wear** to the party on Saturday?
- 'Your hair is dirty.' 'Yes, I know. **I'm going to wash** it.'
- **Are you going to invite** John to your party?

■ You can say that something **is going to happen** when it is clear *now* that it is sure to happen:
- Look at the sky! It**'s going to rain.**
  (black clouds *now* → rain)
- Oh dear! It's 9 o'clock and I'm not ready. **I'm going to be** late.
  (9 o'clock *now* and not ready → late)

It's going
to rain.

■ We also use the *present continuous* (**I am -ing**) for the future, usually for arrangements
(▶ Unit 21):
- **I am playing** tennis with Jack tomorrow.

44

UNIT 22   Exercises

22.1 What are these people going to do?

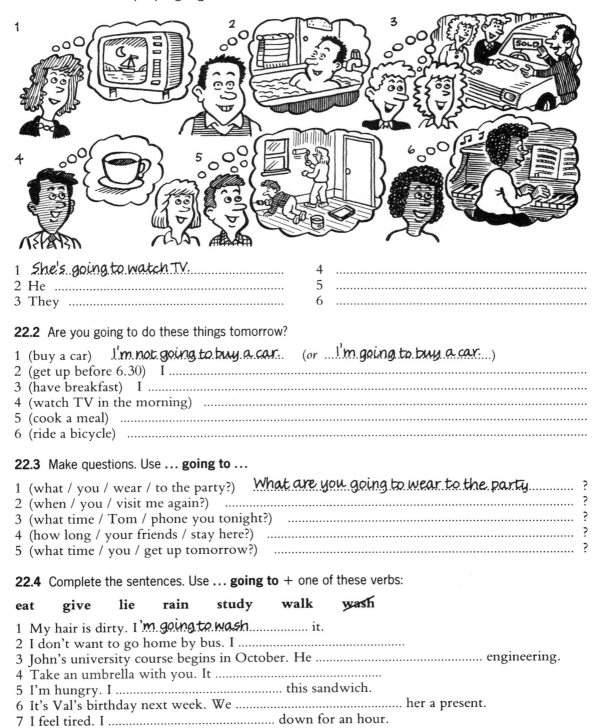

1 *She's going to watch TV.* ....   4 ....
2 He ....   5 ....
3 They ....   6 ....

22.2 Are you going to do these things tomorrow?

1 (buy a car)   *I'm not going to buy a car.*   (or ...*I'm going to buy a car.*...)
2 (get up before 6.30)   I ....
3 (have breakfast)   I ....
4 (watch TV in the morning)   ....
5 (cook a meal)   ....
6 (ride a bicycle)   ....

22.3 Make questions. Use **... going to ...**

1 (what / you / wear / to the party?)   *What are you going to wear to the party* .... ?
2 (when / you / visit me again?)   .... ?
3 (what time / Tom / phone you tonight?)   .... ?
4 (how long / your friends / stay here?)   .... ?
5 (what time / you / get up tomorrow?)   .... ?

22.4 Complete the sentences. Use **... going to** + one of these verbs:

eat   give   lie   rain   study   walk   ~~wash~~

1 My hair is dirty. I *'m going to wash* .... it.
2 I don't want to go home by bus. I ....
3 John's university course begins in October. He .... engineering.
4 Take an umbrella with you. It ....
5 I'm hungry. I .... this sandwich.
6 It's Val's birthday next week. We .... her a present.
7 I feel tired. I .... down for an hour.

45

UNIT 23   will/shall (1)

Bill **is** 24 years old now.

Last year he **was** 23.

Next year he will **be** 25.

■ **will** + *infinitive* (will **be** / will **win** / will **come** etc.):

positive and negative

I/we/you/they he/she/it }	**will (’ll)** **will not (won’t)**	**be** **win** **come** **eat**

question

will	{ I/we/you/they he/she/it	**be?** **win?** **come?** **eat?**

will = **’ll**: **I’ll** (= I will) / you**’ll** / she**’ll** etc.

will not = **won’t**: I **won’t** (= I will not) / you **won’t** / it **won’t** etc.

■ We use **will** for the *future* (**tomorrow** / **next week** etc.):
   – She travels a lot. Today she is in London. Tomorrow she**’ll be** in Rome. Next week
     she**’ll be** in Tokyo.
   – Telephone me this evening. **I’ll be** at home.
   – Leave the old bread in the garden. The birds **will eat** it.
   – We**’ll** probably **go** out this evening.
   – **Will you be** at home this evening?

   – I **won’t be** here tomorrow. (= I will not be here)
   – Don’t drink coffee before you go to bed. You **won’t sleep**.

We often say **I think ... will ...** :
   – **I think** Diana **will pass** the exam.
   – **I don’t think** it **will rain** this afternoon.
   – **Do you think** the examination **will be** difficult?

But do *not* use **will** for things you have *already arranged* to do or *decided* to do   (▶ Units 21–2):
   – We**’re going** to the theatre on Saturday. (*not* ‘we will go’)
   – **Are you working** tomorrow? (*not* ‘will you work’)

■ **shall**
You can say **I shall** (= I will) and **we shall** (= we will):
   – **I shall be** late tomorrow.   *or*   **I will (I’ll) be** late tomorrow.
   – I think **we shall win**.   *or*   I think **we will (we’ll) win**.
But *don’t* use **shall** with **you/they/he/she/it**. (*not* ‘he shall be late’)

▶ Unit 24   **will/shall** (2)

46

UNIT 23   Exercises

23.1 Helen is going on a European tour next month. Look at her plans. Where will she be on these dates?

6 – 9	Paris
9 – 11	Munich
11 – 15	Vienna
16 – 22	Rome
23 – 28	Athens

1 (8th)   She'll be in Paris.
2 (10th) She
3 (25th)
4 (14th)
5 (20th)

23.2 Where will *you* be? Write sentences about yourself. Use **I'll be ... / I'll probably be ... / I don't know where I'll be.**

1 (tomorrow at 10 o'clock)   I'll probably be on the beach.
   (or ...I'll be at work.   or   I don't know where I'll be.   )
2 (one hour from now) I
3 (at midnight)
4 (at 3 o'clock tomorrow afternoon)
5 (two years from now)

23.3 Write the negative.

1 You'll sleep.   You won't sleep.   3 It will happen.
2 I'll forget. I   4 You'll find it.

23.4 Write sentences with **I think ...**   All the sentences are future.

1 (Diana / pass the exam)   I think Diana will pass the exam.
2 (Jack / win the game) I think
3 (Sue / like her present)
4 (the weather / be nice tomorrow)

Now write two sentences with **I don't think ...**

5 (they / get married) I don't
6 (I / be at home this evening)

23.5 The verbs in these sentences are <u>underlined</u>. Which are right? Study Unit 21 before you do this exercise.

1 We ~~'ll go~~ / We are going to the theatre tonight. We've got the tickets.
   (We are going is *right*.)
2 'What <u>will you do</u> / <u>are you doing</u> tomorrow evening?'   'Nothing. I'm free.'
3 <u>I'll go</u> / <u>I'm going</u> away tomorrow morning. My train is at 8.40.
4 I'm sure <u>he'll lend</u> / <u>he's lending</u> you some money. He's very rich.
5 'Why are you putting on your coat?'   '<u>I'll go out</u> / <u>I'm going out</u>.'
6 Do you think Claire <u>will phone</u> / <u>is phoning</u> us tonight?
7 She can't meet us on Saturday. <u>She'll work</u> / <u>She's working</u>.

UNIT 24   will/shall (2)

► Unit 23   **will/shall** (1)

■ You can use **I'll . . .** (= I will) when you *offer* or *decide* to do something:
- 'My case is very heavy.'   **I'll carry** it for you.'
- **'I'll phone** you tomorrow, okay?'   'Okay, goodbye.'

We often say **I think I'll/I don't think I'll . . .** when we decide to do something:
- I'm tired. **I think I'll go** to bed early tonight.
- It's a nice day. **I think I'll sit** in the garden.
- It's raining. **I don't think I'll go** out.

Don't use the present simple (**I go/I phone** etc.) in sentences like these:
- **I'll phone** you tomorrow, okay? (*not* 'I phone you')
- I think **I'll go** to bed early. (*not* 'I go to bed')

Don't use **I'll . . .** for something you decided *before*   (► Units 21–2):
- **I'm working** tomorrow. (*not* 'I'll work')
- **I'm going to watch** TV tonight. (*not* 'I'll watch')
- What **are you doing** at the weekend? (*not* 'what will you do')

■ **Shall I . . . ? / Shall we . . . ?**

Shall I / Shall we . . . ? = Do you think this is a good thing to do? Do you think this is a good idea?
- It's warm in this room. **Shall I open** the window?
- **'Shall I phone** you this evening?'   'Yes, please.'
- I'm going to a party tonight. What **shall I wear**?

- It's a nice day. **Shall we go** for a walk?
- Where **shall we go** for our holidays this year?
- 'Let's go out this evening.'   'Okay, what time **shall we meet**?'   **(Let's ► Unit 48)**

48

UNIT 24   Exercises

24.1 Complete the sentences. Use **I will (I'll)** + one of these verbs:

~~carry~~   do   eat   send   show   sit   stay

1	My case is very heavy.	*I'll carry*... it for you.
2	Enjoy your holiday.	Thank you. I .... you a postcard.
3	I don't want this banana.	Well, I'm hungry. .... it.
4	Are you coming with me?	No, I don't think so. .... here.
5	Did you phone Jack?	Oh no, I forgot. .... it now.
6	Do you want a chair?	No, it's okay. .... on the floor.
7	How do you use this camera?	Give it to me and .... you.

24.2 Complete the sentences. Use **I think I'll ...** or **I don't think I'll ...** + one of these verbs:

buy   ~~go~~   have   play

1 It's cold. *I don't think I'll go*.. out.
2 I'm hungry. I think .... something to eat.
3 I feel tired. I don't .... tennis.
4 This camera is too expensive. I .... it.

24.3 Are the <u>underlined</u> words right or wrong? Correct the sentences that are wrong.

1 <u>I phone</u> you tomorrow morning, okay?   WRONG..I'll phone ....
2 <u>I phone</u> my sister every Friday.   RIGHT...
3 I haven't done the shopping yet. <u>I do</u> it later.   ....
4 'I don't want to drive.' 'Okay, <u>I drive</u>.'   ....
5 'How do you usually go to work?' '<u>I drive</u>.'   ....
6 'I haven't got any money.' '<u>I lend</u> you some.'   ....

24.4 Write sentences with **Shall I ... ?** Choose words from box A and box B.

A	turn on	make
	turn off	~~open~~

B	some sandwiches	the television
	~~the window~~	the light

1	It's warm in this room.	*Shall I open the window*........................... ?
2	This programme isn't very good.	.... ?
3	I'm hungry.	.... ?
4	It's dark in this room.	.... ?

24.5 Write sentences with **Shall we ... ?**   Choose words from box A and box B.

A	what	~~what time~~	where	who

B	buy	go	invite	~~meet~~

1	Let's go out tonight.	Okay, *What time shall we meet*............... ?
2	Let's have a holiday.	Okay, ... ?
3	Let's spend some money.	Okay, ... ?
4	Let's have a party.	Okay, ... ?

49

UNIT 25 can and could

He **can play** the piano.

■ **can** + *infinitive* (can **do** / can **play** / can **come** etc.):

positive and negative

I/we/you/they he/she/it	**can** **can't** (**cannot**)	**do** **play** **come** **see**

question

can	I/we/you/they he/she/it	**do**? **play**? **come**? **see**?

■ **I can do something**. = I *know how* to do it or *it is possible* for me to do it:
  – I **can play** the piano. My brother **can play** the piano too.
  – Ann **can speak** Italian but she **can't speak** Spanish.
  – 'Can you swim?' 'Yes, but not very well.'
  – 'Can you change twenty pounds?' 'I'm sorry I can't.'
  – Bill and Jenny **can't come** to the party next week.

■ In the *past* (**yesterday** / **last week** etc.):

can (do)	→	**could** (do)
can't (do)	→	**couldn't** (do)

  – When I was young, I **could run** very fast.
  – Before she came to Britain, she **couldn't speak** English. Now she **can speak** English very well.
  – I was tired last night but I **couldn't sleep**.
  – Bill and Jenny **couldn't come** to the party last week.

We use **Can you . . . ?** *or* **Could you . . . ?** when we ask people to do things:
  – 'Can (*or* Could) you open the door, please?' 'Yes, sure.'
  – Can (*or* Could) you tell me the time, please?

We use **Can I . . . ?** when we ask if it is okay to do something:
  – 'Tom, **can I take** your umbrella?' 'Yes, of course.'
  – (*on the phone*) Hello. **Can I speak** to Gary, please?

We use **Can I have . . . ?** to ask for something:
  – (*in a shop*) **Can I have** these postcards, please?

UNIT 25   Exercises

25.1 Ask someone if he or she can do these things:

I	2	3	4	5	6
swim	ski	play chess	drive	run ten kilometres	ride a horse

1 ..Can you swim............ ?   3 .... ?   5 .... ?
2 .... you .... ?   4 .... ?   6 .... ?

Can you do these things? Write sentences about yourself. Use **I can** or **I can't** ...

7 I can't swim...................   9 ....   11 ....
8 I ....   10 ....   12 ....

25.2 Complete these sentences. Use **can** or **can't** + one of these verbs:

~~come~~   **find**   **hear**   **see**   **speak**

1 I'm sorry, but we .....can't come........... to your party next Saturday.
2 She got the job because she .... five languages.
3 You are speaking very quietly. I .... you.
4 Have you seen my bag? I .... it.
5 I like this hotel room. You .... the mountains from the window.

25.3 Complete these sentences. Use **can't** or **couldn't** + one of these verbs:

eat   **go**   **go**   **see**   ~~sleep~~   **understand**

1 I was tired but I ..couldn't sleep............
2 She spoke very quickly. I .... her.
3 His eyes are not very good. He .... very well.
4 I wasn't hungry yesterday. I .... my dinner.
5 He .... to the concert next Saturday. He's working.
6 He .... to the meeting last week. He was ill.

25.4 What do you say in these situations? Use **Can you ... ? / Could you ... ? / Can I ... ?**

1 (You are carrying a lot of things. You want me to open the door for you.)
   You say to me: ..Can you open the door (for me) please............................... ?
2 (We are having dinner. You want me to pass the salt.)
   You say to me: .... ?
3 (You want me to turn off the radio.) .... ?
4 (You want to borrow my pen.) .... ?
5 (You are in my house. You want to use my phone.) .... ?
6 (You want me to give you my address.) .... ?

51

UNIT 26   **may** and **might**

I **may go** to Paris.   It **might rain**.
(= Perhaps I will go to Paris.)   (= Perhaps it will rain.)

■ **may** *or* **might** + *infinitive* (may **go** / might **go** / may **play** / might **play** etc.):

		be
I/we/you/they } he/she/it }	**may** (not) **might** (not)	**go** **play** **come**

■ **may/might** = it is possible that something will happen.
You can use **may** *or* **might**:
  – I **may go** to the cinema this evening.
  or I **might go** to the cinema this evening. (= perhaps I will go)
  – 'When is Kay going to phone you?'   'I don't know. She **may phone** this after-
    noon.'
  – Take an umbrella with you. It **might rain**.
  – 'Do you think Jack will come to the party?'   'I'm not sure. **He may**.' (= He may
    come.)
  – 'Are you going out tonight?'   '**I might**.' (= I might go out.)

Study the difference:
  – **I'm playing** tennis tomorrow. *(sure)*
    I **may play** tennis tomorrow. *(possible)*
  – Barbara **is going** to France next week. *(sure)*
    Barbara **might go** to France next week. *(possible)*

■ The negative is **may not** *or* **might not**:
  – I **might not go** to work tomorrow. (= perhaps I will not go)
  – Sue **may not come** to the party. (= perhaps she will not come)

■ **May I .... ?** = Is it okay to do something?:
  – **May I smoke**? (= Is it okay if I smoke? / Can I smoke?)
  – '**May I sit** here?'   'Yes, of course.'

UNIT 26 Exercises

26.1 Write sentences with **may** or **might**.

1 (perhaps I will go to the cinema) ...I may go to the cinema...
2 (perhaps I will see Tom tomorrow) I ....
3 (perhaps Kay will be late) Kay ....
4 (perhaps it will snow today) It ....
5 (perhaps I will wear my new jeans) I ....

These sentences are negative.

6 (perhaps they will not come) ....
7 (perhaps I will not go out tonight) I ....

26.2 Somebody is asking you about your plans. You have some ideas but you are not sure. Use **may** or **might** + one of these:

?	go away this evening	some shoes to a restaurant	Spain tomorrow	fish	?

1 | Where are you going for your holidays next year? | I'm not sure yet. I might go to Spain.
2 | Where are you going tonight? | I don't know yet. I ....
3 | When will you see Ann again? | I'm not sure. ....
4 | What are you going to buy when you go shopping? | I haven't decided yet. ....
5 | What are you doing at the weekend? |
6 | When are you going to phone John? |
7 | What are you going to have for dinner tonight? |

26.3 What are you doing tomorrow? Write *true* sentences about yourself. Use:
I'm (not) -ing   or   **I'm (not) going to...**   or   **I may...**   or   **I might...**

1 (watch television) I'm not going to watch television...
2 (write a letter) ...I might write a letter...
3 (get up early) I ....
4 (go to the cinema) ....
5 (have a bath or shower) ....
6 (buy a newspaper) ....
7 (play tennis) ....
8 (make a telephone call) ....

UNIT 27   must

must + *infinitive* (must **do** / must **see** etc.):

I/we/you/they he/she/it }	**must**	**do** **go** **stop** **write**

■ Use **must** when you think it is necessary or very important to do something:
- The windows are very dirty. I **must clean** them.
- It's a fantastic film. You **must see** it.
- We **must go** to the bank today. We haven't got any money.

must is *present* or *future*:
- I **must go** to the bank now.
- I **must go** to the bank tomorrow.

■ For the *past* (**yesterday** / **last week** etc.), we use **had to** + *infinitive* (**had to go** / **had to do** / **had to write** etc.):
- I **had to go** to the bank yesterday. (= It was necessary for me to go to the bank.)
- We **had to walk** home last night. There was no bus.

▶ Unit 29   **have to ...**

■ **mustn't** (must not)
I **mustn't** do it = it is important *not* to do it, it is a bad thing to do:

- I **must hurry**. I **mustn't be** late.
- I **mustn't forget** to phone George.
  (= I must remember)
- You **mustn't walk** on the grass.
  (= Don't walk on the grass.)

■ **needn't** (need not)
I **needn't** do it = it is *not necessary* to do it, I don't need to do it:
- I **needn't clean** the windows. They aren't dirty.
- You **needn't go** to the bank. I can give you some money.

You can also say **don't need to ...** (= needn't):
- I **don't need to clean** the windows.
- You **don't need to go** to the bank.

UNIT 27   Exercises

27.1 Complete the sentences. Use **must** + one of these verbs:

be   buy   ~~go~~   go   help   hurry   learn   meet   phone   read
wash   win

1 We .....*must go*...... to the bank today. We haven't got any money.
2 I .... I haven't got much time.
3 She's a very interesting person. You .... her.
4 I forgot to phone Dave last night. I .... him today.
5 You .... to drive. It's very useful.
6 This is an excellent book. You .... it.
7 We .... some food. We've got nothing for dinner.
8 My hair is dirty. I .... it.
9 I .... to the post office. I need some stamps.
10 I have a big problem. You .... me.
11 The game tomorrow is very important for us. We ....
12 You can't always have things immediately. You .... patient.

27.2 Put in **must** or **had to**.

1 I ..*had to*.... go to the bank yesterday to get some money.
2 The windows are very dirty. I .... clean them.
3 The windows were very dirty yesterday. I .... clean them.
4 I .... get up early tomorrow. I've got a lot to do.
5 Come on! We .... hurry. We haven't got much time.
6 We arrived home very late last night. We .... wait half an hour for a taxi.
7 These cakes are very nice. You .... have one.
8 Ann came to the party but she didn't stay very long. She .... leave early.
9 He didn't know how to use the machine. I .... show him.
10 I was nearly late for my appointment this morning. I .... run to get there on time.

27.3 Complete the sentences. Use **mustn't** or **needn't** + one of these verbs:

~~be~~   buy   ~~clean~~   hurry   lose   stick   take   tell   wait

1 The windows aren't dirty. You ...*needn't clean*......
   them.
2 I must hurry. I ....*mustn't be*........ late.
3 This letter is very important. You ....
   it.
4 We have lots of time. We ....
5 We .... an umbrella. It's not going to
   rain.
6 This is a secret. You .... anybody.
7 You ....,................... a newspaper. You can have
   mine.
8 I'm not ready yet but you .... for me.
   You go now and I'll come later.
9 (*a parent speaking to a child*) You ....
   your tongue out at people. It's not polite.

UNIT 28   should

You shouldn't smoke so much...

should + *infinitive* (should **do** / should **write** etc.):

I/we/you/they ⎱ he/she/it ⎰	should shouldn't	do go stop write

■ (Someone) **should** do something = It is a good thing to do or the right thing to do:
  – Tom **should go** to bed earlier. He usually goes to bed very late and he's always tired.
  – It's a good film. You **should go** and see it.
  – When you play tennis, you **should** always **watch** the ball.

■ **shouldn't** (*or* **should not**) = It's *not* a good thing to do or it's not the right thing to do:
  – Tom **shouldn't go** to bed so late.
  – You work all the time. You **shouldn't work** so hard.

■ We often use **think** with **should**:

> **I think ... should ...:**
>   – **I think** Carol **should buy** some new clothes.
>   (= I think it's a good idea)
>   – It's late. **I think** we **should go** home now.
>   – 'Shall I buy this coat?'
>   'Yes, **I think** you **should**.'
>
> **I don't think ... should ...:**
>   – **I don't think** you **should work** so hard.
>   (= I don't think it's a good idea)
>   – **I don't think** the police **should carry** guns.
>
> **Do you think ... should ...?:**
>   – **Do you think** I **should buy** this jacket?
>   – What time **do you think** we **should go** home?

Do you think I should buy this hat?

■ **must** (▶ Unit 27) is stronger than **should**:
  – It's a **good** film. You **should** go and see it.
  – It's a **fantastic** film. You **must** go and see it.

■ Another way of saying **should** is **ought to ...**:
  – It's a good film. You **ought to go** and see it. (= You should go and see it.)

UNIT 28   Exercises

28.1 Complete the sentences. Use **should** + one of these verbs:

clean   go   read   visit   ~~watch~~   wear

1. When you play tennis, you *should watch* the ball.
2. You look tired. You .... to bed.
3. You .... your teeth after every meal.
4. The city museum is very interesting. You .... it.
5. When you are driving, you .... a seat-belt.
6. It's a good book. You .... it.

28.2 Make sentences with **shouldn't ... so ...**

1. (you smoke too much) *You shouldn't smoke so much.* ....
2. (you work too hard) You .... so hard.
3. (he eats too much) He .... much.
4. (she watches TV too often) She ....
5. (you talk too much) You ....

28.3 You ask a friend for advice. Make questions with **Do you think I should ...?**

1. (buy this jacket?) *Do you think I should buy this jacket* .... ?
2. (buy a new camera?) Do you think .... ?
3. (get a new job?) Do .... ?
4. (do an English course?) .... ?
5. (learn to drive?) .... ?

28.4 Write sentences with **I think ... should ...** Choose from:

have a holiday   go to university   sell it   ~~go home now~~   go to the doctor

1. It's late. *I think we should go home now.* ....
2. Your car is very old. I think you ....
3. They need a change. I ....
4. He doesn't look well. ....
5. She's very intelligent. ....

Write sentences with **I don't think ... should ...** Choose from:

stay there   ~~phone them now~~   go to work today   get married

6. It's very late. *I don't think you should phone them now.* ....
7. They're too young. I don't think ....
8. That hotel is too expensive for us. I ....
9. You're not very well. ....

28.5 What do you think? Write sentences with **should**.

1. I think everybody should ....
2. I think .... should ....
3. I don't think ....

57

UNIT 29   have to ...

■ **I have to do something** = it is necessary for me to do it, I am obliged to do it:

I/we/you/they **have**	**to do** **to work**
he/she/it **has**	**to go** **to wear**

- I'll be late for work tomorrow. I **have to go** to the dentist.
- Jill starts work at 7.00, so she **has to get** up at 6.00.
- You **have to pass** a test before you can get a driving licence.

■ The *past* (**yesterday / last week** etc.) is **had to . . .**:
- I was late for work yesterday. I **had to go** to the dentist.
- There was no bus, so we **had to walk** home.

■ In *questions* and *negatives* we use **do/does** (*present*) and **did** (*past*):

present

do I/we/you/they } **have to . . . ?**
does he/she/it

I/we/you/they **don't** } **have to . . .**
he/she/it **doesn't**

past

did { I/we/you/they } **have to . . . ?**
        { he/she/it

I/we/you/they } **didn't have to . . .**
he/she/it

- What time **do you have to get** up tomorrow morning?
- **Does Jill have to work** on Saturdays?
- Why **did they have to leave** the party early?

■ I **don't have to** do (something) = it is *not* necessary to do it:·
- I'm not working tomorrow, so I **don't have to get** up early.
- Ian **doesn't have to work** very hard. He's got an easy job.
- We **didn't have to wait** very long. The bus soon came.

■ **have to** and **must**   (must ▶ Unit 27)

Use **must** when you say what *you* think is necessary, when you are giving *your* opinion. Usually, **have to** is also possible:
- It's a fantastic film. You **must** see it. (*or* 'You **have to** see it.')

Use **have to** (*not* **must**) when you are *not* giving your personal opinion:
- Jill won't be here this afternoon. She **has to** go to the doctor. (This is *not* my opinion – it is a fact.)
- In many countries, men **have to** do military service. (This is *not* my opinion – it is the law in those countries.)

UNIT 29   Exercises

29.1 Complete the sentences. Use **have to** or **has to** + one of these verbs:

do   read   speak   travel   ~~wear~~

1 My eyes are not very good. I ...*have to wear*........ glasses.
2 At the end of the course, all the students .... a test.
3 Mary is studying literature. She .... a lot of books.
4 He doesn't understand much English, so I ....,..... very slowly to him.
5 George is not often at home. He .... a lot in his job.

29.2 Complete the sentences. Use **have to** or **had to** + one of these verbs:

answer   buy   change   get   go   ~~walk~~

1 There were no buses yesterday evening. We .....*had to walk*........ home.
2 I'm going to bed early tonight. I .... up early tomorrow morning.
3 It's late. I .... now. I'll see you tomorrow.
4 I went to the supermarket after work because I .... some food.
5 This train doesn't go to London. You .... at Bristol.
6 We did an exam yesterday. We .... six questions out of ten.

29.3 Write questions. Some are present and some are past.

1	I have to get up early tomorrow.	What time *do you have to get up*	?
2	They had to leave early.	Why	?
3	We had to pay a lot of money.	How much .... you	?
4	I have to go home now.	Why	?
5	He had to wait a long time.	How long	?
6	Joy has to work this evening.	Why	?

29.4 Write sentences with **don't/doesn't/didn't have to ...**

1 Why are you going home now?   You *don't have to go home now.*..........................
2 Why is she waiting?   She doesn't ....
3 Why did you get up so early?   You ....
4 Why do you want to decide now?   We ....
5 Why does he work so hard?   He ....

29.5 Put in **have to / has to / had to** or **must**.

1 It's a fantastic film, you .*must (or have to)*. see it.
2 In many countries men ......*have to*............ do military service.
3 Sarah is a nurse. Sometimes she .... work at weekends.
4 I didn't have any money with me, so I .... borrow some.
5 You can't park here for nothing. You .... pay.
6 I eat too much chocolate. I really .... stop.
7 In tennis you .... hit the ball over the net.

59

UNIT 30　Would you like . . . ?

■ **Would you like . . . ?** = Do you want . . . ?
We use **Would you like . . . ?** to *offer* things:
- 'Would you like some coffee?'
  'Yes, please.'
- 'Would you like a cigarette?'
  'No, thank you. I don't smoke.'
- 'What would you like, tea or coffee?'
  'Tea, please.'

We use **Would you like to . . . ?** to *invite* someone:
- Would you like to come to a party?
- 'Would you like to have dinner with me on Sunday?'
  'Yes, I'd love to.' (= I would love to have dinner with you.)
- Where would you like to go this evening?

■ **I'd like** (**I would like**) is a polite way of saying 'I want':
- (*in a restaurant*) I'd like fish, please.
- I'm thirsty. I'd like a drink.
- I'd like to see the film on television this evening.

■ Study the difference:
Would you like . . . ? / I'd like . . .　　　　**Do you like . . . ? / I like . . .**

'Would you like some tea?' = Do you want some tea? (*an offer*)

'Do you like tea?' = Do you think tea is nice?

- 'Would you like to go to the cinema tonight?' (*tonight*)
  'Yes, I'd love to go.'
but　'Do you like going to the cinema?' (*in general*)
  'Yes, I go to the cinema a lot.'

- I'd like an orange. (= I want an orange now.)
but　I like oranges. (*in general*)

▶ Unit 47　**Do you like going . . . ?** and **Would you like to go . . . ?**

UNIT 30   Exercises

30.1 Look at the pictures. What are the people saying? Use **Would you like ... ?** + one of these:
an apple / a biscuit / some cake / some cheese / a cup of coffee / a sandwich.

1 ..Would you like.. ..a cup of coffee.. ?
2 .... ?
3 .... ?
4 .... ?
5 .... ?
6 .... ?

30.2 Invite people to do things. Use **Would you like to ... ?**

1 (invite someone to come to a party next Friday)
  Would you like to come to a party next Friday .... ?
2 (invite someone to go to a concert on Sunday)
  .... on Sunday?
3 (invite someone to play tennis tomorrow)
  .... ?
4 (invite someone to dance) .... ?

30.3 Choose the correct form.

1 'Do you like / Would you like a cigarette?'   'Yes, please.'
  Would you like is *right*.
2 'Do you like / Would you like a banana?'   'No, thank you.'
3 'Do you like / Would you like bananas?'   'Yes, I love them.'
4 'What do you like / would you like to drink?'   'Water, please.'
5 'Do you like / Would you like to go out for a walk?'   'Not now. Perhaps later.'
6 I like / I'd like ice-cream but I don't eat it very often.
7 I'm tired. I like / I'd like to go to sleep.
8 'Do you like / Would you like something to eat?'   'No, thanks. I'm not hungry.'

61

UNIT 31   there is   there are

There's a man on the roof.

There's a train at 10.30.

There are seven days in a week.

singular:

there is . . .	**(there's)**
there is not . . .	**(there isn't** *or* **there's not)**
is there . . . ?	

– **There's** a big tree in the garden.
– **There's** a good film on TV this evening. I'm going to watch it.
– Excuse me **is there** a hotel near here?
– 'Have you got any money?' 'Yes, **there's** some in my bag.'
– We can't go skiing. **There isn't** any snow.

plural:

there are . . .	
there are not . . .	**(there aren't)**
are there . . . ?	

– **There are** some big trees in the garden.
– **Are there** any letters for me today?
– This is a modern town. **There aren't** many old buildings here.
– **How many players are there** in a football team?
– **There are 11 players** in a football team.

■ there is and it is

there is

There's a book on the table.
(*not* 'It's a book on the table.')

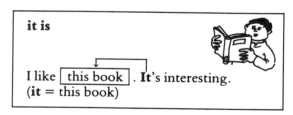

it is

I like this book . **It**'s interesting.
(**it** = this book)

Compare:
– A: What's that noise ?   B: **It**'s a train. (**it** = that noise)

There's a train at 10.30.   **It**'s a fast train. (**it** = the 10.30 train)

– **There is** a lot of salt in this soup.

I don't like this soup . **It**'s too salty. (**it** = this soup)

UNIT 31   Exercises

31.1 What's in the box? Ask questions with **Is there ... ?** and **Are there ... ?**

1 (any cigarettes?) *Are there any cigarettes in the box* ?
2 (any books?) .... in the box ?
3 (a man?) .... ?
4 (any money?) .... ?
5 (any clothes?) .... ?
6 (a key?) .... ?

31.2 Dunford is a small town. Look at the information in the box and write sentences with **There is/ isn't/are/aren't ...**

sports centre	Yes	1	*There is a sports centre in Dunford.*
swimming-pool	No	→ 2	.... in Dunford.
hospital	Yes	3	....
cinemas	Yes (two)	4	....
university	No	5	....
big hotels	No	6	....
cathedral	Yes	7	....

31.3 Put in **there is / there isn't / is there? / there are / there aren't / are there?**

1 Dunford is a very modern town. *There aren't* many old buildings.
2 Look! .... a photograph of George in the newspaper!
3 Excuse me, ... a restaurant near here?
4 .... five people in my family: my parents, my two sisters and me.
5 We can't take any photographs. .... a film in the camera.
6 How many students .... in your class?
7 Where can we sit? .... any chairs.
8 .... a bus from the city centre to the airport?

31.4 Write sentences with **There are ...**   Choose the right number: 7 9 15 26 30 50.

1 (days / a week)   *There are seven days in a week.*
2 (states / the USA)   ....
3 (players / a rugby team)   ....
4 (planets / the solar system) ....
5 (letters / the English alphabet) ....
6 (days / September)   ....

31.5 Put in **there** or **it**.

1 *There*'s a train at 10.30.   *It*'s a fast train.
2 I'm not going to buy this shirt.   ....'s very expensive.
3 'What's wrong?' '.............'s something in my eye.'
4 ....'s a car in front of the house. Is .... your car?
5 'Is .... anything on TV?'   'Yes, ...'s a film at 8.15.'
6 ....'s a letter on the floor. Is .... for you?

63

UNIT 32   there was / were / has been / will be

there	is/are was/were has been / have been will be	► Unit 31 **was/were** ► Unit 11 **has/have been** ► Units 15–17 **will** ► Unit 23

---

there was/were

The time is now 11 o'clock.

There was a train at 10.30.

Compare:

there is/are (*present*)
- **There is** a good film on TV this evening.
- We are staying at a very big hotel. **There are** 250 rooms.
- I'm hungry but **there isn't** anything to eat.

- **Are there** any letters for me this morning?

there was/were (*past*)
- **There was** a good film on TV yesterday evening.
- We stayed at a very big hotel. **There were** 250 rooms.
- When I arrived home, I was hungry but **there wasn't** anything to eat.
- **Were there** any letters for me yesterday morning?

---

there has been / there have been

There's been an accident.

- Look! **There's been** an accident. (there**'s** been = there **has** been)
- This road is very dangerous. **There have been** many accidents on it.

but There **was** an accident **last night**. (*not* 'has been . . . last night' ► Unit 19)

---

there will be

- Do you think **there will be** a lot of people at the party on Saturday?
- (*from the weather forecast*) Tomorrow the weather will be cold. **There will be** some rain in the afternoon.

UNIT 32 Exercises

32.1 Look at the two pictures. Now the room is empty but before it was full of things. Write sentences about the things in the list. Use **There was/were...**

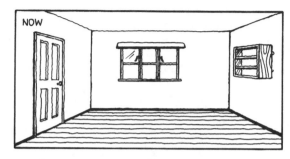

an armchair   some books   a carpet   a clock   some flowers
some pictures   a sofa   a small table

1 .....There was a clock... on the wall near the window.
2 .... on the floor.
3 .... on the wall near the door.
4 .... in the middle of the room.
5 .... on the table.
6 .... on the shelves.
7 .... in the corner near the door.
8 .... opposite the door.

32.2 Put in **there was / there wasn't / was there? / there were / there weren't / were there?**

1 I was hungry but ..there wasn't... anything to eat.
2 .Were there....... any letters for me yesterday?
3 .... a football match on TV last night but I didn't see it.
4 'We stayed at a nice hotel.'   'Did you?   .... a swimming-pool?'
5 The suitcase was empty.   .... any clothes in it.
6 I found a wallet in the street but .... any money in it.
7 '........................... many people at the meeting?'   'No, very few.'
8 We didn't visit the museum.   .... enough time.
9 I'm sorry I'm late.   .... a lot of traffic.
10 The radio wasn't working because .... any batteries in it.

32.3 Put in **there is / there are / there was / there were / there has been / there will be**.

1 .There was.......... a good film on TV yesterday evening.
2 Look! .There has been.. an accident. Call an ambulance!
3 .... 24 hours in a day.
4 .... a party at the club last Friday but I didn't go.
5 Look! This bag is empty.   .... nothing in it.
6 'Why are those policemen outside the bank?'   '........................... a robbery.'
7 When we arrived at the cinema, ... a long queue outside.
8 .... somebody at the station to meet you when you arrive tomorrow.
9 Ten years ago .... 500 children at the school. Now .... over a
  thousand.

UNIT 33   it...

■ **it** for *time/day/distance/weather*

time		What time is **it**? **It**'s half past ten. (10.30) **It**'s late. **It**'s time to go home.
day		What day is **it**? **It**'s 16 March. **It**'s Thursday today. **It**'s my birthday today.
distance		How far is **it** from London to Bristol? **It**'s a long way from here to the airport. We can walk home. **It** isn't far.★ **It**'s 20 miles from our village to the nearest town. ★ Use **far** in *questions* (**is it far?**) and *negatives* (**it isn't far**). Use **a long way** in *positive sentences* (**it's a long way**).
weather		**It**'s raining. **It** isn't raining. Is **it** snowing? **It** rains/snows/rained/snowed. **It**'s warm/hot/cold/fine/cloudy/windy/sunny/foggy/dark etc. **It**'s a nice day today.

Compare **it** and **there**:
- **It rains** a lot in winter. (**rains** is a *verb*)

but **There is a lot of rain** in winter. (**rain** is a *noun*)
- **It** was very **windy.** (**windy** is an *adjective*)

but **There was a** strong **wind** yesterday. (**wind** is a *noun*)

there is and **it is** ▶ Unit 31

■ **it's nice to** ... etc.

It's	easy/difficult/impossible/dangerous/safe/stupid/ cheap/expensive/nice/good/wonderful/terrible etc.	to ...

- **It** 's nice **to see** you again . (**it** = to see you again)
- **It's impossible to understand** her. (**it** = to understand her)
- **It wasn't easy to find** your house. (**it** = to find your house)

■ Don't forget **it**:
- **It**'s raining again. (*not* 'Is raining again.')
- Is **it** true that you are married? (*not* 'Is true that ... ?')

UNIT 33   Exercises

33.1 Put in **it is (it's)** or **is it?**

1 What time .*is it*.. ?
2 ..*It's*... raining again.
3 .... very late. We must go home.
4 '............ cold out?'   'Yes, put on your coat.'
5 .... true that Bill can fly a helicopter?
6 'What day .... today? .... Thursday?'   'No, Friday.'
7 .... about three miles from the airport to the city centre.
8 .... possible for me to phone you at your office?
9 'Shall we walk to the restaurant?'   'I don't know. How far .... ?'
10 .... Jack's birthday today. He's 27.
11 .... a pity that Ann can't come to the party on Saturday.
12 I don't believe it!   .... impossible!

33.2 Write questions with **How far ... ?**

1 (here / the airport?)   .*How far is it from here to the airport*.............................. ?
2 (New York / Washington?)   How .... Washington?
3 (your house / the station?)   .... ?
4 (the hotel / the beach?)   .... ?

33.3 Put in **it** or **there**.

1 ...*It*...... rains a lot in winter.
2 .*There*. was a strong wind yesterday.
3 Look!   ....'s snowing.
4 We can't go skiing.   .... isn't any snow.
5 'Did .... rain yesterday?'   'No, ... was fine.'
6 ....'s dark in this room. Can you turn on the light?
7 ....'s a big black cloud in the sky.   ....'s going to rain.
8 .... was a storm last night. Did you hear it?
9 ....'s a long way from here to the nearest shop.

33.4 Complete the sentences. Use **it's** + (*box 1*) + **to** + (*box 2*).

it's	box 1		to	box 2	
	difficult	dangerous		see you again	meet people
	~~easy~~	impossible		wear	go out alone
	easy	nice		~~understand him~~	sleep
		stupid			save

1 .*It's easy to understand him*.. because he speaks very slowly.
2 ...., Jill. How are you?
3 .... at night. There is always a lot of noise.
4 A lot of cities are not safe.   .... at night.
5 If you haven't got a well-paid job, ... money.
6 .... warm clothes in hot weather.
7 Everybody is very friendly in this town. ....

67

UNIT 34   go/going   work/working   play/playing etc.

■ **go/work/play** etc. (*infinitive*)
We use the *infinitive* (**go/work/play/be** etc.) after:

will	Tom **will be** here tomorrow.	▶ Units 23–4
shall	**Shall** I **open** the window?	▶ Units 23–4
can	I **can't play** tennis.	▶ Unit 25
could	**Could** you **pass** the salt, please?	▶ Unit 25
may	**May** I **smoke**?	▶ Unit 26
might	I **might be** late tonight.	▶ Unit 26
must	It's late. I **must go** now.	▶ Unit 27
should	You **shouldn't work** so hard.	▶ Unit 28
would	**Would** you **like** some coffee?	▶ Unit 30

We use the *infinitive* with **do/does/did**:

do	**Do** you **work**?	I **don't work**.
does	How much **does** it **cost**?	She **doesn't play** tennis.
did	What time **did** they **leave**?	We **didn't sleep** very well.

do/does (*present simple*) ▶ Units 6–7   **did** (*past simple*) ▶ Unit 10

■ **to go / to work / to play** etc. (**to** + *infinitive*)
We use **to . . .** (**to go / to work / to play / to be** etc.) after:

(I'm) **going** (**to . . .**)	**I'm going to play** tennis tomorrow. What **are** you **going to do**?	▶ Unit 22
(I) **have** (**to . . .**)	I **have to go** now. Everybody **has to eat**.	▶ Unit 29
(I) **want** (**to . . .**)	Do you **want to go** out? They don't **want to come** with us.	▶ Unit 47
(I) **would like** (**to . . .**)	**I'd like to be** rich. **Would you like to go** out?	▶ Unit 30

■ **going/working/playing** etc.
We use **-ing** with **am/is/are/was/were**:

am/is/are **was/were**	} + **-ing**	*present continuous*	▶ Units 3–4, 21
		past continuous	▶ Unit 12

– Please be quiet. **I'm working**.
– Tom **isn't working** today.
– What time **are** you **going** out?
– We didn't go out because it **was raining**.
– What **were** you **doing** at 11 o'clock yesterday morning?

▶ Unit 47   **to . . . (I want to do)** and **-ing (I enjoy doing)**

68

UNIT 34   Exercises

34.1 Finish each of these sentences. Write '... **phone Jack**' or '... **to phone Jack**'.

1 I'll .phone. Jack.
2 I'm going .to. phone. Jack.
3 Can you .... Jack?
4 Shall I .... ?
5 I'd like ....

6 I have ....
7 You should ....
8 I want ....
9 I might ....
10 You must ....

34.2 Complete the sentences with a verb from the box. Sometimes you need the infinitive (**go/work** etc.) and sometimes you need **-ing** (**going/working** etc.).

do/doing	drive/driving	eat/eating	get/getting	go/going
listen/listening	rain/raining	~~sleep/sleeping~~	stay/staying	wait/waiting
watch/watching	wear/wearing	~~work/working~~		

1 Please be quiet. I'm .working..
2 I feel tired. I didn't .sleep....... very well last night.
3 What time do you usually .... up in the morning?
4 'Where are you .... ?' 'To the shop.'
5 Did you .... television last night?
6 Put up your umbrella. It's ....
7 The police stopped her because she was .... the car too fast.
8 You can turn off the radio. I'm not .... to it.
9 They didn't .... anything because they weren't hungry.
10 'What are you .... this evening?' 'I'm .... at home.'
11 'Does she always .... glasses?' 'No, only for reading.'
12 My friends were .... for me when I arrived.

34.3 Put in the correct form. Choose the infinitive (**go/open** etc.), **to** + infinitive (**to go / to open** etc.) or **-ing** (**going/opening** etc.).

1 Shall I ...open.... the window? (open)
2 It's late. I have ..to.go.... now. (go)
3 Tom isn't ....working........ this week. He's on holiday. (work)
4 Do you want .... out this evening? (go)
5 'Where are you .... for your holidays this year?' (go)
    'We're not sure, but we may .... to Italy.' (go)
6 I'm afraid I can't .... you. (help)
7 It's a really good film. You must .... it. (see)
8 What time do you have .... tomorrow morning? (leave)
9 Do you think it will .... this afternoon? (rain)
10 I'm hungry. I'm going .... something to eat. (have)
11 My brother is .... physics at university. (study)
12 He spoke very quietly. I couldn't .... him. (hear)
13 I'm very tired. I must .... down for a few minutes. (lie)
14 I was very tired. I had .... down for a few minutes. (lie)
15 Would you like .... out for dinner this evening? (go)
16 You don't look well. I don't think you should .... out. (go)

69

UNIT 35   be/have/do in *present* and *past tenses*

■ **be (am/is/are/was/were) –ing (cleaning/working/doing** etc.)**
present continuous and past continuous

am/is/are –ing *present continuous* ▶ Units 3–4, 21

- Please be quiet. **I'm working**.
- It **isn't raining** at the moment.
- What **are** you **doing** this evening?

was/were –ing *past continuous* ▶ Unit 12

- I **was working** when she arrived.
- It **wasn't raining**, so we went out.
- What **were** you **doing** at 3 o'clock?

■ **be (am/is/are/was/were) +** *past participle* **(cleaned/made/eaten** etc.)
passive

am/is/are + *past participle* *present passive* ▶ Unit 20

- The room **is cleaned** every day.
- I **am** never **invited** to parties.
- Oranges **are imported** into Britain.

was/were + *past participle* *past passive* ▶ Unit 20

- The room **was cleaned** yesterday.
- These houses **were built** 100 years ago.
- How **was** the window **broken**?

■ **have/has +** *past participle* **(cleaned/lost/eaten/been/gone** etc.)
present perfect

have/has + *past participle* *present perfect* ▶ Units 15–17

- I **have cleaned** my room.
- Tom **has lost** his passport.
- Barbara **hasn't been** to Canada.
- Where **have** they **gone**?

■ **do/does/did +** *infinitive* **(clean/like/eat/go** etc.)
present simple and past simple – negatives and questions

do/does + *infinitive* *present simple negatives* *and questions*   ▶ Units 6–7

- I like coffee but I **don't like** tea.
- Tom **doesn't smoke**.
- What **do** you usually **do** at weekends?
- **Does** Barbara **live** alone?

did + *infinitive* *past simple negatives* *and questions*   ▶ Unit 10

- I **didn't watch** TV yesterday.
- It **didn't rain** last week.
- What time **did** Barbara **go** out?

UNIT 35 Exercises

35.1 Put in **is/are/do/does**.

1 ..*Do*.... you clean your teeth every day?
2 Where .*are*. they going?
3 Why .... you looking at me?
4 .... Bill live in London?
5 .... you like dancing?
6 .... the sun shining?
7 What time .... the shops close?

8 .... you working tomorrow?
9 .... Alice work on Saturdays?
10 What .... this word mean?
11 What time .... you going out?
12 What time .... you usually go out?
13 .... it raining?
14 .... you feeling all right?

35.2 Put in **am not / isn't / aren't / don't / doesn't**. All these sentences are negative.

1 Tom .*doesn't*............. smoke.
2 It .....*isn't*.............. raining at the moment.
3 I .... want to go out this evening.
4 I .... going out this evening.
5 George .... working this week.
6 My parents .... watch television very often.
7 Tom and Ann .... coming to the party next week.
8 Barbara .... speak a foreign language.
9 I'm sorry, I .... understand. Can you say that again, please?
10 You can turn off the television. I .... watching it.

35.3 Put in **was/were/did/have/has**.

1 Where .*were*.. your shoes made?
2 ..*Did*... you go out last night?
3 What .... you doing at 10.30?
4 Where .... he buy his new coat?
5 Where .... she born?
6 Where .... you born?
7 .... Chris gone home?

8 What time .... she go?
9 What .... she wearing yesterday?
10 When .... this road built?
11 Why .... they go home early?
12 How long .... they been married?
13 .... you see Jim last night?
14 .... you ever seen a ghost?

35.4 Put in **is/are/was/were/have/has**.

1 Oranges ...*are*... imported into Britain.
2 Joe ...*has*... lost his passport.
3 Glass .... made from sand.
4 I .... made some coffee. Would you like some?
5 This shopping centre .... built ten years ago.
6 The streets in this town .... cleaned every day.
7 .... you finished your work?
8 Jill .... gone to Italy for a holiday.
9 These are very old photographs. They .... taken a long time ago.
10 George and Linda are here. They .... just arrived.
11 She's Italian but she .... born in France.
12 Can you tell me how this word .... pronounced?

UNIT 36 *Regular* and *irregular verbs*

■ *Past simple* and *past participle*
The past simple and past participle of *regular* verbs is **-ed**:
clean → clean**ed**   live → liv**ed**   paint → paint**ed**   study → stud**ied**

past simple (▶ Unit 9):
- — I **cleaned** my shoes yesterday.
- — Charlie **studied** engineering at university.

We use the *past participle* for the *present perfect* and the *passive*.
present perfect = **have**/**has** + *past participle* (▶ Units 15–17):
- — I **have cleaned** my shoes.
- — Joan **has lived** in London for ten years.

passive = **be** (**am**/**is**/**are**/**was**/**were**) + *past participle* (▶ Unit 20):
- — These rooms **are cleaned** every day.
- — My car **was repaired** last week.

■ *Irregular verbs*
The past simple and past participle of *irregular* verbs are *not* **-ed**:

	make	break	cut
past simple	**made**	**broke**	**cut**
past participle	**made**	**broken**	**cut**

Sometimes the past simple and past participle are the same. For example:

	make	find	buy	cut
past simple	**made**	**found**	**bought**	**cut**
past participle	**made**	**found**	**bought**	**cut**

- — I **made** a cake yesterday. (*past simple*)
- — I **have made** some coffee. (*past participle – present perfect*)
- — Butter **is made** from milk. (*past participle – present passive*)

Sometimes the past simple and past participle are different. For example:

	break	know	begin	go
past simple	**broke**	**knew**	**began**	**went**
past participle	**broken**	**known**	**begun**	**gone**

- — Somebody **broke** this window last night. (*past simple*)
- — Somebody **has broken** this window. (*past participle – present perfect*)
- — This window **was broken** last night. (*past participle – past passive*)

▶ Appendix 1   List of irregular verbs   ▶ Appendix 2   Irregular verbs in groups

UNIT 36   Exercises

36.1 Write the past simple / past participle of these verbs. (The past simple and past participle are the same for all the verbs in this exercise.)

1 make	..made..........	6 sit	....	11 hear	....
2 cut	..cut...........	7 leave	....	12 cost	....
3 get	....	8 build	....	13 catch	....
4 think	....	9 put	....	14 lose	....
5 pay	....	10 buy	....	15 understand	....

36.2 Write the past simple and past participle of these verbs.

1 break	.broke...	broken.	6 run	....	11 take	....
2 begin	....		7 speak	....	12 go	....
3 eat	....		8 write	....	13 know	....
4 drink	....		9 come	....	14 throw	....
5 give	....		10 drive	....	15 forget	....

36.3 Put the verb into the right form.

1 I **washed**. my hands because they were dirty.   (wash)
2 Somebody has **broken**... this window.   (break)
3 I feel good. I .... very well last night.   (sleep)
4 We .... a very good film yesterday.   (see)
5 It .... a lot when we were on holiday.   (rain)
6 I've .... my bag.   (lose)   Have you .... it?   (see)
7 George's bicycle was .... last week.   (steal)
8 I .... to bed early because I was tired.   (go)
9 Have you .... your book yet?   (finish)
10 These houses were .... about 20 years ago.   (build)
11 Ann .... to drive when she was 18.   (learn)
12 I've never .... a horse in my life.   (ride)
13 Yesterday I .... off my bicycle and .... my leg.   (fall/hurt)
14 She's a good friend of mine. I've .... her a long time.   (know)

36.4 Complete these sentences with a verb from the list. Put the verb into the correct form, past simple or past participle.

cost	drive	fly	make	meet	sell	speak	swim	tell	wake

1 I have **made**. some coffee. Would you like some?
2 I know Gary but I've never .... his wife.
3 We were .... up by a loud noise in the middle of the night.
4 She jumped into the river and .... to the other side.
5 Many different languages are .... in the Philippines.
6 Our holiday .... a lot of money because we stayed in an expensive hotel.
7 Have you ever .... a very fast car?
8 All the tickets for the concert were .... very quickly.
9 Have you .... John about your new job?
10 A bird .... in through the open window while we were having our dinner.

UNIT 37   I am / I don't etc.

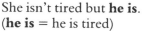

She isn't tired but **he is**.
(**he is** = he is tired)

He smokes but **she doesn't**.
(**she doesn't** = she doesn't smoke)

am/is/are	was/were	have/has	do/does/did	
can will	must	may	might would	should

■   We use these verbs with other verbs (**am going** / **has seen** / **can't come** etc.) but you can
also use them alone:
  – I haven't got a car but my sister **has**. (= my sister has got a car)
  – 'Please help me.'   'I'm sorry, I **can't**.' (= I can't help you)
  – 'Are you tired?'   'I **was**, but I'**m not** now.' (= I was tired but I'm not tired now.)
  – 'Do you think Ann will come?'   'She **might**.' (= She might come.)
  – 'Are you going now?'   'Yes, I'm afraid I **must**.' (= I must go)

■ You can use these verbs in this way with **Yes . . .** and **No . . .**:
  – 'Is it raining?'   'Yes, it **is**. / No, it **isn't**.'
  – 'Have you ever been to Canada?'   'Yes, I **have**. / No, I **haven't**.'
  – 'Will Alan be here tomorrow?'   'Yes, he **will**. / No, he **won't**.'

■ Use **do/does** for the *present simple*:
  – I don't like hot weather but Sue **does**. (= Sue likes hot weather)
  – She works very hard but I **don't**. (= I don't work very hard)
  – 'Do you enjoy your work?'   'Yes, I **do**.'

Use **did** for the *past simple*:
  – 'Did you and John enjoy the film?'   'I **did** but John **didn't**.'
    (= I enjoyed it but John didn't enjoy it.)
  – 'Did it rain yesterday?'   'No, it **didn't**.'

■ You cannot use the short forms **'m/'s/'re/'ve/'ll** *at the end* of a sentence. Use the full forms
am/is/are/have/will etc.:
  – 'Are you tired?'   'Yes, **I am**.' (*not* 'Yes, I'm.')

74

UNIT 37   Exercises

37.1 Complete these sentences with **do/does/did**.

1 I don't like hot weather but Sue *does.*
2 You don't know John very well but I ....
3 I didn't enjoy the party but my friends ....
4 I don't want to go out this evening but Peter ....
5 Ann doesn't smoke but all her friends ....
6 My mother doesn't wear glasses but my father ....

37.2 Complete these sentences with **don't/doesn't/didn't**.

1 Sue likes hot weather but I *don't.*
2 I like football but my brother ....
3 I wanted to go out last night but Jan ....
4 Kate lives in London but her parents ....
5 The workers in the factory work hard but the manager ....
6 Val played tennis last weekend but Tom ....

37.3 Complete these sentences. Use only one verb each time (**is/have/can** etc.).

1 Kay wasn't hungry but we *were.*
2 You haven't met Jack's parents but I ....
3 Bill can't drive but all his friends ....
4 I'm not intelligent but you ....
5 I'm not going to the party tomorrow night but George ....
6 Their house wasn't very big but the garden ....
7 I wasn't very tired but Philip and Joy ....
8 Diana won't be here tomorrow but I ....
9 I don't smoke but my brother ....
10 I haven't got a video camera but I know somebody who ....

37.4 Complete these sentences with a negative verb (**isn't/haven't/can't** etc.).

1 My sister can play the piano but I *...can't......*
2 Tom's house is big but my house ....
3 I'll be here tomorrow but Chris ....
4 I've already seen the film but Ian ....
5 One of the men was wearing a coat but the other man ....
6 I got up early this morning but James ....
7 My friends are going out tonight but I ....
8 Julia watches television a lot but I ....

37.5 Answer these questions about yourself. Use **Yes, I have / No, I'm not** etc.

1 Are you British?   *No, I'm not.*
2 Have you got a car? ....
3 Is it raining? ....
4 Do you feel well? ....
5 Are you tired? ....
6 Do you like chocolate? ....
7 Will you be in Paris tomorrow? ....
8 Have you ever played tennis? ....
9 Did you buy anything yesterday? ....
10 Were you born in Europe? ....

UNIT 38   Have you? / Are you? / Don't you? etc.

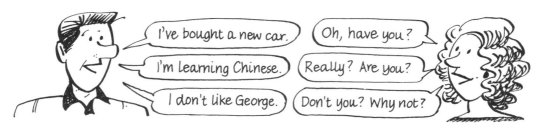

■ In conversation, you can say **have you?** / **is it?** / **can't he?** etc. to show that you are interested or surprised. You can use these verbs in this way:

am/is/are   was/were   have/has   do/does/did   can   will.

    – 'You're late.'   'Oh, **am I?** I'm sorry.'
    – 'I was ill last week.'   '**Were you?** I didn't know that.'
    – 'It's raining again.'   '**Is it?** It was sunny five minutes ago.'

    – 'Bill can't drive.'   '**Can't he?** I didn't know that.'
    – 'I'm not hungry.'   '**Aren't you?** I am.'
    – 'Sue isn't at work today.'   '**Isn't she?** Is she ill?'

Use **do/does** for the *present simple*, **did** for the *past simple*:
    – 'I speak four languages.'   '**Do you?** Which ones?'
    – 'Tom doesn't eat meat.'   '**Doesn't he?** Does he eat fish?'
    – 'Linda got married last week.'   '**Did she?** Really?'

■ *Question tags*
You can use **... have you?** / **... is it?** /
... can't she? etc. at the end of a sentence.
These 'endings' are *question tags*
(= mini-questions).

A *positive* sentence → a *negative* question tag
A *negative* sentence → a *positive* question tag

positive → *negative*

It's a beautiful day, **isn't it?**	Yes, it's lovely.
She lives in London, **doesn't she?**	Yes, that's right.
You closed the window, **didn't you?**	Yes, I think so.
Those shoes are nice, **aren't they?**	Yes, very nice.
Tom will be at home tomorrow, **won't he?**	Yes, I think so.

negative → *positive*

That isn't your car, **is it?**	No, my car is white.
You don't smoke, **do you?**	No, never.
You haven't met my mother, **have you?**	No, I haven't.
You won't be late, **will you?**	No, don't worry.

UNIT 38 Exercises

38.1 Answer with **Do you? / Doesn't she? / Did they?** etc.

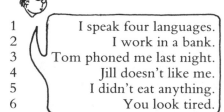

1	I speak four languages.	...........Do you................... ?	Which ones?
2	I work in a bank.	.... ?	I work in a bank too.
3	Tom phoned me last night.	.... ?	What did he say?
4	Jill doesn't like me.	.... ?	Why not?
5	I didn't eat anything.	.... ?	Weren't you hungry?
6	You look tired.	.... ?	I don't feel tired.

38.2 Answer with **Have you? / Haven't you? / Did she? / Didn't she?** etc.

1	I've bought a new car.	...Have you...... ?	What make is it?
2	Tim doesn't eat meat.	...Doesn't he...... ?	Does he eat fish?
3	I've lost my key.	.... ?	When did you last have it?
4	Sue was born in Rome.	.... ?	I didn't know that.
5	I can't swim.	.... ?	You must learn.
6	I didn't sleep well last night.	.... ?	Was the bed uncomfortable?
7	This ring is gold.	.... ?	It's very beautiful.
8	I'm not coming with you.	.... ?	Why not?
9	I met Pam last week.	.... ?	How is she?
10	She works in a factory.	.... ?	What kind of factory?
11	I won't be here next week.	.... ?	Where will you be?
12	The clock isn't working.	.... ?	It was working this morning.

38.3 Complete these sentences with a question tag (**isn't it? / haven't you?** etc.).

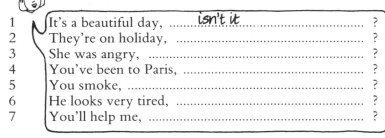

1	It's a beautiful day,	......isn't it........... ?	Yes, it's lovely.
2	They're on holiday,	.... ?	Yes, they're in Portugal.
3	She was angry,	.... ?	Yes, very angry.
4	You've been to Paris,	.... ?	Yes, many times.
5	You smoke,	.... ?	Yes, but not often.
6	He looks very tired,	.... ?	Yes, he works too hard.
7	You'll help me,	.... ?	Yes, of course I will.

38.4 Complete these sentences with a question tag, positive (**is it? / do you?** etc.) or negative (**isn't it? / don't you?** etc.).

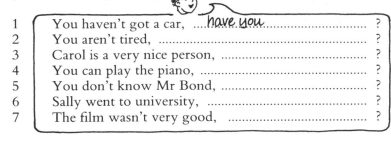

1	You haven't got a car,	....have you............ ?	No, I can't drive.
2	You aren't tired,	.... ?	No, I'm fine.
3	Carol is a very nice person,	.... ?	Yes, I like her very much.
4	You can play the piano,	.... ?	Yes, but not very well.
5	You don't know Mr Bond,	.... ?	No, I've never met him.
6	Sally went to university,	.... ?	Yes, she studied history.
7	The film wasn't very good,	.... ?	No, it was terrible.

UNIT 39   too / either   so am I / neither do I etc.

---

too and either

We use **too** and **either** at the end of a sentence.

We use **too** after a *positive* verb:
  – 'I'm happy.' '**I'm** happy **too**.'
  – 'I enjoyed the film.' 'I **enjoyed** it **too**.'
  – Mary is a doctor. Her husband **is** a doctor **too**.

We use **either** after a *negative* verb (am **not** / is**n't** / ca**n't** etc.):
  – 'I'm not happy.' 'I'm **not** happy **either**.' (*not* 'I'm not happy too')
  – 'I can't cook.' 'I ca**n't either**.'
  – Bill doesn't watch TV. He does**n't** read newspapers **either**.

So am I / Neither do I etc.

	am/is/are ...
	was/were ...
so	do/does ...
	did ...
	have/has ...
neither	can ...
	will ...
	must ...

So am I (= I am too), **So have I** (= I have too) etc.:
  – '**I'm** tired.' '**So am I**.' (*not* 'So I am.')
  – '**I was** late for work today.' '**So was John**.'
  – '**I work** in a bank.' '**So do I**.'
  – '**We went** to the cinema last night.' '**Did you? So did we**.'

Neither am I (= I'm not either), **Neither have I** (= I haven't either) etc.:
  – '**I haven't** got a key.' '**Neither have I**.' (*not* 'Neither I have.')
  – '**Ann can't** cook.' '**Neither can Tom**.'
  – '**I won't** (= will not) be here tomorrow.' '**Neither will I**.'
  – '**I never eat** meat.' '**Neither do I**.'

You can also use **Nor ...** (= **Neither**):
  – '**I'm not** married.' '**Nor** am I.' (= Neither am I.)

am/was/do etc.   ▶ Unit 37

UNIT 39 Exercises

39.1 Put in **too** or **either**.

1	I'm happy.	I'm happy ...too............................
2	I'm not hungry.	I'm not hungry ....
3	I'm tired.	I'm tired ....
4	It rained on Saturday.	It rained on Sunday ....
5	Ann can't drive a car.	She can't ride a bicycle ....
6	I don't smoke.	I don't smoke ....
7	Jane's mother is a teacher.	Her father is a teacher ....

39.2 Answer with **So ... I** (**So am I** / **So do I** / **So can I** etc.).

1	I went to bed late last night.	.....So did I........................
2	I'm hungry.	....
3	I've been to Rome.	....
4	I want to go home now.	....
5	I'll be late tomorrow.	....
6	I was surprised at the news.	....

Answer with **Neither ... I**.

7	I can't play the piano.	....
8	I didn't buy a newspaper.	....
9	I haven't got any money.	....
10	I'm not working tomorrow.	....
11	I don't know them very well.	....

39.3 You are talking to Maria. Write *true* answers about *yourself*. Where possible, use **So ... I** or **Neither ... I**. Look at the examples carefully.

MARIA: I'm tired. / I can't play tennis. you can answer: So am I. or I'm not (tired). / Neither can I. or I can (play tennis). YOU

1	I'm learning English.	....
2	I can ride a bicycle.	....
3	I'm not tired.	....
4	I like dancing.	....
5	I don't like cold weather.	....
6	I slept well last night.	....
7	I've never been to India.	....
8	I don't go to the cinema very often.	....
9	I'm going out tomorrow evening.	....
10	I haven't got a headache.	....
11	I didn't watch TV last night.	....
12	I need a holiday.	....

79

UNIT 40 *Negatives:* **isn't/haven't/don't** etc.

■ We use **not** (**n't**) in negative sentences:

positive → *negative*	
am	**am not** (**'m not**)	I'**m not** tired.
is	**is not** (**isn't** *or* **'s not**)	It **isn't** (*or* It'**s not**) raining.
are	**are not** (**aren't** *or* **'re not**)	They **aren't** (*or* They'**re not**) here.
was	**was not** (**wasn't**)	Jack **wasn't** hungry.
were	**were not** (**weren't**)	The shops **weren't** open.
have	**have not** (**haven't**)	I **haven't** finished my work.
has	**has not** (**hasn't**)	Sue **hasn't** got a car.
will	**will not** (**won't**)	They **won't** be here tomorrow.
would	**would not** (**wouldn't**)	I **wouldn't** like to be an actor.
can	**cannot** (**can't**)	George **can't** drive.
could	**could not** (**couldn't**)	I **couldn't** sleep last night.
should	**should not** (**shouldn't**)	You **shouldn't** work so hard.
must	**must not** (**mustn't**)	I **mustn't** forget to phone Ann.

■ *Present simple* negative   (▶ Unit 6):
I/we/you/they **do not** (**don't**) } + *infinitive* (**work/live/go** etc.)
he/she/it **does not** (**doesn't**)

Past simple negative   (▶ Unit 10):
I/they/he/she etc. **did not** (**didn't**)   + *infinitive*

positive	→	*negative*
I **smoke**.	→	I **don't smoke**.
They **work** hard.	→	They **don't work** hard.
Tom **plays** the guitar.	→	Tom **doesn't play** the guitar.
She **likes** her job.	→	She **doesn't like** her job.
I **got** up early.	→	I **didn't get** up early.
We **worked** hard.	→	We **didn't work** hard.
They **saw** the film.	→	They **didn't see** the film.
She **had** a bath.	→	She **didn't have** a bath.

■ The negative of '**Look!**', '**Go away!**' etc. is '**Don't . . . !**':
Look! → **Don't look!**
Go away! → **Don't go** away!

■ **Do** can also be the main verb (**don't do** / **didn't do** etc.):

positive	→	*negative*
Do it.	→	**Don't do** it.
He **does** a lot of work.	→	He **doesn't do** much work.
I **did** the examination.	→	I **didn't do** the examination.

UNIT 40　Exercises

40.1 Make these sentences negative.

1 I'm tired. _I'm not tired._
2 He's got a car. _He hasn't got a car_
3 They are married. ....
4 I've had dinner. ....
5 It's cold today. ....
6 I can see you. ....

7 We were late. ....
8 I'm going out. ....
9 She has gone out. ....
10 I'll be late tonight. ....
11 It was expensive. ....
12 You should go. ....

40.2 Make negatives with **don't/doesn't/didn't**.

1 He saw me. _He didn't see me._
2 Do it! _Don't do it_
3 I like fish. ....
4 She smokes. ....
5 Look at me! ....
6 I got up early. ....

7 They understood. ....
8 Phone me tonight. ....
9 I did the shopping. ....
10 He lives near here. ....
11 It rained yesterday. ....
12 They did the work. ....

40.3 Make these sentences negative.

1 It's raining. _It isn't raining._
2 She saw the film. _She didn't see the film._
3 She can swim. ....
4 They're on holiday. ....
5 He speaks German. ....
6 I enjoyed the film. ....
7 It's important. ....

8 We watched TV. ....
9 They were angry. ....
10 He'll be pleased. ....
11 I went to the bank. ....
12 She's got a camera. ....
13 Open the door. ....
14 I could hear them. ....

40.4 Complete these sentences with a negative verb (**isn't/haven't/don't** etc.).

1 The sun is shining. It _isn't_ raining.
2 She isn't rich. She _hasn't_ got much money.
3 'Would you like something to eat?' 'No, thank you. I .... hungry.'
4 I .... hear you. Please speak louder.
5 George .... write letters very often. He prefers to phone.
6 I don't like this book. It .... very interesting.
7 'Where is Jill?' 'I .... know. I .... seen her today.'
8 She .... go to work yesterday because she .... very well, but she's better today.
9 Be careful! .... fall!
10 We .... take an umbrella with us because the weather was fine.
11 I've been to Spain many times but I .... been to Portugal.
12 When we were in London, we stayed with friends. We .... stay at a hotel.
13 She .... be here tomorrow. She's going away.
14 'Who broke that window?' 'Not me! I .... do it.'
15 The box was too heavy. We tried to lift it but we ....
16 We didn't see what happened. We .... looking at the time.

UNIT 41   *Questions (1):* **is it ... ? have you ... ? do they ... ?** etc.

positive | you | ✕ | are | **You are** eating.
question | are | ✕ | you | **Are you** eating?   What **are you** eating?

■ In questions, the first verb (**is/are/have** etc.) is *before* the subject:

positive		*question*		
subject + verb			*verb + subject*	
I **am** late.	→		**Am**	I late?
That seat **is** free.	→		**Is**	that seat free?
She **was** angry.	→	Why	**was**	she angry?
David **has** gone.	→	Where	**has**	David gone?
You **have** got a car.	→		**Have**	you got a car?
They **will** be here.	→	When	**will**	they be here?
Tom **can** swim.	→		**Can**	Tom swim?

■ Be careful with word order: the subject is after the first verb:
– Where **has David** gone? (*not* 'Where has gone David?')
– Why **are those people** waiting? (*not* 'Why are waiting those people?')

■ *Present simple* questions: **do** (I/we/you/they) ⎫
(▶ Unit 7)   **does** (he/she/it)   ⎬ + *infinitive* (**work/live/go** etc.)
Past simple questions: **did** (you/they/she etc.) + *infinitive*
(▶ Unit 10)

positive			*question*		
You	**smoke**.	→		**Do you**	**smoke**?
They	**live** in London.	→	Where	**do they**	**live**?
Jack	**smokes**.	→		**Does Jack**	**smoke**?
She	**gets** up early.	→	What time	**does she**	**get** up?
They	**worked** hard.	→		**Did they**	**work** hard?
You	**had** dinner.	→	What	**did you**	**have** for dinner?
She	**got** up early.	→	What time	**did she**	**get** up?

Do can also be the main verb (**do you do / did she do** etc.):
– What **do you** usually **do** at weekends?
– 'What **does your sister do**?' 'She works in a bank.'
– 'I broke my leg.' 'How **did you do** that?' (*not* 'How did you that?')

■ *Negative questions* with **Why ... ?** (**Why isn't ...?** / **Why don't ...?** etc.):
Be careful with word order in these questions:
– Where's John? **Why isn't he** here? (*not* 'Why he isn't here?')
– **Why can't Paula** come to the meeting? (*not* 'Why Paula can't ...')
– **Why didn't you** phone me last night?

▶ Units 42–3 *Questions (2–3)*

82

UNIT 41   Exercises

41.1 Write questions.

1	I can swim.	(and you?)	...Can.you.swim.. ?
2	I smoke.	(and Jim?)	...Does.Jim.smoke..................................... ?
3	I was late this morning.	(and you?)	.... ?
4	I've got a key.	(and Ann?)	.... ?
5	I'll be here tomorrow.	(and you?)	.... ?
6	I'm going out this evening.	(and Tom?)	.... ?
7	I've finished my work.	(and you?)	.... ?
8	I like my job.	(and you?)	.... ?
9	I live near the city centre.	(and Pam?)	.... ?
10	I enjoyed my holiday.	(and you?)	.... ?
11	I had a shower this morning.	(and you?)	.... ?

41.2 You are asking somebody questions. Write the full questions.

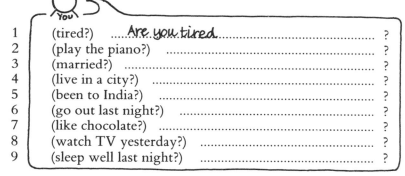

1	(tired?)	....Are.you.tired................................ ?	Yes, a little.
2	(play the piano?)	.... ?	Yes, but not very well.
3	(married?)	.... ?	No, I'm single.
4	(live in a city?)	.... ?	No, in a small village.
5	(been to India?)	.... ?	No, never.
6	(go out last night?)	.... ?	No, I stayed at home.
7	(like chocolate?)	.... ?	Yes, I love it.
8	(watch TV yesterday?)	.... ?	No, I never watch TV.
9	(sleep well last night?)	.... ?	No, not very well.

41.3 Ask questions.

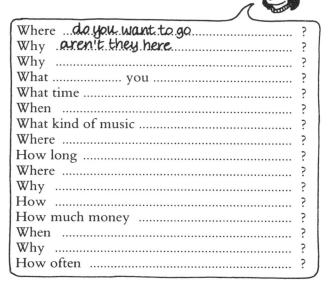

1	I want to go.	Where ...do.you.want.to.go................ ?
2	They aren't here.	Why ...aren't.they.here...................... ?
3	It's important.	Why .... ?
4	I'm reading.	What .... you .... ?
5	Jan went home.	What time .... ?
6	Dave and Mary are going away.	When .... ?
7	I like music.	What kind of music .... ?
8	I met Tim.	Where .... ?
9	He is going to stay here.	How long .... ?
10	The children have gone.	Where .... ?
11	I can't come to the party.	Why .... ?
12	I broke the window.	How .... ?
13	I need some money.	How much money .... ?
14	She did her driving test.	When .... ?
15	I don't like her.	Why .... ?
16	It rains a lot.	How often .... ?

UNIT 42   *Questions (2):* **Who saw you? Who did you see?**

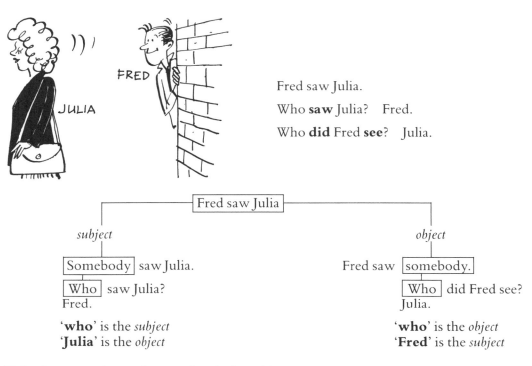

Fred saw Julia.

Who **saw** Julia?   Fred.

Who **did** Fred **see**?   Julia.

Fred saw Julia

subject

Somebody saw Julia.

Who saw Julia?
Fred.

'**who**' is the *subject*
'**Julia**' is the *object*

object

Fred saw somebody.

Who did Fred see?
Julia.

'**who**' is the *object*
'**Fred**' is the *subject*

■ In these questions **who** or **what** is the *subject*:
- **Who lives** in that house? (= Somebody lives there – who?)
  (*not* 'Who does live . . . ?')
- **What happened**? (= Something happened – what?)
  (*not* 'What did happen?')
- **What's** (= **What is**) **burning**?
- **Who's got** (= **Who has got**) my key?

■ In these questions **who** or **what** is the *object*:
- **Who did you meet** yesterday? (= You met somebody – who?)
- **What did she say**? (= She said something – what?)
- **Who are you phoning**?
- **What was he wearing**?

Compare:
- George likes eggs.   → **Who likes** eggs?   George.
                          What does George **like**?   Eggs.
- Jill won some money. → **Who won** some money?   Jill.
                          What did Jill **win**?   Some money.

■ Use **who** for people (somebody), **what** for things, ideas etc. (something):
- **Who** is your favourite singer?
- **What** is your favourite song?

UNIT 42   Exercises

42.1 Make questions with **who** and **what**. In these sentences **who/what** is the subject.

1 Somebody broke the window.   Who broke the window ?
2 Something happened.   What happened ?
3 Somebody is coming.   Who .... ?
4 Somebody took my umbrella.   .... your umbrella ?
5 Something made me angry.   .... you angry ?
6 Somebody wants to see you.   .... me ?
7 Somebody told me about the accident. .... you .... ?
8 Something went wrong.   .... ?

42.2 Make questions with **who** and **what**. In these sentences **who/what** is the object.

1 I met somebody.   Who did you meet ?
2 I'm doing something.   What are you doing ?
3 I'm reading something.   What .... you .... ?
4 I saw somebody.   Who .... ?
5 I want something.   .... ?
6 I phoned somebody.   .... ?
7 I'm going to cook something.   .... ?
8 I bought something.   .... ?

42.3 Make questions with **who** and **what**. Sometimes **who/what** is the subject, sometimes **who/what** is the object.

1   Somebody lives in that house.   Who lives in that house ?
2   Tom said something.   What did Tom say ?
3   They have lost something.   What .... ?
4   Somebody cleaned the kitchen.   Who .... ?
5   I asked somebody for money.   Who .... you .... money ?
6   Somebody asked me for money.   Who .... ?
7   Something happened last night.   What .... ?
8   Jack bought something.   What .... ?
9   Somebody telephoned me yesterday. Who .... ?
10 I telephoned somebody yesterday.   Who .... ?
11 Somebody knows the answer.   Who .... ?
12 Something woke me up this morning. What .... ?
13 Somebody has got my pen.   Who .... pen ?
14 Tom and Ann saw something.   What .... ?
15 Somebody saw the accident.   Who .... ?
16 Somebody did the washing-up.   Who .... ?
17 Jill did something.   What .... ?
18 This word means something.   What .... ?

85

UNIT 43   *Questions (3):* Who is she talking to?
                              What is it like?

Julia is talking | **to** someone |.

Who?

| **Who** | is Julia talking | **to** | ?

■ Questions (**Who . . . ?**/**What . . . ?**/**Where . . . ?**/**Which . . . ?**) often end with a *preposition*
(**to**/**for**/**about**/**with** etc.):
  – 'I'm thinking.'   '**What** are you thinking **about**?'
  – 'I'm afraid.'   'Why? **What** are you afraid **of**?'
  – '**Where** is your friend **from**?'   'She's from Germany.'
  – '**Who** does this book belong **to**?'   'It's mine.'
  – '**Who** did she go on holiday **with**?'   'With her parents.'
  – '**What** does he look **like**?'   'He's got a beard and wears glasses.'
  – 'This book is very good.'   'Is it? **What** is it **about**?'
  – 'Tom's father is in hospital.'   '**Which hospital** is he **in**?'

■ **What (is/are/was/were) . . . like?**

'**What is it like?**' = Tell me something about it; is it good or bad, big or small, old or
new? etc.
When we say '**What . . . like?**', **like** is a *preposition*. It is *not* the verb **like** (**Do you like
music?** etc.).

  – A: I went to the new restaurant last night.
    B: Oh, did you? **What**'s it **like**? Good?
    A: Yes, excellent.

  – A: **What**'s your new teacher **like**?
    B: She's very good. We learn a lot.

  – A: I met Linda's parents yesterday.
    B: Oh, **what** are they **like**?
    A: They're very friendly.

  – A: **What** was the weather **like** when you were on holiday?
    B: Very nice.

UNIT 43 Exercises

43.1 Write questions.

1	I'm thinking about something.	What *are you thinking about* ?
2	He went out with somebody.	Who *did he go out with* ?
3	I'm waiting for somebody.	Who are you .... ?
4	She danced with somebody.	Who did she .... ?
5	He's interested in something.	What .... ?
6	I had dinner with somebody.	Who .... ?
7	They're looking for something.	What .... ?
8	George was with somebody.	Who .... ?
9	I gave the money to somebody.	Who .... ?
10	I'm looking at something.	What .... ?
11	They were talking about something.	What .... ?
12	I dreamt about somebody.	Who .... ?
13	He was afraid of something.	What .... ?
14	They're going to a restaurant.	Which restaurant .... ?
15	She spoke to somebody.	Who .... ?
16	I stayed at a hotel.	Which hotel .... ?

43.2 You are talking to somebody from another country. You want some information about the country. Ask questions with **What is/are ... like?**

1 (the houses)   *What are the houses like* .... ?
2 (the food)   What .... ?
3 (the weather)   .... ?
4 (the people)   .... ?
5 (your city)   .... ?
6 (the shops)   .... ?
7 (the schools)   .... ?
8 (TV programmes) .... ?

43.3 Ask questions with **What was/were ... like?**

1 Your friend has just come back from holiday. Ask about the weather.
What was the weather like .... ?
2 Your friend has just come back from the cinema. Ask about the film.
What .... ?
3 Your friend has just arrived at the airport. Ask about the flight.
.... ?
4 Your friend has just been to a concert. Ask about the concert.
.... ?
5 Your friend has just finished an English course. Ask about the lessons.
.... ?
6 Your friend has just come back from holiday. Ask about the hotel.
.... ?

UNIT 44   What...?   Which...?   How...?

■ **What ...?**

What + *noun* (**What colour ... ?** / **What kind ... ?** etc.):

    – **What colour** is your car?   **What colour** are your eyes?

    – **What size** is this shirt?   **What kind** of job do you want?

    – **What make** is your TV set?   **What time** is it?

What *without a noun*:

    – **What**'s your favourite colour?

    – **What** do you want to do this evening?

What and Who ▶ Unit 42

■ **Which ...?**

Which + *noun* (*things or people*):

    – **Which train** did you catch – the 9.50 or the 10.30?

    – **Which doctor** did you see – Doctor Ellis, Doctor Gray or Doctor Hill?

Which *without a noun* (*not people*):

    – **Which** is bigger – Canada or Australia?

but   **Who** is taller – Bill or Jerry? (**Who** *for people*)

Which one(s) ▶ Unit 69

■ **What ...?** and **Which ...?**

We say **Which** when we are thinking about a small number (perhaps two, three or four things):

    – We can go this way or that way.
      Which way shall we go?

    – There are four umbrellas here.
      Which is yours?

WHICH?

Use **What** in other situations:

    – **What** is the capital of Italy?

    – **What sort** of music do you like? (*not* 'Which sort ... ?')

Compare:

    – **What colour** are your eyes? (*not* 'Which colour ... ?')

but   **Which colour** do you prefer, **pink or yellow**?

■ **How ...?**

    – '**How** was the party last night?'   'It was great!'

    – '**How** do you usually go to work?'   'By bus.'

How + *adjective/adverb* (**how old** / **how big** / **how fast** etc.):

    – **How old** is your father?   **How tall** are you?   **How big** is the house?

    – **How far** is it to the shops from here?

    – **How often** do you go on holiday?

44.1 Write questions with **Which**.

1	He stayed at a hotel.
2	We're going to a restaurant.
3	She reads a newspaper.
4	I'm going to learn a language.
5	They visited many places.
6	I'm waiting for a bus.

1 *Which hotel did he stay at* .... ?
2 .... to ?
3 .... ?
4 .... ?
5 .... ?
6 .... ?

44.2 Put in **what/which/who**.

1 *What* is that man's name?
2 *Which* way shall we go? This way or the other way?
3 You can have tea or coffee. .... do you want?
4 'I can't find my umbrella.' '.......... colour is it?'
5 .... is your favourite sport?
6 This is a very nice house. .... room is yours?
7 .... is more expensive, meat or fish?
8 .... is older, Ann or George?
9 .... is your telephone number?
10 .... kind of TV programmes do you like watching?
11 'She's got three cars.' '.......... car does she use most?'
12 '.......... nationality are you?' 'I'm Brazilian.'

44.3 Write questions with **What ... ?** or **How ... ?**

1 Are his eyes blue? Green? Brown? *What colour are his eyes* .... ?
2 Did you get up at 7 o'clock? 7.30? 8.15? .... ?
3 Are you 20 years old? 21? 22? .... ?
4 Is the door red? Blue? Yellow? .... ?
5 Do you watch TV every day? Once a week? Never?

.... ?
6 Are these shoes size 37? 38? 39? .... ?
7 Is it 1000 miles from Paris to Moscow? 1500? 2000?

.... ?
8 Is your room very big? Quite big? Not very big? .... ?
9 Do you like classical music? Rock? Folk music?

.... ?
10 Can you run one kilometre? Five? Ten? .... ?
11 Is your pullover size 38? 40? 42? .... ?
12 Are you 1.75 metres? 1.80? 1.85? .... ?
13 Is it Monday? Tuesday? Wednesday? .... ?
14 Is this box one kilogram? One and a half? Two? .... ?
15 Can this plane fly at 500 miles an hour? 600? 700?

.... ?
16 Do you like horror films? Science fiction films? Thrillers? Comedies?

.... ?

UNIT 45   How long does it take?

How long **does it take** by plane from London to Madrid?

It takes two hours.

I started reading the book two weeks ago. I finished it today.

It took me two weeks to read it.

How long **does it take**	by plane by train by car	from . . . to . . . ?

It takes	two hours ten minutes a long time	by plane by train by car	from . . . to . . .

- **How long does it take** by train from London to Manchester?
  It takes two hours by train from London to Manchester.
- **How long does it take** by car from your house to the station?
  It takes ten minutes by car from my house to the station.

How long	**did does will**	**it take**	(you) (Ann) (them)	**to** (do something)?

It	**took takes will take**	(me) (Ann) (them)	a week a long time three hours	**to** (do something).

- **How long does it take to cross** the Atlantic Ocean by ship?
- **How long will it take me to learn** to drive?
- 'I came by train.' 'Did you? **How long did it take**?'
- **Did it take you a long time to find** a job?
- **It takes a long time to learn** a language.
- **It takes me 20 minutes to get** to work in the morning.
- **It took Tom an hour to do** his shopping.
- **It will take me an hour to cook** the dinner.
- **It doesn't take long to cook** an omelette.

UNIT 45 Exercises

45.1 Write questions with **How long does it take ... ?**

1 (by plane / London / Madrid) How long does it take by plane from London to Madrid ?
2 (by car / Rome / Milan) .... ?
3 (by bus / the city centre / the airport) ....

.... ?
4 (by plane / Cairo / London) .... ?
5 (by taxi / the station / the hotel) .... ?
6 (by train / Paris / Geneva) .... ?
7 (by boat / Dover / Ostend) .... ?
8 (by bicycle / your house / your work) ....

.... ?

45.2 Look at the timetable of flights from London. How long does it take to get to each place? Write
sentences with **It takes ...**

from LONDON	depart	arrive
to EDINBURGH	07.10	08.20
MANCHESTER	07.15	08.05
NEWCASTLE	07.30	08.30
CORK	11.15	12.30
ABERDEEN	09.25	10.50
BELFAST	08.30	09.40

How long does it take to fly to:
1 Edinburgh? It takes an hour and ten minutes
2 Manchester? It ....
3 Newcastle? ....
4 Cork? ....
5 Aberdeen? ....
6 Belfast? ....

45.3 Write questions with **How long did it take ... ?**

1 She found a job. How long did it take her to find a job .... ?
2 I walked to the station. .... you .... ?
3 They cleaned the house. .... ?
4 I learnt to swim. .... ?
5 He found an apartment. .... ?

45.4 Write sentences with **It took ...**

1 (he read the book / two weeks) It took him two weeks to read the book. ....
2 (we walked home / an hour) ....
3 (I learnt to drive / a long time) ....
4 (they repaired the car / all day) ....
5 *Write a true sentence about yourself:* ....

45.5 How long does it take (you) to do these things? Write full sentences.

1 (run five kilometres?) It takes me about 30 minutes to run five kilometres. ....
2 (have a shower?) ....
3 (fly to London from your country?) ....

....
4 (study to be a doctor in your country?) ....

....
5 (walk from your house to the nearest shop?) ....

....

91

UNIT 46   Can you tell me where ...?
         Do you know what ...? etc.

Excuse me, can you tell me where the station is, please?

We say: Where **is** the station?
but
Can you tell me where **the station** **is** ?

(*not* 'Can you tell me where is the station?')
also:

I know
I don't know
Do you know   } **where the station is** (?)
I can't remember
I wonder
(etc.)

Who **are those people**?	who **those people are**
Where **have they** gone?	where **they've** gone (?)
How old **is Tom**?	how old **Tom is**
What time **is the bus**?	what time **the bus is**
When **is Ann** going away?	when **Ann is** going away (?)
How much **is this camera**?	how much **this camera is**
Why **were they** late?	why **they were** late
What **was he** wearing?	what **he was** wearing

but

Do you know
I don't know
I know
Can you tell me
I can't remember

■ Questions with **do/does/did** (*present simple* and *past simple*):

            Where **does he live** ?
                        ↓
Do you know where **he lives** ?   (*not* 'Do you know where does he live?')

How **do aeroplanes fly**?	how **aeroplanes fly** (?)
What **does she want**?	what **she wants**
Why **did she go** home?	why **she went** home
Where **did I put** the key?	where **I put** the key

but

Do you know
I don't know
I know
I can't remember

■ Questions beginning **Is ...? / Do ...? / Can ...?** etc. (*yes/no questions*):

Is Jack at home?	**Jack is** at home	
Have they got a car?	**they've** got a car	
Can he help us?	if	**he can** help us (?)
Does Ann smoke?	*or*	**Ann smokes**
Did anybody see you?	whether	**anybody saw** me

but

Do you know
I don't know

You can use **if** or **whether** in these sentences:
    – Do you know **if** she smokes?   *or*   Do you know **whether** she smokes?

92

UNIT 46   Exercises

46.1 You are a tourist. Ask **Excuse me, can you tell me where ... ?**

1 (the station)   *Excuse me, can you tell me where the station is* .... ?
2 (the museum)   Excuse me, ... ?
3 (the information centre)   .... ?
4 (the nearest bank)   .... ?

46.2 Answer these questions with **I don't know where/when/why ...** etc.

| Have they gone to London? | (where) *I don't know where they've gone.* |

1	Is he in the garden?	(where) I don't know where ....
2	Are they leaving tomorrow?	(when) .... when
3	Was he angry because I was late?	(why) I don't know ....
4	Are they from Australia?	(where) I ....
5	Is the house very old?	(how old) ....
6	Will he be here soon?	(when) ....

46.3 Write sentences with **Do you know ... ?** / **I don't remember ...** etc.

1 (How do aeroplanes fly?)   Do you know *how aeroplanes fly* .... ?
2 (Where does Susan work?)   I don't know ....
3 (Where do they live?)   Do you know .... ?
4 (What did he say?)   Do you remember .... ?
5 (What time does the concert begin?) Do you know .... ?
6 (Why did they leave early?)   I don't know ....
7 (How did the accident happen?) I don't remember ....

46.4 Ask questions with **Do you know if** (or **whether**) ... ?

1 (Have they got a car?)   *Do you know if they've got a car* .... ?
2 (Are they married?)   Do you know .... ?
3 (Does she like her job?)   Do you know .... ?
4 (Will George be here tomorrow?)   Do .... ?
5 (Did he pass his examination?)   .... ?

46.5 Write new questions beginning **Do you know ... ?**

1 (What does she want?)   *Do you know what she wants* .... ?
2 (Where is Ann?)   Do you know where .... ?
3 (Is Pat working today?)   Do you .... ?
4 (What time do they start work?) Do .... ?
5 (Do they work on Sundays?)   .... ?
6 (Why were they so nervous?)   .... ?
7 (Where did Stella go?)   .... ?
8 (Are the shops open tomorrow?) .... ?

UNIT 47   to ... (I want to do) and -ing (I enjoy doing)

■ *verbs +* **to ...** (I **want to do**)

want	decide	hope	try
need	offer	expect	forget
plan	refuse	promise	learn

+ **to ...** (**to do** / **to work** / **to be** etc.)

- – What do you **want to do** this evening?
- – I **hope to go** to university next year.
- – We have **decided to leave** tomorrow morning.
- – You **forgot to switch** off the light when you went out.
- – My brother is **learning to drive**.
- – I **tried to work** but I was too tired.

■ *verbs +* **-ing** (I **like doing**)

like	love	suggest	stop
enjoy	hate	mind	finish

+ **-ing** (**do**ing/work**ing**/be**ing** etc.)

- – I **enjoy** danc**ing**. (*not* 'enjoy to dance')
- – Do you **like** driv**ing**?
- – I **hate** gett**ing** up in the morning.
- – Ann **loves** go**ing** to the cinema.
- – Has it **stopped** rain**ing**?
- – Mary **suggested** go**ing** to the cinema.
- – I don't **mind** be**ing** alone.

but:

would like	would hate
would love	would prefer

+ **to ...** (**to do** / **to work** / **to be** etc.)

- – Jan **would like to meet** you. (*not* 'would like meeting')
- – I'**d love to go** to Australia. (**I'd** = I would)
- – '**Would** you **like to sit** down?'   'No, I'**d prefer to stand**, thank you.'
- – I **wouldn't like to be** a teacher.

would like   ▶ Unit 30

■ *verbs +* **to ...** *or* **-ing**:

start	continue
begin	prefer

+ **to ...** (**to do** etc.)
or **-ing** (**do**ing etc.)

- – It **started raining.** *or* It **started to rain.**
- – I **prefer travelling** by car. *or* I **prefer to travel** by car.
  (*but* **would** prefer **to do** something)

UNIT 47   Exercises

47.1 Put the verb in the right form, **to ...** or **-ing**.

1 I enjoy ..*dancing*.. (dance).
2 Where do you want ....*to go*...... (go)?
3 What have you decided .... (do)?
4 I learnt .... (swim) when I was five years old.
5 I'm trying .... (work). Please stop .... (talk).
6 Have you finished .... (clean) the kitchen?
7 I'm tired. I want .... (go) to bed.
8 The weather was nice, so I suggested .... (go) for a walk by the river.
9 Don't forget .... (send) me a postcard when you're on holiday.
10 Where's Bill? He promised .... (be) here on time.
11 Do you enjoy .... (read) books?
12 I don't mind .... (travel) by train but I prefer .... (fly).
13 We invited Jane to the party but she didn't want .... (come).
14 Goodbye. I hope .... (see) you again soon.
15 You must stop .... (work) so hard. It's bad for you.
16 They were very angry and refused .... (speak) to me.
17 Where is Ann? I need .... (talk) to her.
18 Why did you start .... (cry)?
19 I enjoy .... (visit) other countries.

47.2 Ask questions with **Do you like ... ?**

1 I often get up early.   *Do you like getting up early* .... ?
2 I often write letters.   Do you like .... ?
3 I often travel by train.   Do .... ?
4 I often visit museums.   .... ?
5 I often eat in restaurants.   .... ?

Do *you* like doing these things? Use **I like / don't like / hate / don't mind...**

6 *I don't mind getting up early*........... (*or* **I like ... / I don't like ... / I hate ...**)
7 I .... letters.
8 .... train.
9 ....
10 ....

47.3 Put the verb in the right form, **to ...** or **-ing**.

1 Pam would like ..*to meet*.... (meet) you.
2 Do you like ...*driving*... (drive)?
3 I like your house. Do you like .... (live) here?
4 What would you like .... (do) this evening?
5 I'd love .... (help) you but it's impossible.
6 I travel a lot. I love .... (travel).
7 My brother is a teacher but he doesn't like .... (teach) very much.
8 This ring is very beautiful. I'd hate .... (lose) it.
9 Would you prefer .... (leave) now or later?
10 He wasn't happy when he lost the game. He hates .... (lose).

UNIT 48   I want you to ... / I told you to ...

The woman **wants to go**.

The man **doesn't want the woman to go.**
He **wants her to stay**.

> (I) **want to ...**

> (I) **want (somebody) to ...**

■ We say **I want (you) to ...**:
  - I **want you to be** happy. (*not* 'I want that you are happy.')
  - They didn't **want anybody to know** their secret.

We also use this structure (*verb* + somebody + **to ...**) with:

tell					
ask	I	**told**	**you**	**to be**	careful.
advise	She	**asked**	**her friend**	**to help**	her.
persuade	What do you	**advise**	**me**	**to do**?	
expect	We	**persuaded**	**George**	**to come**	with us.
teach	I didn't	**expect**	**you**	**to be**	here.
	I	**taught**	**my brother**	**to swim**.	

■ I **told** (somebody) **to ...** / I **told** (somebody) **not to ...**:

  - Tom said (to Ann): '**Wait** for me!'
    → Tom **told** Ann **to wait** for **him**.

  - Tom said (to Ann): '**Don't wait** for me.'
    → Tom **told** Ann **not to wait** for **him**.

■ **make** and **let**
After **make** and **let** we do *not* use **to**:
  - He's very funny. He **makes us laugh**. (*not* 'makes us to laugh')
  - I don't want you to go alone. **Let me go** with you. (*not* 'Let me to go')

Let's (**do** something)
You can say **Let's ...** (= **let us**) when you want people to do things with you:
  - Come on! **Let's dance**!
  - 'Shall we go out tonight?'   'No, I'm tired. **Let's stay** at home.'

■ **help**
You can say **help** somebody **do** *or* **help** somebody **to do**:
  - Tom **helped me carry** the box. *or* Tom **helped me to carry** the box.

UNIT 48   Exercises

48.1 Write sentences beginning **I (don't) want you ... / Do you want me ... ?**

1 (you must come with me)   *I want you to come with me.*
2 (shall I come with you?)   *Do you want me to come with you* .... ?
3 (listen carefully)   I want ....
4 (please don't be angry)   I don't ....
5 (shall I wait for you?)   Do you .... ?
6 (don't phone me tonight)   ....
7 (you must meet Sarah)   ....
8 (shall I make some coffee?) .... ?

48.2 Write sentences with **advised/persuaded/let** etc.

1 (George came with us / we persuaded him)   *We persuaded George to come with us.*
2 (I stayed in bed / the doctor advised me)   The doctor ....
3 (she phoned me / I asked her)   I ....
4 (I went to the party / Tom persuaded me)   Tom ....
5 (I used their phone / they let me)   They ....
6 (Ann plays the piano / her mother taught her)   Ann's ....

48.3 Write sentences with **told**.

1 Tom said to Ann: 'Wait for me!'   *Tom told Ann to wait for him.*
2 I said to you: 'Don't wait for me.'   *I told you not to wait for me.*
3 The man said to me: 'Get into the car!' The man told ....
4 I said to the children: 'Be quiet.'   I ....
5 She said to me: 'Don't lose the key.'   She ....
6 Tom said to me: 'Phone me later.'   ....
7 I said to Tom: 'Don't say anything.'   ....

48.4 Complete these sentences with the verbs in the list. Sometimes **to** is necessary (**to get /
to arrive** etc.) and sometimes **to** is not necessary (**get/arrive** etc.).

arrive   clean   cry   do   explain   ~~go~~   get   hear   know   sleep
wait   walk

1 Please stay with me. I don't want you ...*to go.*......
2 Kevin's parents didn't want him .... married.
3 She didn't understand the story, so she asked me .... it to her.
4 Don't wake me up tomorrow morning. Let me ....
5 Talk quietly. I don't want anybody .... us.
6 'Do you want to go by car?'   'No, let's .... '
7 You're here early. I expected you .... later.
8 It was a very sad film. It made me ....
9 Please don't tell Sarah about my plan. I don't want her ....
10 The kitchen is very dirty. Can you help me .... it?
11 'Shall we begin?'   'No, let's .... a few minutes.'
12 What do you think about my problem? What do you advise me .... ?

97

UNIT 49   He said that . . . / He told me that . . .

He said that he was tired.

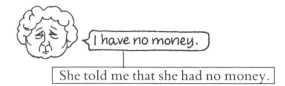

She told me that she had no money.

■ After **said that** / **told** (somebody) **that** . . . a verb is usually *past*:

am/is → was	(she said) '**I'm** working.' → She said that she **was** working. (they said to us) 'The hotel **isn't** very good.' → They told us that the hotel **wasn't** very good.
are → were	(I said) 'The shops **are** open.' → I said that the shops **were** open.
have/has → had	(I said to him) '**I've** finished my work.' → I told him that I **had** finished my work.
can → could	(Tom said) 'I **can't** come to the party.' → Tom said that he **couldn't** come to the party.
will → would	(my friends said to me) 'The exam **will** be easy.' → My friends told me that the exam **would** be easy.
do/does → did	(I said) 'It **doesn't** matter.' → I said that it **didn't** matter. (he said) 'I **don't** know your address.' → He said that he **didn't** know my address.
like → liked	(Mary said) 'I **like** tomatoes.' → Mary said that she **liked** tomatoes.
go → went (etc.)	(they said) 'We often **go** to the cinema.' → They said that they often **went** to the cinema.

■ **say** (→ **said**) and **tell** (→ **told**)
say something (**to** somebody): They **said that** . . . (*not* 'They said me that . . .')
tell somebody something: They **told me that** . . . / They **told Ann that** . . .
       – He **said** that he was tired. (*not* 'He said *me* that he was tired.')
  but   He **told me** that he was tired. (*not* 'He told that he was tired.')
       – What did he **say to you**? (*not* 'say you')
  but   What did he **tell you**? (*not* 'tell to you')

■ '**that**' is not necessary in these sentences. You can say:
       – He said **that** he was tired. *or* He said he was tired. (*without* '**that**')

98

UNIT 49   Exercises

49.1 A is talking to B about other people. Finish A's second sentence.

1 A: She likes you.   B: Does she? Are you sure?
   A: Yes, she told me that ....*she liked you*..............
2 A: He is married.   B: Is he? Are you sure?
   A: Yes, he told me that he ....
3 A: She can play tennis.   B: Can she? Are you sure?
   A: Yes, she said that ....
4 A: They are from Italy.   B: Are they? Are you sure?
   A: Yes, they told me that ....
5 A: She has got a job.   B: Has she? Are you sure?
   A: Yes, she told me that ....
6 A: They will help us.   B: Will they? Are you sure?
   A: Yes, they said that ....
7 A: He is going to India.   B: Is he? Are you sure?
   A: Yes, he said that ....
8 A: She works in a bank.   B: Does she? Are you sure?
   A: Yes, she told me that ....
9 A: They live in London.   B: Do they? Are you sure?
   A: Yes, they told me that ....
10 A: She is studying art.   B: Is she? Are you sure?
   A: Yes, she said that ....

49.2 Read what these people say and then write sentences with **She/He said that ...**

1 I'm tired
   ....*He said that he was tired*..........

2 I'll phone later.
   She said that she ....

3 I don't want to study.
   He said ....

4 I haven't been to London.
   He ....

5 I've lost my key.
   ....

6 I'm learning German.
   ....

7 I can't drive a car.
   ....

8 I know the answer.
   ....

9 I'm not going out.
   ....

10 I've got a lot of problems.
   ....

49.3 Put in **say/said** or **tell/told**.

1 She ..*said*...... that she was tired.   6 Did Lucy .... that she would be late?
2 He ..*told*..... me that he was tired.   7 I didn't .... the police anything.
3 I .... her that it was important.   8 The man .... us he was a reporter.
4 Jack .... me you were ill.   9 He .... he was a reporter.
5 She .... she didn't like Peter.   10 Did they .... you their names?

99

UNIT 50   I went to the shop to buy ...

Ann didn't have any bread.
But she wanted some bread.
So she went to the shop.

Why did she go to the shop?
To buy some bread.

She went to the shop **to buy**
some bread.

■ **to ...** (**to do** / **to buy** / **to see** etc.) tells us *why* a person does something (*the purpose*):
    – 'Why are you going out?'   '**To buy** a newspaper.'
    – George went to the station **to meet** his friend.
    – She turned on the TV **to watch** the news.
    – I'd like to go to Spain **to learn** Spanish.

money/time to (do something):
    – We need some **money to buy** food.
    – I haven't got **time to watch** television.

■ **to ...** and **for ...** :

to + *verb*:   **to buy** / **to have** / **to see** etc.
for + *noun*:   **for some bread** / **for dinner** / **for a holiday** etc.
    – She went to the shop **to buy** some bread. (**to** + *verb*)
  but   She went to the shop **for some bread**. (**for** + *noun*)
    – They are going to Scotland **to see** their grandmother. (*not* 'for to see')
  but   They are going to Scotland **for a holiday**.
    – We need some money **to buy** food. (*not* 'for buy')
  but   We need some money **for food**.

■ **wait**

wait for somebody/something:
    – Are you **waiting for the bus**?
    – Please wait **for me**.

wait for somebody/something **to ...** :
    – I can't go out yet. **I'm waiting for John to phone**.
    – I was having dinner when they arrived. They **waited for me to finish** my meal.

enough/too + **to ...**   ▶ Units 85–6

UNIT 50 Exercises

50.1 Write sentences with **I went to the ... to ...** Choose from:

get some medicine	meet a friend	~~catch a train~~	buy some food
get some stamps	get some money		

1 (the station)   I went to the station to catch a train.
2 (the bank)   I went ....
3 (the supermarket)   I ....
4 (the post office)   ....
5 (the chemist)   ....
6 (the café)   ....

50.2 Finish the sentences with the best ending. Choose from:

to open this door	to let some fresh air into the room	to wake them up
~~to watch the news~~	to tell him about the party	to get some petrol
to see the Pyramids	to read the newspaper	to clean it
to see who it was		

1 I turned on the television   to watch the news.
2 She sat down in an armchair ....
3 Do I need a key .... ?
4 The house is dirty but they don't have time ....
5 She opened the window ....
6 I knocked on their bedroom door ....
7 We stopped at a petrol station ....
8 A lot of people go to Egypt ....
9 I phoned Tom ....
10 The doorbell rang, so I looked out of the window ....

50.3 Put in **to** or **for**.

1 She went to the shop .to... buy some bread.
2 We stopped at a petrol station .... some petrol.
3 I'm going to walk home. I haven't got any money .... a taxi.
4 We went to a restaurant .... have dinner.
5 He wants to go to university .... study economics.
6 I'm going to London .... an interview next week.
7 I'm going to London .... visit a friend of mine.
8 I got up late this morning. I didn't have time .... wash.
9 Everybody needs money .... live.
10 The office is very small. There's space only .... a table and a chair.

50.4 Finish these sentences. Use the words in brackets ( ).

1 I can't go out yet. I'm waiting   for John to phone. .... (John / phone).
2 We're not going out yet. We're waiting .... (the rain / stop).
3 We called the police and then we waited .... (them / come).
4 I sat down in the cinema and waited .... (the film / begin).

UNIT 51　get

■ **get something/somebody** = receive/buy/fetch/find

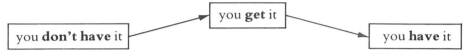

you **don't have** it → you **get** it → you **have** it

- Did you **get my letter** last week? (= *receive*)
- I like your pullover. Where did you **get it**? (= *buy*)
- (*on the phone*) 'Hello, can I speak to Ann, please?'　'One moment. I'll **get her**.' (= *fetch*)
- Is it difficult to **get a job** in your country? (= *find*)

■ **get cold/hungry/tired/better** etc. (**get** + *adjective*) = become

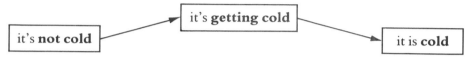

it's **not cold** → it's **getting cold** → it is **cold**

- Drink your coffee. It**'s getting cold**.
- If you don't eat, you **get hungry**.
- I'm sorry he's ill. I hope he **gets better** soon.

also: **get married** and **get lost**:
- Linda and Frank **are getting married** next month.
- I went for a walk and **got lost**. (= I lost my way)

■ **get to** a place (**get to work** / **get to London** / **get home** etc.) = arrive
- I usually **get to work** before 8.30. (= *arrive at work*)
- We went to Oxford yesterday. We left London at 8.00 and **got to Oxford** at 9.00.
- Can you tell me how to **get to the city centre**?

but **get home** (*not* 'get to home'):
- What time did you **get home** last night?

■ **get in/out/on/off**
get in (a car)
get out (of a car)

get on
get off } (a bus, a train, a plane)

- She **got in the car** and drove away. (*you can also say* 'got **into** the car')
- A car stopped and a man **got out**. (*but* 'got out **of the car**')
- They **got on** the bus outside the hotel and **got off** in Cross Street.

UNIT 51　Exercises

51.1 Finish these sentences. Use **get(s)** + the best ending.

your shoes　~~my letter~~　**some milk**　**a ticket**　**a doctor**　**the job**
some petrol　**a very good salary**

1 I wrote to you last week. Did you .get.my.letter... ?
2 We stopped at the petrol station to ....
3 Quick! This man is ill. We must ....
4 Where did you .... ?　They're very nice.
5 'Are you going to the concert?'　'Yes, if I can .... ,
6 I had an interview with the manager but I didn't ....
7 When you go to the shop, can you .... ?
8 She's got a good job. She ....

51.2 Complete these sentences. Use **getting** + one of these words:

dark　**late**　~~cold~~　**ready**　**married**

1 Drink your coffee. It's .getting.cold..
2 It's .... It's time to go home.
3 'I'm .... next week.'　'Oh, are you? Congratulations!'
4 'Where's Sally?'　'She's in her room. She's .... to go out.'
5 Turn on the light. It's ....

51.3 Complete the sentences. Use **get/got** + one of these words:

tired　**old**　~~hungry~~　**married**　**better**　**wet**　**lost**

1 If you don't eat, you .get.hungry...
2 If you work very hard, you ....
3 Don't go out in the rain. You'll ....
4 My brother .... last month. His wife's name is Julia.
5 We didn't know the way home, so we ....
6 Everybody wants to stay young, but we all ....
7 The beginning of the film wasn't very good but it ....

51.4 Write sentences with **I left ... and got to ...**

1 (home / 7.30 → work / 8.15)　.I.left.home.at.7.30.and.got.to.work.at.8.15.......................
2 (London / 10.15 → Bristol / 11.45)　I left London at 10.15 and ....

....

3 (home / 8.30 → the airport / 9.30)　I left home ....

....

4 (the party / 11.15 → home / midnight)　I ....

....

51.5 Put in **got** + **in/out (of)/on /off**.

1 She .....got.in........ the car and drove away.
2 I .... the bus and walked to my house from the bus-stop.
3 She .... the car, shut the door and went into a shop.
4 I made a stupid mistake. I .... the wrong train.

UNIT 52 go

■ **go to . . .** (**go to London** / **go to work** / **go to a concert** etc.)
— I'm **going to France** next week.
— What time do you usually **go to work**?
— Tom didn't want to **go to the concert**.
— I **went to the dentist** on Friday.
— What time did you **go to bed** last night?

also: **go to sleep** (= start to sleep):
— I went to bed and **went to sleep** very quickly.

go home (*without* **to**):
— I'm **going home** now. (*not* 'going to home')

■ **go on**   **holiday** / **a trip** / **an excursion** / **a cruise**
— We **go on holiday** (**to** Scotland) every year.
— When we were on holiday, we **went on** a lot of excursions **to** different places.
— Schoolchildren often **go** away **on school trips**.

■ **go for**   **a walk** / **a run** / **a swim** / **a drink** / **a meal** / **a holiday**
— The sea looks nice. Let's **go for a swim**.
— Last night we **went** out **for a meal**. The restaurant was very good.
— 'Where's Ann?'   'She**'s gone for a walk** in the park.'
— They've **gone to** Scotland **for a holiday**.
   (We say '**on holiday**' *but* '**for a** holiday')

■ **go swimming** / **go shopping** etc.

We use **go –ing** for sporting activities (**go swimming** / **go skiing** / **go jogging** / **go fishing** etc.) and also **shopping** (**go shopping**):

I **go**	shopp**ing**
he **is going**	swimm**ing**
we **went**	fish**ing**
they **have gone**	sail**ing**
she wants **to go**	ski**ing**
	etc.

— We live near the mountains. In winter we **go skiing** every weekend.
— She has a small boat and she often **goes sailing**.
— Are you **going shopping** this afternoon?
— It's a nice day. Let's **go swimming**. (*or* Let's **go for a swim**.)
— George **went fishing** last Sunday. He caught a lot of fish.

UNIT 52   Exercises

52.1 Put in **to/on/for** where necessary.

1 I'm going ..to.. France next week.
2 She has a small boat, so she often goes .—... sailing. (*no preposition*)
3 Sue went .... New York last year.
4 Would you like to go .... the cinema this evening?
5 Jack goes .... jogging every morning before breakfast.
6 I'm going out .... a walk. Do you want to come?
7 I'm tired because I went .... a party last night and went .... bed very late.
8 They're going .... holiday .... Italy next week.
9 The weather was warm and the river was clean, so we went .... a swim.
10 Excuse me, I must go .... the toilet.
11 It's late. I must go .... home now.
12 I need some stamps, so I'm going .... the post office.
13 One day, I'd like to go .... a trip round the world.
14 She isn't feeling well, so she's gone .... the doctor.

52.2 What did these people do yesterday afternoon? Look at the pictures and write a sentence with **went -ing**.

George   Diane   Peter   Harry   Linda   Sheila

1 George went sailing...........................   4 ....
2 Diane ....   5 ....
3 ....   6 ....

52.3 Use the words in the list to finish these sentences. Use **to/on/for** if necessary.

home   shopping   ~~a swim~~   Portugal   riding   holiday   the bank
sleep   fishing   a walk

1 The sea looks nice. Let's go for a swim...
2 George went .... and caught a lot of fish.
3 I went .... in the cinema because the film was very boring.
4 'Is Ann at home?' 'No, she's gone .... to get some money.'
5 He has three horses. He often goes ....
6 The weather is nice. Shall we go .... in the park?
7 I'm going .... I have to buy a lot of things.
8 It's late and I'm tired. I'm going .... Goodnight.
9 'Are you going .... soon?' 'Yes, next month. We're going .... '

UNIT 53   I/me   he/him   they/them etc.

■ *people*

subject	**I**	**we**	**you**	**he**	**she**	**they**
object	**me**	**us**	**you**	**him**	**her**	**them**

subject			*object*
I	**I** like Ann.	Ann likes **me**.	**me**
we	**We** like Ann.	Ann likes **us**.	**us**
you	**You** like Ann.	Ann likes **you**.	**you**
he	**He** likes Ann.	Ann likes **him**.	**him**
she	**She** likes Ann.	Ann likes **her**.	**her**
they	**They** like Ann.	Ann likes **them**.	**them**

Use **me/him/her** etc. (*object*) after *prepositions* (**for/to/at/with** etc.):
- This letter isn't **for you**. It's **for me**.
- Where's Alan? I want to talk **to him**.
- Who is that woman? Why are you looking **at her**?
- We're going to the cinema. Do you want to come **with us**?
- They are going to the cinema. Do you want to go **with them**?

■ *things*

> It's nice. I like it.

> They're nice. I like them.

subject	**it**	**they**
object	**it**	**them**

- I want **that book**. Please give **it** to me.
- I want **those books**. Please give **them** to me.
- Diane never drinks **milk**. She doesn't like **it**.
- I never go to **parties**. I don't like **them**.
- 'Where's **the newspaper**?'   'You're sitting **on it**.'

UNIT 53   Exercises

53.1 Finish the sentences with **him/her/them**.

1 I don't know those girls. Do you know ....them......... ?
2 I don't know that man. Do you know .... ?
3 I don't know those people. Do you know .... ?
4 I don't know Fred's wife. Do you know .... ?
5 I don't know his friends. Do you know .... ?
6 I don't know the woman in the black coat. Do you know .... ?
7 I don't know Mr Stevens. Do you know .... ?
8 I don't know those students. Do you know .... ?

53.2 Finish the sentences. Use **I/me/we/us/you/he/him/she/her/they/them**.

1 **I** want to see **her** but ....she........ doesn't want to see ....me.........

2 **I** want to see **him** but .... doesn't want to see ....
3 **They** want to see **me** but .... don't want to see ....
4 **We** want to see **them** but .... don't want to see ....
5 **She** wants to see **him** but .... doesn't want to see ....
6 **They** want to see **her** but .... doesn't want to see ....
7 **I** want to see **them** but .... don't want to see ....
8 **He** wants to see **us** but .... don't want to see ....
9 **You** want to see **her** but .... doesn't want to see ....

53.3 Finish the sentences. Use **me/us/him/her/it/them**.

1 Who is that woman? Why are you looking at ......her............ ?
2 'Do you know that man?'   'Yes, I work with ....'
3 I'm talking to you. Please listen to ....
4 These photographs are nice. Do you want to look at .... ?
5 I like that camera. I'm going to buy ....
6 Where are the tickets? I can't find ....
7 We're going out. You can come with ....
8 I don't like dogs. I'm afraid of ....
9 Where is she? I want to talk to ....
10 Those apples are bad. Don't eat ....

53.4 Put in **it/them** + **me/us/him/her/them**.

1 I want those books. Please give .....them......... to ....me.........
2 He wants the key. Please give .... to ....
3 She wants the keys. Please give .... to ....
4 I want the letter. Please give .... to ....
5 They want the money. Please give .... to ....
6 We want the photographs. Please give .... to ....

UNIT 54   my/his/their etc.

I → **my**	I like	**my**	job.
we → **our**	We like	**our**	jobs.
you → **your**	You like	**your**	job.
he → **his**	He likes	**his**	job.
she → **her**	She likes	**her**	job.
they → **their**	They like	**their**	jobs.
it → **its**	Oxford (= it) is famous for **its** university.		

We use **my/your/his/her** etc. + *a noun*:

my hands	**his mother**	**her** new **car**
our house	**your** best **friend**	**their room**

■ **his/her/their**:

■ **its** and **it's**:

its   Oxford is famous for **its** university.
it's (= it **is**)   I like Oxford. **It's** a nice city. (= It **is** nice.)

108

UNIT 54   Exercises

54.1 Finish these sentences.

1 He .... *lives with his parents.*...............
2 They live with .... parents.
3 We .... parents.
4 Ann lives ....

5 I .... parents.
6 John ....
7 Do you live .... ?
8 Most children ....

54.2 Finish these sentences.

1 I ...*'m going to wash my hands.*................
2 She's going to wash ....
3 We're going to ....

4 He's going to ....
5 They're going ....
6 Are you going .... ?

54.3 Look at the family tree and finish the sentences.

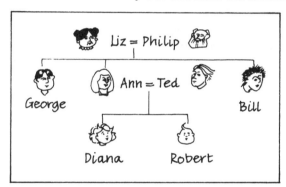

1 I saw Liz with ..*her*. husband, Philip.
2 I saw Ann and Ted with .... children.
3 I saw Ted with .... wife, Ann.
4 I saw George with .... brother, Bill.
5 I saw Ann with .... brother, Bill.
6 I saw Liz and Philip with .... son, Bill.
7 I saw Ann with .... parents.
8 I saw Diana and Robert with .... parents.

54.4 Put in **my/our/your/his/her/their/its**.

1 I like .*my*. job.
2 Do you like .... job?
3 Does your father like .... job?
4 Sally is married. .... husband works in a bank.
5 I know Mr Watson but I don't know .... wife.
6 Put on .... coat when you go out. It's very cold.
7 .... favourite sport is tennis. I play a lot in summer.
8 My sister plays tennis too but .... favourite sport is athletics.
9 We're staying at a very nice hotel. .... room is very comfortable.
10 Mr and Mrs Baker live in London but .... son lives in Australia.
11 Thank you for .... letter. It was good to hear from you again.
12 We are going to invite all .... friends to the party.
13 John is a teacher but .... sister is a nurse.
14 Do you think that most people are happy in .... jobs?
15 I gave the money to my mother and she put it in .... bag.
16 I often see that man but I don't know .... name.
17 They've got two children but I don't remember .... names.
18 The company has offices in many places but .... head office is in New York.

UNIT 55　Whose is this? It's mine.

| mine | ours | yours | his | hers | theirs |

I	→	my	→	mine
we	→	our	→	ours
you	→	your	→	yours
he	→	his	→	his
she	→	her	→	hers
they	→	their	→	theirs

It's **my money**.	It's **mine**.
It's **our money**.	It's **ours**.
It's **your money**.	It's **yours**.
It's **his money**.	It's **his**.
It's **her money**.	It's **hers**.
It's **their money**.	It's **theirs**.

■ **my/our/your/her/their** + *a noun* (**my hands / your book** etc.):
  - **My hands** are cold.
  - Is this **your book**?
  - Ann gave me **her umbrella**.
  - It's **their problem**, not **our problem**.

■ **mine/ours/yours/hers/theirs** *without a noun*:
  - These books are **mine** but this newspaper is **yours**. (= your newspaper)
  - I didn't have an umbrella, so Ann gave me **hers**. (= her umbrella)
  - It's their problem, not **ours**. (= our problem)
  - 'Is that their car?' 'No, **theirs** is green.' (= their car)

■ **his** *with or without a noun*:
  - Is this **his camera**?
  - It's a nice camera. Is it **his**?

■ We say: a friend **of mine** / a friend **of his** / some friends **of yours** etc.:
  - I went out to meet **a friend of mine**. (*not* 'a friend of me')
  - Are those people **friends of yours**? (*not* 'friends of you')

■ **Whose . . . ?**
  - **Whose book** is this? (= Is it your book? his book? my book? etc.)

You can use **whose** with or without a noun:
  - **Whose money** is this? } It's mine.
    Whose is this?
  - **Whose shoes** are these? } They're John's.
    Whose are these?

110

UNIT 55   Exercises

55.1 Finish the sentences with **mine/yours** etc.

1 It's your money.   It's _yours_.
2 It's my bag.   It's ....
3 It's our car.   It's ....
4 They're her shoes.   They're ....

5 It's their house.   ....
6 They're your books.   ....
7 They're my glasses.   ....
8 It's his coat.   ....

55.2 Choose the right word.

1 Is this your/~~yours~~ book? (your is *right*)
2 It's their/~~theirs~~ problem, not ~~your~~/ours. (their and ours are *right*)
3 Are these your/yours shoes?
4 Is this camera your/yours?
5 That's not my/mine umbrella. My/Mine is yellow.
6 They know our/ours address but we don't know their/theirs.
7 They've got two children but I don't know their/theirs names.
8 My/Mine room is bigger than her/hers, but her/hers is nicer.

55.3 Finish these sentences with ... **friend(s) of mine/yours** etc.

1 I went to the cinema with a _friend of mine_.
2 They went on holiday with some _friends of theirs._
3 She's going out with a friend ....
4 We had dinner with some ....
5 I played tennis with a ....
6 He's going to meet a ....
7 Do you know that man? Is he a .... ?

55.4 Look at the pictures. Write questions with **Whose ... ?**

1 _Whose book is this_ ?
2 Whose .... ?
3 .... ?
4 .... ?
5 .... ?
6 .... ?

7 .... ?
8 .... ?
9 .... ?
10 .... ?
11 .... ?
12 .... ?

UNIT 56   I/me/my/mine

I etc.	**me** etc.	**my** etc.	**mine** etc.
I know Tom.	Tom knows **me**.	It's **my** car.	It's **mine**.
We know Tom.	Tom knows **us**.	It's **our** car.	It's **ours**.
You know Tom.	Tom knows **you**.	It's **your** car.	It's **yours**.
He knows Tom.	Tom knows **him**.	It's **his** car.	It's **his**.
She knows Tom.	Tom knows **her**.	It's **her** car.	It's **hers**.
They know Tom.	Tom knows **them**.	It's **their** car.	It's **theirs**.
▶ Unit 53	▶ Unit 53	▶ Unit 54	▶ Unit 55

- 'Do **you** know that man?'   'Yes, **I** know **him** but **I** can't remember **his name**.'
- She was very happy because **we** invited **her** to stay with **us** at **our house**.
- 'Where are the children? Have **you** seen **them**?'   'Yes, **they** are playing with **their friends** in the garden.'
- That pen is **mine**. Can **you** give it to **me**, please?
- 'Is this **your umbrella**?'   'No, it's **yours**.'
- **He** didn't have an umbrella, so **she** gave **him hers**. (= she gave her umbrella to him)
- **I** gave **him my address** and **he** gave **me his**. (= he gave his address to me)

UNIT 56 Exercises

56.1 Finish the sentences in the same way.

1. Do you know that man?
Yes, I *know him but I can't remember his name.*

2. Do you know that woman?
Yes, I know ...., but I can't remember ....

3. Do you know these people?
Yes, I .... but I .... names.

4. Do you know me?
Yes, I .... but ....

56.2 Finish these sentences in the same way.

1 We invited her *to stay with us at our house.* ....
2 He invited us to stay with .... house.
3 They invited me to stay with .... house.
4 I invited her to stay ....
5 We invited them to ....
6 You invited him ....
7 She invited me ....

56.3 Finish the sentences.

1 It's hers. Give *it to her.* ....
2 They're mine. Give *them to me.* ....
3 It's his. Give it ....
4 They're hers. Give them ....
5 It's ours. Give ....
6 It's theirs. Give ....
7 They're his. Give ....
8 It's mine. Give ....

56.4 Finish the sentences in the same way.

Here's my address. And here's mine.

1 I gave him *my address and he gave me his.* ....
2 I gave her .... address and she gave me ....
3 He gave me .... address and I gave ....
4 We gave her .... address and she gave ....
5 I gave them .... address and they ....
6 She gave us .... address and ....
7 You gave him .... address and ....
8 We gave them .... address and ....
9 They gave you .... address and ....
10 She gave him .... address and ....

UNIT 57 myself/yourself/himself etc.

Jack is looking at Tom.
He is looking at **him**.

Tom is looking in the mirror.
He is looking at **himself**.

He is looking at **him** .
——different people——

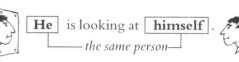

He is looking at **himself** .
——the same person——

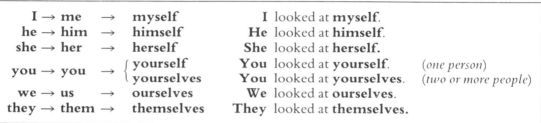

I → me →	**myself**	I looked at **myself**.	
he → him →	**himself**	He looked at **himself**.	
she → her →	**herself**	She looked at **herself**.	
you → you → {	**yourself**	You looked at **yourself**.	(one person)
	yourselves	You looked at **yourselves**.	(two or more people)
we → us →	**ourselves**	We looked at **ourselves**.	
they → them →	**themselves**	They looked at **themselves**.	

- **I cut myself** with a knife. (*not* 'I cut me')
- She fell off her bicycle but **she** didn't **hurt herself**.
- Do **you** sometimes **talk to yourself** when you are alone?
- If you want some more food, **help yourselves**.
- Did **they pay for themselves** or did you pay for them?
- 'Did you all have a nice time?' 'Yes, **we enjoyed ourselves**.'

■ **by myself/by yourself** etc. = alone
- **I** went on holiday **by myself**. (= I went on holiday alone.)
- She wasn't with her friends. **She** was **by herself**.

■ **-selves** and **each other**
- I looked at **myself** and Tom looked at **himself**.
  = We looked at **ourselves** (*in the mirror*).
- *but* I looked at Tom and he looked at me.
  = We looked at **each other**.

We looked at ourselves.

- Jill and Ann are good friends. They know **each other** very well.
  (= Jill knows Ann and Ann knows Jill.)
- Paul and I live near **each other**.
  (= Paul lives near me and I live near him.)

We looked at each other.

UNIT 57   Exercises

57.1 Finish the sentences with **myself/yourself** etc.

1 He enjoyed .himself........................
2 I enjoyed ....
3 She enjoyed ....
4 We enjoyed ....

5 Did you enjoy .... ? (one person)
6 Bill and I enjoyed ....
7 The children enjoyed ....
8 Jack didn't enjoy ....

57.2 Finish the sentences with **myself/yourself** etc.

1 I cut .myself..... with a knife.
2 Be careful! That plate is very hot. Don't burn ....
3 I'm not angry with you. I'm angry with ....
4 They never think about other people. They only think about ....
5 I got out of the bath and dried .... with a towel.
6 When people are alone, they often talk to ....
7 The police say that the woman shot .... with a gun.
8 Don't pay for me. I want to pay for ....
9 He fell off the ladder but he didn't hurt ....
10 I'd like to know more about you. Tell me about .... (one person)
11 Goodbye! Have a good holiday and look after ....! (two people)

57.3 Make sentences with **by myself / by yourself** etc.

1 I went on holiday alone.   I went on holiday by myself.
2 John lives alone.   John lives ....
3 Do you live alone?   Do you ....
4 She went to the cinema alone.   She ....
5 When I saw him, he was alone.   When I saw him, ...
6 Don't go out alone.   Don't ....
7 I had dinner alone.   I ....

57.4 Finish the sentences. Use **each other**.

1 I looked at Bill and Bill looked at me.   Bill and I looked at each other. ....
2 I know him and he knows me.   We ....
3 She likes him and he likes her.   They ....
4 You can help me and I can help you.   We can ....
5 He understands her and she understands him.
   They ....
6 He gives her presents and she gives him presents.
   They ....
7 Tom didn't see Jill and Jill didn't see Tom.
   Tom and Jill ....
8 I didn't speak to her and she didn't speak to me.
   We ....
9 She often writes letters to him and he often writes letters to her.
   ....

UNIT 58   -'s (Ann's camera / my brother's car etc.)

Ann's camera
(**her** camera)

my brother's car
(**his** car)

the manager's office
(**his** or **her** office)

■ We normally use **-'s** (*not* **of . . .**) for *people*:
- – I stayed at **my sister's** house. (*not* 'the house of my sister')
- – Have you met **Mr Kelly's** wife? (*not* 'the wife of Mr Kelly')
- – Are you going to **James's** party?
- – Ann is **a girl's** name.

You can use **-'s** without a noun:
- – Mary's hair is longer than **Ann's**. (= Ann's hair)
- – 'Whose umbrella is this?'   'It's **my mother's**.' (= my mother's umbrella)
- – 'Where were you last night?'   'At **John's**.' (= John's house)

■ friend's and friends'

my friend's house = *one friend*
(= **his** house *or* **her** house)

my friends' house = *two or more friends*
(= **their** house)

We write **-'s** after **friend/student/mother** etc. (*singular*):
my mother's car (*one mother*)   my father's car (*one father*)

We write **-'** after friend**s**/student**s**/parent**s** etc. (*plural*):
my parent**s'** car (*two parent**s***)

■ We use **of . . .** (*not usually* **-'s**) for *things, places* etc.:

the roof **of the building** (*not* 'the building's roof')
the beginning **of the film** (*not* 'the film's beginning')
the time **of the next train**   the name **of this town**
the capital **of Spain**   the cause **of the problem**
the meaning **of this word**   the back **of the car**

UNIT 58 Exercises

58.1 Look at the family tree and finish the sentences. Use **-'s**.

Liz and Philip are married.
They have two children, Charles and Ann.
Ann is married to Ted.
Ann and Ted have a son, Robert.

1 Philip is .....Liz's..... husband.
2 Liz is .... wife.
3 Charles is .... brother.
4 Charles is .... uncle.
5 Ann is .... wife.

6 Liz is .... grandmother.
7 Ann is .... sister.
8 Ted is .... husband.
9 Ted is .... father.
10 Robert is .... nephew.

58.2 Look at the big picture and then answer the questions.

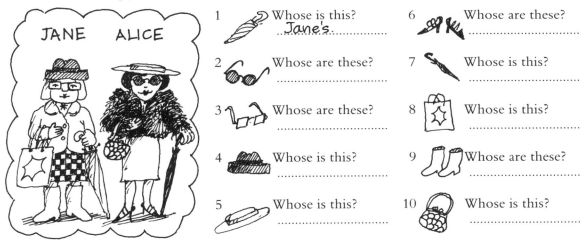

JANE   ALICE

1 Whose is this?
...Jane's...........

2 Whose are these?
....

3 Whose are these?
....

4 Whose is this?
....

5 Whose is this?
....

6 Whose are these?
....

7 Whose is this?
....

8 Whose is this?
....

9 Whose are these?
....

10 Whose is this?
....

58.3 Complete the sentences. Sometimes you need **-'s**, sometimes **of** ...

1 I like ...Ann's camera.. (the camera / Ann)
2 What is ...the name of this town.................................... ? (the name / this town)
3 When is .... ? (the birthday / your sister)
4 Do you like .... ? (the colour / this coat)
5 Write your name at .... (the top / the page)
6 What is .... ? (the address / Jill)
7 What was .... ? (the cause / the accident)
8 .... is near the city centre. (the house / my parents)
9 .... is very good. (the spoken English / Maria)
10 For me the morning is .... (the best part / the day)
11 .... very interesting. (the job / my brother)
12 The car stopped at .... (the end / the street)
13 .... is blue. (the favourite colour / Pat)
14 .... are very thin. (the walls / this house)

UNIT 59   a/an

He's got **a** camera.

She's waiting for **a** bus.

It's **a** nice day.

■ **a** = 'one'. Don't forget **a**:
  – Do you want **a cup** of tea? (*not* 'Do you want cup of tea?')
  – Alice works in **a bank**. (*not* 'in bank')
  – I want to ask **a question**. (*not* 'ask question')
  – When I was **a child**, I liked reading stories.
  – Birmingham is **a** large **city** in central England.

■ **an** (*not* **a**) before **a/e/i/o/u**:
  – They live in **an o**ld house. (*not* 'a old house.')
  – **A m**ouse is **an a**nimal. It's **a s**mall animal.
  – Can you give me **an e**xample, please?
  – This is **an i**nteresting book.
  – I bought **a h**at and **an u**mbrella.

  also **an hour** (**h** is not pronounced: an (h)our)
  but   **a university**   **a European** country
  (these words are pronounced '*yuniversity*', '*yuropean*')

■ We use **a/an** for jobs etc.:
  – 'What's your job?'
    'I'm **a dentist**.' (*not* 'I'm dentist.')
  – 'What does she do?'   'She's **an engineer**.'
  – Would you like to be **a teacher**?
  – Beethoven was **a composer**.
  – Picasso was **a** famous **painter**.
  – Are you **a student**?

I'm a dentist.

■ **another** (an + other) is one word (*not* 'an other'):
  – Can I have **another cup** of coffee?
  – Open **another window**. It's very hot.

UNIT 59   Exercises

59.1 Write **a** or **an**.

1 .a.... book	7 .... organisation	13 .... question
2 an.. old book	8 .... restaurant	14 .... important question
3 .... window	9 .... Chinese restaurant	15 .... hamburger
4 .... horse	10 .... Indian restaurant	16 .... hour
5 .... airport	11 .... accident	17 .... economic problem
6 .... university	12 .... bad accident	18 .... nice evening

59.2 What are these things? Choose your answer from the list and write a sentence.

animal   ~~**bird**~~   **flower**   **fruit**   **musical instrument**   **planet**   **river**
tool   **game**   **vegetable**

1 a duck? It 's a bird.	6 a hammer? It ....
2 the Nile? It	7 a carrot? It ....
3 a rabbit? It	8 Mars? It ....
4 tennis? It	9 a trumpet? It ....
5 a rose? It	10 a pear? It ....

59.3 What are their jobs? Look at the pictures and finish the sentences. The jobs are: **nurse /
photographer / private detective /dentist / taxi-driver / road-sweeper / shop assistant**.

1 She 's a dentist.	5 She ....
2 He's	6 He ....
3 He	7 She ....
4 She	8 And you? I'm ....

59.4 Write sentences from the words in brackets (   ). Write **a** or **an** where necessary.

1 (I bought newspaper) I bought a newspaper.
2 (we went to party last night) We went ....
3 (my brother is artist) ....
4 (it's beautiful day today) ....
5 (I ate sandwich and apple) ....
6 (Britain is industrial country) ....
7 (I had bath this morning) ....
8 (Barbara works in office) ....
9 (it's very difficult question) ....
10 (we stayed at expensive hotel) ....

UNIT 60   flower/flowers (*singular* and *plural*)

■ The plural of a noun is usually **–s**:

singular (= one)   *plural* (= two or more)

            a flower → **some** flower**s**

            a week → **six** week**s**

            a baby → **two** babie**s**

    a nice place → **many** nice place**s**

a flower   **some** flowers

Spelling of plural endings   ▶ Appendix 4 (4.1 and 4.2):

-es after **-s/-sh/-ch/-x**:

    bu**s** → bu**ses**   di**sh** → di**shes**   chur**ch** → chur**ches**   bo**x** → bo**xes**

    also: potato → potato**es**   tomato → tomato**es**

-y → -ies:

    ba**by** → ba**bies**   par**ty** → par**ties**   dictiona**ry** → dictiona**ries**

    but   **-ay → -ays** / **-ey → -eys** / **-oy → -oys** / **-uy → -uys**

    d**ay** → d**ays**   monk**ey** → monk**eys**   b**oy** → b**oys**   g**uy** → g**uys**

-f/-fe → -ves:

    shel**f** → shel**ves**   kni**fe** → kni**ves**   wi**fe** → wi**ves**

■ These things are plural in English:

scissors   **glasses**   **trousers**   **jeans**   **shorts**   **pyjamas**   **tights**

    – Do you wear **glasses**?

    – I need the **scissors**. Where **are they**?

You can also say **a pair of . . .** with these words:

a pair of scissors   **a pair of jeans**   **a pair of tights** etc.

    – I need **a new pair of jeans**. *or* I need **some** new **jeans**. (*but not* 'a new jeans')

■ Some plurals do *not* end in **-s**:

---

    a **man** → two men   a **woman** → some wom**en**

    a **child** → many child**ren**

  one **foot** → two feet   a **tooth** → all my te**e**th

    a **mouse** → some m**ice**

    a **sheep** → two **sheep**   a **fish** → many **fish**

---

also: a **person** → **two people** / **some people** / **many people** etc.

    – **She**'s **a** nice **person**. *but* **They** are nice **people**. (*not* 'nice persons')

    – **Some people are** very stupid. (*not* 'Some people is')

Police is a plural word:

    – **The police are** coming. (*not* 'The police is coming.')

UNIT 60   Exercises

60.1 Write the plural.

1 flower ......*flowers*.......   8 woman ....   15 umbrella ....
2 man   ...*men*...............   9 address ....   16 person ....
3 boat   ....   10 sheep ....   17 family ....
4 language ....   11 tooth ....   18 holiday ....
5 watch ....   12 leaf ....   19 sandwich ....
6 country ....   13 child ....   20 city ....
7 knife   ....   14 foot ....   21 mouse   ....

60.2 Put in **is** or **are**.

1 ..*Is*.... the shop open?   6 Where .... my camera?   11 Who .... those men?
2 ..*Are*. the shops open?   7 Where .... my glasses?   12 Who .... that woman?
3 My hands .... cold.   8 Where .... the children?   13 Who .... those people?
4 My nose .... cold.   9 Your coat .... dirty.   14 Mice .... small animals.
5 My feet .... cold.   10 Your jeans .... dirty.   15 Where .... the scissors?

60.3 Some of these sentences are right and some are wrong. Correct the sentences that are wrong.
Write 'okay' if the sentence is right.

1 She's a very nice person. .*okay*..
2 I need a new jeans. *I need a new pair of jeans. OR I need some new jeans.*...........
3 I've got two brother and four sister. ....
4 It's a lovely park with a lot of beautiful tree. ....
5 There are a lot of sheep in that field. ....
6 Do you make many mistake when you speak English? ....
7 She's married and she has three childs. ....
8 Most of my friend are students. ....
9 He put on his pyjama and went to bed. ....
10 We went fishing but we didn't catch many fish. ....
11 There were three persons in the car, two women and a man. ....
12 I like your trouser. Where did you get it? ....
13 The town centre is usually full of tourist. ....
14 This scissor isn't very sharp. ....

60.4 Which is right? Complete the sentences.

1 It's a nice place. Many people .....*go*....... there for a holiday.   (**go** or **goes**?)
2 Some people .... always late.   (**is** or **are**?)
3 The president is not popular. The people .... like him.   (**don't** or **doesn't**?)
4 A lot of people .... television every day.   (**watch** or **watches**?)
5 Three people .... killed in the accident.   (**was** or **were**?)
6 How many people .... in that house?   (**live** or **lives**?)
7 .... the police carry guns in your country?   (**Do** or **Does**?)
8 The police .... looking for the stolen car.   (**is** or **are**?)
9 I need my glasses, but I can't find ....   (**it** or **them**?)
10 I'm going to buy .... new trousers today.   (**a** or **some**?)

121

UNIT 61   a car / some money (*countable/uncountable 1*)

A noun can be *countable* or *uncountable*.

Countable nouns   For example:

(a) **car**   (a) **hat**   (a) **flower**   (a) **man**   (a) **house**   (a) **party**   (an) **idea**

You can use **one/two/three . . .** + *countable nouns* (you can *count* them):

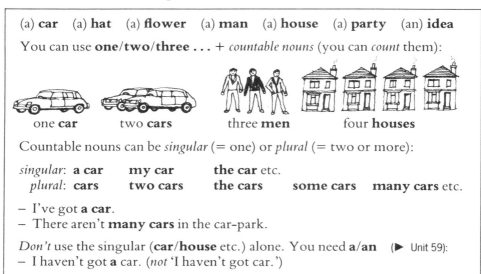

one **car**   two **cars**   three **men**   four **houses**

Countable nouns can be *singular* (= one) or *plural* (= two or more):

singular: **a car**   **my car**   **the car** etc.
plural: **cars**   **two cars**   **the cars**   **some cars**   **many cars** etc.

– I've got **a car**.
– There aren't **many cars** in the car-park.

Don't use the singular (**car/house** etc.) alone. You need **a/an**   (▶ Unit 59):
– I haven't got **a** car. (*not* 'I haven't got car.')

Uncountable nouns   For example:

water   rain   air   rice   salt   oil   plastic   money   music   tennis

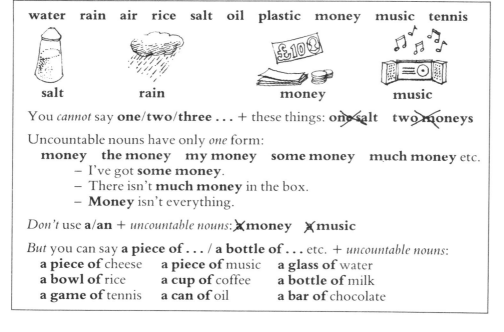

salt   **rain**   **money**   **music**

You *cannot* say **one/two/three . . .** + these things: one salt   two moneys

Uncountable nouns have only *one* form:
   money   the money   my money   some money   much money etc.
      – I've got **some money**.
      – There isn't **much money** in the box.
      – **Money** isn't everything.

Don't use **a/an** + *uncountable nouns*: money   music

But you can say **a piece of . . . / a bottle of . . .** etc. + *uncountable nouns*:
   a piece of cheese   **a piece of** music   **a glass of** water
   a bowl of rice   **a cup of** coffee   **a bottle of** milk
   a game of tennis   **a can of** oil   **a bar of** chocolate

▶ Unit 62 *countable/uncountable 2*

UNIT 61   Exercises

61.1 What are these things? Some are countable and some are uncountable. Write **a/an** if necessary. The names of the things are:

bucket   cup   sand   tea   toothpaste   credit card   money   hat   ~~salt~~
soap   toothbrush   ~~umbrella~~

1	2	3	4	5	6

7	8	9	10	11	12

1 .salt............   4 ....   7 ....   10 ....
2 .an umbrella......   5 ....   8 ....   11 ....
3 ....   6 ....   9 ....   12 ....

61.2 Some of these sentences need **a/an**. Some of the sentences are right. Put in **a/an** where necessary.

1 I haven't got car.   .a car.......................
2 Salt is not expensive.   okay.....................
3 Ann never wears hat.   ....
4 Are you looking for job?   ....
5 Mary doesn't eat meat.   ....
6 I'm going to party tonight.   ....
7 Do you like cheese?   ....

8 Do you want cup of coffee?   ....
9 I never drink milk.   ....
10 Britain is island.   ....
11 Jack made very bad mistake.   ....
12 Everybody needs food.   ....
13 Can you drive car?   ....
14 I've got very good idea.   ....

61.3 What are these things? Look at the pictures and write **a ... of ...** for each picture. Use the words in the boxes.

a	bar	cup	loaf	of	bread	~~milk~~	tea
	~~bottle~~	glass	piece		chocolate	paper	water
	bowl	jar	piece		honey	soup	wood

1	2	3	4	5	6	7	8	9

1 .a bottle of milk..........   4 ....   7 ....
2 ....   5 ....   8 ....
3 ....   6 ....   9 ....

UNIT 62   a car / some money (*countable/uncountable 2*)

▶ Unit 61   *countable/uncountable 1*

a/an and **some**

---

a/an + *singular countable nouns* (**car/apple/shoe** etc.):
   – I need **a** new **car**.
   – Would you like **an apple**?

some + *plural countable nouns* (**cars/apples/shoes** etc.):
   – I need **some** new **shoes**.
   – Would you like **some apples**?
   (= two or more apples)

some + *uncountable nouns* (**water/money/music** etc.):
   – I need **some money**.
   – Would you like **some cheese**?
   (*or* Would you like **a piece of** cheese?)

Compare **a/an** and **some**:
   – She bought **a hat**, **some shoes** and **some perfume**.
   – I read **a newspaper**, wrote **some letters** and listened to **some music**.

an apple

some apples

some cheese
or a piece of cheese

Many nouns are *sometimes countable* and *sometimes uncountable*. For example:

a cake   some cakes   some cake *or* a piece of cake

a chicken   some chickens   some chicken *or* a piece of chicken

---

■ Be careful with these words – they are usually uncountable in English:
bread   weather   information   advice   hair   furniture   paper   news
   – I'm going to buy **some bread** (*or* **a loaf of** bread). (*not* 'a bread')
   – It's nice **weather** today. (*not* 'It's a nice weather')
   – I need **some information** about hotels in London.
   – They have **some** very nice **furniture** in their house. (*not* 'furnitures')
   – She's got long **hair**. (*not* 'long hairs')
   – I want to make a list. Can you give me **some paper** (*or* **a piece of** paper / **a sheet of** paper)? (*not* 'a paper' – 'a paper' = a newspaper)
   – I've just had **some** good **news** about my holiday. (*not* 'a good news')

▶ Unit 59   **a/an**   ▶ Unit 70   **some   any**

UNIT 62   Exercises

62.1 What did you buy? Use the pictures to make sentences (**I bought ...**).

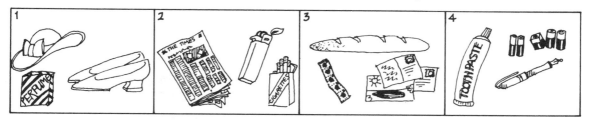

1 I bought a hat, some shoes and some perfume.
2 I bought ....
3 I ....
4 ....

62.2 Write sentences with **Would you like a/an ...?** or **Would you like some ...?**

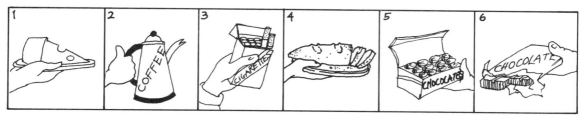

1 Would you like some cheese .... ?   4 .... ?
2 Would you like .... ?   5 .... ?
3 Would .... ?   6 .... ?

62.3 Put in **a/an** or **some**.

1 I read ...*a*.. newspaper, wrote ..*some*. letters and listened to ..*some*.. music.
2 I need .... money. I want to buy .... food.
3 We met .... interesting people at the party.
4 I'm going to open .... window to get .... fresh air.
5 She didn't eat much for lunch – only .... apple and .... bread.
6 We live in .... big house. There's .... nice garden with .... beautiful trees.
7 I'm going to make .... table. First, I need .... wood.
8 We talked to her and she gave us .... very good advice.
9 I want to write .... letter. I need .... pen and .... paper.
10 We had .... nice weather when we were on holiday.

62.4 Look at the <u>underlined</u> words in these sentences. Which is right?

1 I'm going to buy some new shoe/<u>shoes</u>.   (shoes is *right*)
2 They are going to buy some new <u>chair/chairs</u>.
3 They are going to buy some new <u>furniture/furnitures</u>.
4 He's got big blue <u>eye/eyes</u>.
5 He's got short fair <u>hair/hairs</u>.
6 The tourist guide gave us some <u>information/informations</u> about the town.

125

UNIT 63   a/an and the

a/an

- They've got **a car**. (*there are many cars and they've got one*)

- I'm writing **a letter**. (*there are many letters and I'm writing one*)

- When we were in London, we stayed at **a** small **hotel**. (*there are many small hotels in London*)

- Rome is **a** big **city** in Italy. (*there are many big cities in Italy and Rome is one*)

- Britain is **an island**. (*there are many islands and Britain is one*)

the

- I'm going to clean **the car** tomorrow. (= my car)

- I wrote to her but **the letter** never arrived. (= the letter that I wrote)

- We didn't enjoy our holiday. **The hotel** was terrible. (= our hotel)

- Rome is **the capital** of Italy. (*there is only one capital of Italy*)

- What is **the** largest **island** in **the world**?

■ We say **the . . .** when it is clear which thing we mean. For example:

the door / the ceiling / the floor / the carpet / the light etc. (*of a room*)
the roof / the garden / the kitchen / the bathroom etc. (*of a house*)
the centre / the station / the airport / the town hall etc. (*of a town*)

- 'Where's Tom?'   'In **the garden**.' (= the garden of this house)
- I turned off **the light**, opened **the door** and went out. (= the light and the door of the room)
- Do you live very far from **the centre**? (= the centre of your town)
- I'd like to speak to **the manager**, please. (= the manager of this shop)

UNIT 63   Exercises

63.1 Put in **a/an** or **the**.

1 I wrote to her but .*the*. letter never arrived.
2 Britain is ..*an*. island.
3 What is .... name of this village?
4 Jane is .... very nice person. You must meet her.
5 Montreal is .... large city in Canada.
6 What is .... largest city in Canada?
7 'What time is it?' 'I don't know. I haven't got .... watch.'
8 When I went to Rome, I stayed with .... Italian friend of mine.
9 You look very tired. You need .... holiday.
10 Don't sit on .... floor. It's very dirty.
11 'Let's go to .... restaurant this evening.'
    'That's .... good idea. Which restaurant shall we go to?'
12 Can you turn on .... radio, please? I want to listen to some music.
13 Tom is in .... bathroom. He's having .... bath.
14 This is a nice room, but I don't like .... colour of .... carpet.
15 We live in .... old house near .... station. It's two miles from .... centre.

63.2 Put in **a/an** or **the** where necessary in these sentences.

1 I turned off_light, opened_door and went out. ...*the light   the door*...............................
2 Excuse me, can I ask question, please? ....
3 Alan is best player in our football team. ....
4 How far is it from here to airport? ....
5 Enjoy your holiday and don't forget to send me postcard! ....
6 Have you got ticket for concert tomorrow night? ....
7 What is name of director of film we saw last night? ....
8 Yesterday I bought jacket and shirt. Jacket was cheap but shirt was expensive.
....
9 Peter and Mary have two children, boy and girl. Boy is seven years old and girl is three.
....

63.3 Complete the sentences. Use **a/an** or **the** + one of these:

bicycle   ~~capital~~   cigarette   play   difficult language   kitchen   nice day
next train   roof   ~~small hotel~~

1 Rome is ...*the capital*... of Italy.
2 When we were in London, we stayed at ...*a small hotel*...
3 Can you ride .... ?
4 What's that man doing on .... of that house? Is he repairing something?
5 We went to the theatre last night but .... wasn't very good.
6 Do you think English is .... for people to learn?
7 'Would you like .... ?' 'No, thanks. I don't smoke.'
8 'Where's Jack?' 'He's in .... He's cooking something.'
9 Excuse me, what time is .... to London?
10 It's .... today. Let's go out.

127

UNIT 64　the

■ **the** ... = it is clear which thing or person we mean　(▶ Unit 63):
- Rome is **the capital of Italy**. (*there is only one capital*)
- What is **the name of this village**? (*the village has only one name*)
- Excuse me, where is **the nearest bank**?
- Who is **the President of the United States**?
- Can you tell me **the time**, please? (= the time now)
- My office is on **the first floor**. (= the first floor of the building)

Don't forget **the**:
- Do you live near **the city centre**? (*not* 'near city centre')
- Which is **the best restaurant** in this town? (*not* 'Which is best')

■ **the top of** ... / **the end of** ... etc.
- Write your name at **the top of the page**.
- **The beginning of the film** was not very good.
- My house is at **the end of this street**.
- The table is in **the middle of the room**.
- Do you drive on **the left** or on **the right** in your country?

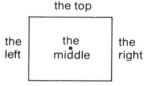

■ **the same** ...
- We live in **the same street**. (*not* 'in same street')
- These books are not different. They are **the same**. (*not* 'They are same.')

Note that we say:

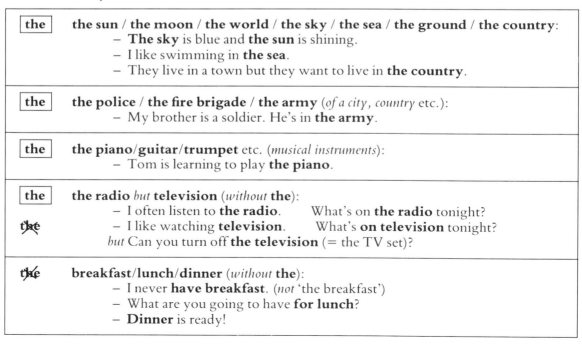

the	the sun / the moon / the world / the sky / the sea / the ground / the country: – **The sky** is blue and **the sun** is shining. – I like swimming in **the sea**. – They live in a town but they want to live in **the country**.
the	the police / the fire brigade / the army (*of a city, country* etc.): – My brother is a soldier. He's in **the army**.
the	the piano/guitar/trumpet etc. (*musical instruments*): – Tom is learning to play **the piano**.
the t~~he~~	the radio *but* television (*without* **the**): – I often listen to **the radio**.　　What's on **the radio** tonight? – I like watching **television**.　　What's **on television** tonight? *but* Can you turn off **the television** (= the TV set)?
t~~he~~	breakfast/lunch/dinner (*without* **the**): – I never **have breakfast**. (*not* 'the breakfast') – What are you going to have **for lunch**? – **Dinner** is ready!

UNIT 64   Exercises

64.1 Put in **the** where necessary. Write 'okay' if the sentence is correct.

1 Sky is blue and sun is shining.   *The sky ... the sun* ....
2 What are you going to have for lunch?   *okay* ....
3 Our apartment is on third floor.   ....
4 Help! Fire! Somebody call fire brigade.   ....
5 Who was first man to walk on moon?   ....
6 Which city is capital of your country?   ....
7 What is largest city in world?   ....
8 Would you like to be in army?   ....
9 Do you live near sea?   ....
10 After dinner we watched television.   ....
11 'Where is your dictionary?'   'It's on top shelf on right.'   ....
12 We live in country, about five miles from nearest village.   ....
13 Ann is coming to see us at end of May or beginning of April.   ....
14 'Is this book cheaper than that one?'   'No, they're same price.'   ....
15 Prime Minister is most important person in British government.   ....
16 I don't know everybody in this photograph. Who is man on left?   ....
17 It was a very nice hotel but I don't remember name.   ....
18 I didn't like her first time I met her.   ....
19 What do you usually have for breakfast?   ....
20 'Have you got any milk?'   'Yes, there's some in fridge.'   ....

64.2 Complete these sentences. Use **the same** + one of these words:

age   colour   day   problem   ~~street~~   time

1 I live in King Street and you live in King Street. We live in   *the same street.* ....
2 I arrived at 8.30 and you arrived at 8.30. We arrived at   ....
3 I've got no money and you've got no money. We've got   ....
4 He's 25 and she's 25. They are   ....
5 My shirt is dark blue and my jacket is dark blue. They are   ....
6 I'm leaving on Monday and you're leaving on Monday. We're leaving on   ....

64.3 Complete these sentences. Use the words in the list. Use **the** if necessary.

breakfast   ~~dinner~~   guitar   lunch   police   radio   sky   sun
television   ~~time~~

1 'Can you tell me   *the time* .... please?'   'Yes, it's half past six.'
2 We had   *dinner* .... at a restaurant last night.
3 .... is a star. It gives us light and warmth.
4 Did you see the film on   .... last night?
5 I was hungry this morning because I didn't have   ....
6 .... stopped me because I was driving too fast.
7 'Can you play   .... ?'   'No, I can't play any musical instruments.'
8 'What did you have for   .... ?'   'Just a salad.'
9 When I'm working at home I like listening to   ....
10 .... is very clear tonight. You can see all the stars.

UNIT 65   go home / go to work / go to the cinema

She's **at work**.   They're going **to school**.   He's **in bed**.

~~the~~ (*without* **the**)

---

go to work / get to work / be at work / start work / finish work etc.
- What time do you **go to work** in the morning? (*not* 'to the work')
- I **finish work** at 5 o'clock every day.

go to school / be at school / start school / leave school etc.
- What did you **learn at school** today? (*not* 'at the school')

go to university / be at university etc.
- After she **leaves school**. (*not* 'leaves the school') she wants to **go to university**. (*not* 'go to the university')

go to church / be at (*or* **in**) **church**
- Don usually **goes to church** on Sundays. (*not* 'to the church')

go to bed / be in bed
- I'm tired. I'm **going to bed**. (*not* 'to the bed')

go to hospital / be in hospital
- Jack is very ill. He**'s in hospital**. (*not* 'in the hospital')

go to prison / be in prison
- I wouldn't like to **be in prison**. (*not* 'in the prison')

go home / get home / arrive home / come home / walk home / leave home etc.
be at home / stay at home etc.
- I'm tired. I'm **going home**. (*not* 'to home')
- Are you going out or are you **staying at home**?

---

the (*with* **the**)

---

the cinema	Do you often **go to the cinema**?
the theatre	We're **going to the theatre** this evening.
the bank	I must **go to the bank** today.
the post office	Are you **going to the post office**?
the doctor	You're ill. You must **go to the doctor**.
the dentist	I'm **going to the dentist** tomorrow.
the toilet	Excuse me, I must **go to the toilet**.

also **the station / the airport / the city centre** etc.   (▶ Unit 63)

UNIT 65 Exercises

65.1 Where are these people? Look at the pictures and complete the sentences. Sometimes you need **the**.

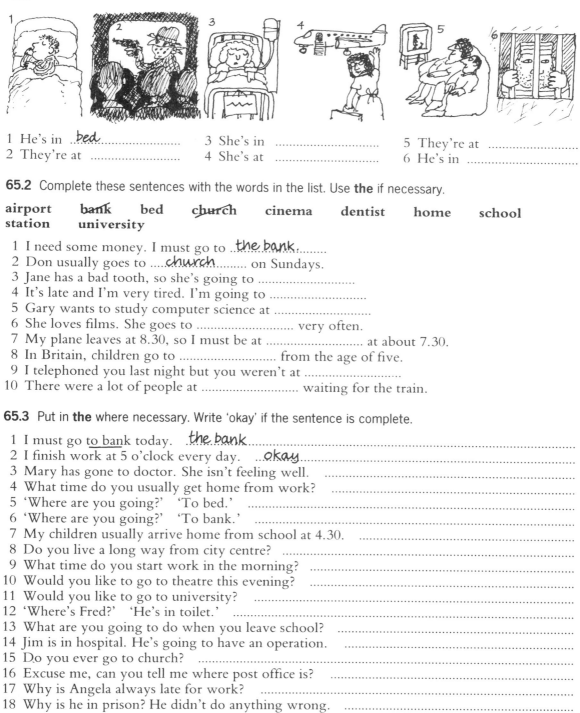

1 He's in ..*bed*..................
2 They're at ....
3 She's in ....
4 She's at ....
5 They're at ....
6 He's in ....

65.2 Complete these sentences with the words in the list. Use **the** if necessary.

airport   ~~bank~~   bed   ~~church~~   cinema   dentist   home   school
station   university

1 I need some money. I must go to ..*the bank.*........
2 Don usually goes to ....*church*......... on Sundays.
3 Jane has a bad tooth, so she's going to ....
4 It's late and I'm very tired. I'm going to ....
5 Gary wants to study computer science at ....
6 She loves films. She goes to .... very often.
7 My plane leaves at 8.30, so I must be at .... at about 7.30.
8 In Britain, children go to .... from the age of five.
9 I telephoned you last night but you weren't at ....
10 There were a lot of people at .... waiting for the train.

65.3 Put in **the** where necessary. Write 'okay' if the sentence is complete.

1 I must go <u>to bank</u> today.   ..*the bank*............................
2 I finish work at 5 o'clock every day.   ..*okay*...................................
3 Mary has gone to doctor. She isn't feeling well.   ....
4 What time do you usually get home from work?   ....
5 'Where are you going?'   'To bed.'   ....
6 'Where are you going?'   'To bank.'   ....
7 My children usually arrive home from school at 4.30.   ....
8 Do you live a long way from city centre?   ....
9 What time do you start work in the morning?   ....
10 Would you like to go to theatre this evening?   ....
11 Would you like to go to university?   ....
12 'Where's Fred?'   'He's in toilet.'   ....
13 What are you going to do when you leave school?   ....
14 Jim is in hospital. He's going to have an operation.   ....
15 Do you ever go to church?   ....
16 Excuse me, can you tell me where post office is?   ....
17 Why is Angela always late for work?   ....
18 Why is he in prison? He didn't do anything wrong.   ....

131

UNIT 66   I like **music**
I hate **examinations**

(*not* 'the music')   (*not* 'the examinations')   (*not* 'the cold weather')

~~the~~

> Do *not* say 'the' for *general ideas*:
> - I like **music**. (= music in general)
> - I like **classical music**. (= classical music in general)
> - We don't eat **meat** very often. (*not* 'the meat')
> - **Life** is not possible without **water**. (*not* 'the life / the water')
> - I hate **examinations**. (= examinations in general)
> - Do they sell **foreign newspapers** in that shop?
> - I'm not very good at writing **letters**.
>
> Do *not* say '**the**' for *games and sports*:
> - My favourite sports are **tennis** and **skiing**. (*not* 'the tennis / the skiing')
>
> Do *not* say '**the**' for *languages or academic subjects* (**history/geography/biology/physics** etc.):
> - Do you think **English** is difficult? (*not* 'the English')
> - Tom's brother is studying **physics** and **chemistry**.

the and ~~the~~

> - **Flowers** are beautiful. (= flowers in general)
> *but*   Your garden is very nice. **The flowers** are beautiful. (= the flowers in your garden)
>
> - I don't like **cold weather**. (= cold weather in general)
> *but*   **The weather** isn't very nice today. (= the weather today)
>
> - Are you interested in **history**?
> *but*   Are you interested in **the history of your country**?
>
> - Everybody needs **food**. (= food in general)
> *but*   It's a nice hotel and **the food** is very good.

UNIT 66   Exercises

66.1 What do you think about these things? Begin your sentences with:
I love... / **I like...** / **I don't mind...** (= it's okay) / **I don't like...** / **I hate...**

1 (examinations)   *I hate examinations.*
2 (dogs) ....
3 (hard work) ....
4 (Italian food) ....
5 (loud music) ....
6 (small children) ....
7 (hot weather) ....
8 (staying in hotels) ....
9 (opera) ....
10 (big cities) ....

66.2 Are you interested in these things? Write sentences with:

I'm very interested in ...	**I know a lot about ...**
I'm interested in ...	**I don't know much about ...**
I'm not interested in ...	**I don't know anything about ...**

1 (history)   *I'm very interested in history.*
2 (politics)   I ....
3 (sport) ....
4 (art) ....
5 (astronomy) ....
6 (economics) ....

66.3 Look at the underlined words in these sentences. Which is right (**the** or ~~**the**~~)?

1 Potatoes / ~~The potatoes~~ are not expensive. (Potatoes is *right*.)
2 This is a good meal. ~~Potatoes~~ / The potatoes are very nice. (The potatoes is *right*.)
3 Everybody needs friends / the friends.
4 I never drink coffee / the coffee.
5 'Where's coffee / the coffee?'   'It's in the cupboard.'
6 Jan doesn't go to parties / the parties very often.
7 Tennis / The tennis is a very popular sport.
8 We went for a swim in the river. Water / The water was very cold.
9 I don't like swimming in cold water / the cold water.
10 You must visit the art gallery. Paintings / The paintings are very beautiful.
11 Money / The money doesn't always bring happiness / the happiness.
12 English / The English is the language of international business.
13 Children / The children learn things / the things very quickly.
14 Excuse me, can you pass salt / the salt, please?
15 I enjoy eating in restaurants / the restaurants.
16 Do you think that capitalism / the capitalism is a good economic system?
17 I enjoy taking photographs / the photographs. It's my hobby.
18 I must show you photographs / the photographs I took when I was on holiday.

UNIT 67   the (*names of places*)

Places (continents/countries/states/islands/cities/towns/villages etc.)

> ~~the~~ Usually we do *not* say '**the**' + names of places:
> - **France** is a very large country. (*not* 'the France')
> - **Cairo** is the capital of **Egypt**.
> - **Corsica** is an island in the Mediterranean.
>
> *But* we say **the** + republic/states/kingdom:
> | the | the **Republic** of Ireland / the Irish **Republic**
> the United **States** (of America) (**the USA**)   the United **Kingdom** (**the UK**)

Places in towns (streets/buildings etc.)

> ~~the~~ Usually we do *not* say '**the**' + names of streets, squares etc.:
> - Kevin lives in **Coronation Street**.
> - Where is **Highfield Road**, please?
> - **Trafalgar Square** is in the centre of London.
>
> ~~the~~ We *do not* say '**the**' + name of place + airport/station/university/castle etc.:
> | **Munich Airport**   **Paddington Station**   **Cambridge University**
> | **Westminster Abbey**   **Edinburgh Castle**   **London Zoo**
>
> *But* we usually say **the** + names of hotels/restaurants/pubs/cinemas/theatres/museums:
> | the | the **Hilton (Hotel)**   the **Star of India** (restaurant)
> the **Science Museum**   the **Odeon** (cinema)
> the **National Theatre**   the **Tate Gallery** (art gallery)

Seas, rivers etc.

> We say **the** + names of oceans/seas/rivers/canals:
> | the | the **Atlantic (Ocean)**   the **Mediterranean (Sea)**
> the **(River) Nile**   the **Suez Canal**

the ... of ...

> We say **the** + names with ... **of** ...:
> | the | the Republic **of** Ireland   the Bank **of** England
> the Great Wall **of** China   the Tower **of** London
>
> **the north/south/east/west/middle (of ...)**:
> - I've been to **the north of Italy** but not to **the south**.

the –s (*plural names*)

> We say **the** + *plural names* (**the –s**) of countries/islands/mountains:
> | the | the Netherlands   the Canary Islands   the Philippines   the Andes

UNIT 67 Exercises

67.1 These are geography questions. Choose your answer from the box. Sometimes you need to use 'The'.

Alps	**Amazon**	**Atlantic**	**Bahamas**	**Cairo**	**Kenya**	**Red Sea**
Asia	**Andes**	**Pacific**	**Malta**	**Tokyo**	**Rhine**	**Switzerland**
United States						

1 ..*Cairo*.................... is the capital of Egypt.
2 ..*The Atlantic*........... is between Africa and America.
3 .... is a country in the middle of Europe.
4 .... is a river in South America.
5 .... is the largest continent in the world.
6 .... is the largest ocean.
7 .... is a river in Europe.
8 .... is between Canada and Mexico.
9 .... is in East Africa.
10 .... are mountains in South America.
11 .... is the capital of Japan.
12 .... is an island in the Mediterranean.
13 .... are mountains in central Europe.
14 .... is between Saudi Arabia and Africa.
15 .... are a group of islands near Florida.

67.2 Put in **the** where necessary. If the sentence is correct, write 'okay'.

1 Kevin lives in Coronation Street. ..*okay*.......
2 Have you ever been to National Theatre? *the National Theatre* ....
3 'Where are you staying?' 'At Intercontinental Hotel.' ....
4 Milan is a large city in north of Italy. ....
5 Brussels is the capital of Belgium. ....
6 Manila is the capital of Philippines. ....
7 National Gallery is in Trafalgar Square in London. ....
8 Most of the best shops are in Merrion Street. ....
9 Rocky Mountains are in North America. ....
10 In London, Houses of Parliament are beside River Thames. ....
11 Have you ever been to British Museum? ....
12 Texas is famous for oil and cowboys. ....
13 Last night we saw a play at Royal Theatre. ....
14 You must visit Museum of Modern Art. It's very interesting. ....
15 Alan studied chemistry at London University. ....
16 When I finish my studies, I'm going to United States for a year. ....
17 Panama Canal joins Atlantic Ocean and Pacific Ocean. ....
18 There are two cinemas in our town – Regal and Plaza. ....
19 If you sail from Britain to Denmark, you cross North Sea. ....
20 Mary comes from a small village in west of Ireland. ....
21 Europe is not a large continent but it has a large population. ....
22 Have you ever been to USA? ....

135

UNIT 68　this/that/these/those

> **this** (*singular*)
> **this** **house/picture/man** etc.

"Do you like this picture?"

> **these** (*plural*)
> **these** houses/flower**s**/**men** etc.

"These flowers are for you."

> **that** (*singular*)
> **that** **house/picture/man** etc.

"Do you like that picture?"

> **those** (*plural*)
> **those** houses/flowers/**people** etc.

"Who are those people?"

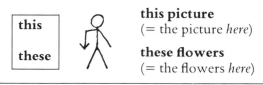

| this | | **this picture** (= the picture *here*) |
| these | | **these flowers** (= the flowers *here*) |

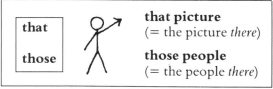

| that | | **that picture** (= the picture *there*) |
| those | | **those people** (= the people *there*) |

■ We use **this/that/these/those** *with a noun* (**this hotel** / **that girl** etc.) *or without a noun* (**this/that** etc.):

- **This hotel** is expensive but it's very nice.
- 'Who's **that girl**?'　'I don't know.'
- Do you like **these shoes**? I bought them last week.
- Don't eat **those apples**. They're bad.

- **This** is a nice hotel but it's very expensive.
- 'Excuse me, is **this** your bag?'　'Oh, yes. Thank you very much.'
- 'Who's **that**?' (= Who's that girl/woman?)　'I don't know. I've never seen her before.'
- Which shoes do you like most? **These** or **those**?

this one / that one ▶ Unit 69

UNIT 68   Exercises

68.1 Put in **this** or **these**.

1 ..*this*.. chair   3 .... sandwich   5 .... children   7 .... houses
2 ..*these*.. chairs   4 .... things   6 .... place   8 .... trousers

Put in **that** or **those**.

9 .... picture   11 .... men   13 .... eggs   15 .... room
10 .... socks   12 .... tree   14 .... woman   16 .... plates

68.2 Write questions: **Is this/that your ... ?** or **Are these/those your ... ?**

68.3 Complete the sentences. Use **this/that/these/those** + these words:

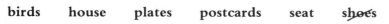

birds   house   plates   postcards   seat   shoes

1 Do you like *these shoes* ?
2 Who lives in .... ?
3 Look at .... !
4 How much are .... ?
5 Excuse me is .... free?
6 .... are dirty.

137

UNIT 69   one/ones

■ **one** (= a . . .)

These chocolates are nice. Would you like one?

Would you like | **one** | ?

= Would you like | **a chocolate** | ?

> **one = a/an . . . (a chocolate / a book / an apple etc.)**

– I need **a pen**. Have you got **one**? (**one = a pen**)
– A: Is there **a bank** near here?
  B: Yes, there's **one** at the end of this street. (**one = a bank**)

■ **one** and **ones**

one (*singular*)

Which one do you want? This one.

Which **one**? (= Which **hat**?)

> **one = hat/book/girl** etc.

this one / that one
– Which **car** is yours? **This one** or **that one**? (= this/that **car**)

the one . . .
– A: Which **hotel** did you stay at?
  B: **The one near the station**.

the . . . one
– I don't like the black **coat** but I like **the brown one**.
– Don't buy that **camera**. Buy **the other one**.

a/an . . . one
– This **cup** is dirty. Can I have **a clean one**?
– That **biscuit** was nice. I'm going to have **another one**.   (another ▶ Unit 59)

ones (*plural*

Which ones do you want? The white ones.

Which **ones**? (= Which **flowers**?)

> **ones = flowers/books/girls** etc.

We use **these/those** alone (*not usually* 'these ones / those ones'):
– Which **flowers** do you want? **These** or **those**?

the ones . . .
– A: Which **cigarettes** are yours?
  B: **The ones on the table**.

the . . . ones
– I don't like the red **shoes** but I like **the green ones**.
– Don't buy those **apples**. Buy **the other ones**.

(some) . . . ones
– These **cups** are dirty. Can we have **some clean ones**?
– My **shoes** are very old. I must buy **some new ones**.

UNIT 69   Exercises

69.1 A asks B some questions. Use the information in the box to write B's answers. Use **one** (*not* **'a/an...'**) in the answers.

B doesn't need a car	B has just had a cup of coffee
there's a chemist in Mill Road	B can't ride a bicycle
~~B hasn't got a pen~~	B hasn't got an umbrella

1 A: Can you lend me a pen?   B: I'm sorry, *I haven't got one.*
2 A: Would you like to have a car?   B: No, I don't ....
3 A: Have you got a bicycle?   B: No, I can't ....
4 A: Can you lend me an umbrella?   B: I'm sorry, ...
5 A: Is there a chemist near here?   B: Yes, ...
6 A: Would you like a cup of coffee? B: No thank you, ...

69.2 Complete the sentences. Use **a/an ... one**. Use these words in your answers:

clean   **better**   **big**   **different**   **new**   **old**

1 This cup is dirty. Can I have *a clean one* .... ?
2 I'm going to sell my car and then I'm going to buy ....
3 That's not a very good photograph but this is ....
4 This box is too small. I need ....
5 I want today's newspaper. This is ....
6 Why do we always go to the same restaurant? Let's go to ....

69.3 Use the information in the box to complete these conversations. Use **one/ones**.

the coat is black	the pictures are on the wall
the girl is tall with long hair	the books are on the top shelf
~~the hotel is near the station~~	the flowers are yellow
the house has got a red door	the shoes are green
I took the photographs on the beach last week	the man has got a moustache and glasses

1 A: We stayed at a hotel.
   B: *Which one* .... ?
   A: *The one near the station.* ....
2 A: Those shoes are nice.
   B: .... ?
   A: ....
3 A: That's a nice house.
   B: .... ?
   A: .... with ....
4 A: I like that coat.
   B: .... ?
   A: ....
5 A: I like those pictures.
   B: .... ?
   A: ....

6 A: Are those your books?
   B: .... ?
   A: ....
7 A: Do you know that girl?
   B: .... ?
   A: ....
8 A: Those flowers are beautiful.
   B: .... ?
   A: ....
9 A: Who's that man?
   B: .... ?
   A: ....
10 A: Have you seen my photographs?
   B: .... ?
   A: ....

UNIT 70   some   any

some

Use **some** in *positive* sentences:
– I'm going to buy **some** eggs.
– There is **some** ice in the fridge.
– They made **some** mistakes.
– She said **something**.
– I saw **somebody** (*or* **someone**).

any

Use **any** in *negative* sentences:
– I'm **not** going to buy **any** eggs.
– There is**n't any** ice in the fridge.
– They did**n't** make **any** mistakes.
– She did**n't** say **anything**.
– I did**n't** see **anybody** (*or* **anyone**).

any and **some** in *questions*

In most questions (but not all) we use **any**:
  – Is there **any** ice in the fridge?
  – Did they make **any** mistakes?
  – Are you doing **anything** this evening?
  – I can't find Ann. Has **anybody** seen her?

We normally use **some** (*not* **any**) when we
offer things (**Would you like some . . . ?**):
  – A: Would you like **some** coffee?
    B: Yes, please.
  – A: Would you like **something** to eat?
    B: No, thank you. I'm not hungry.
or ask for things (**Can I have some . . . ?** /
Can you lend me some . . . ? etc.):
  – 'Can I have **some** soup, please?'   'Yes, of course. Help yourself.'
  – 'Can you lend me **some** money?'   'I'm sorry, I can't.'

■ Compare **some** and **any**:
  – We've got **some** cheese but we have**n't** got **any** bread.
  – I did**n't** take **any** photographs but Ann took **some**. (= some photographs)
  – You can have **some** coffee, but I do**n't** want **any**. (= any coffee)
  – I've just made **some** coffee. **Would you like some?** (= some coffee)
  – I have**n't** got **any** money. **Can you lend me some?** (= some money)

something/somebody/anything/anybody ▶ Unit 73

UNIT 70   Exercises

70.1 Put in **some** or **any**.

1 I'm going to buy ...*some*... eggs.
2 They didn't make ..*any*.... mistakes.
3 I can pay. I've got .... money.
4 There aren't ....:....... shops in this part of the town.
5 George and Alice haven't got .... children.
6 Have you got .... brothers or sisters?
7 There are .... beautiful flowers in the garden.
8 Are there .... letters for me this morning?
9 I haven't got .... stamps but Ann's got ....
10 Do you know .... good hotels in London?
11 'Would you like .... tea?'   'Yes, please.'
12 Don't buy .... rice. We don't need ....
13 We haven't got .... bread, so I'm going out to buy ....
14 When we were on holiday, we visited .... very interesting places.
15 I went out to buy .... milk but they didn't have .... in the shop.
16 I'm thirsty. Can I have .... water, please?

70.2 Complete the sentences. Use **some** or **any** + one of these words:

air   batteries   chairs   cheese   friends   languages   milk   ~~money~~
photographs   problems   shampoo   stamps

1 I can't buy you a drink. I haven't got ...*any money*.................
2 I want to wash my hair. Is there .... ?
3 I'm going to the post office to get ....
4 Can you speak .... foreign .... ?
5 I haven't got my camera, so I can't take ....
6 Sorry we're late. We had .... with the car.
7 Everybody was standing because there weren't .... in the hall.
8 It's hot in this office. I'm going out for .... fresh ....
9 Why isn't the radio working? Are there .... in it?
10 Can I have .... in my coffee, please?
11 Yesterday evening I went to a restaurant with .... of mine.
12 'Would you like ....?'   'No, thank you. I've had enough to eat.'

70.3 Put in **somebody** (or **someone**) / **something** / **anybody** (or **anyone**) / **anything**.

1 She said ..*something*........ but I didn't understand it.
2 'What's wrong?'   'There's .... in my eye.'
3 Do you know .... about politics?
4 I went to the shop but I didn't buy ....
5 .... has broken the window. I don't know who.
6 There isn't .... in the box. It's empty.
7 I'm looking for my keys. Has .... seen them?
8 Would you like .... to drink?
9 I didn't eat .... because I wasn't hungry.
10 I can do this job alone. I don't need .... to help me.

UNIT 71   not + any   no   none

He **hasn't** got **any** money.

He's got **no** money.

A: How much money has he got?
B: **None**.

■ **not (n't) + any**
- I'm **not** going to do **any** work this evening.
- There are**n't any** good hotels in the town.
- Ann took some photographs but I did**n't** take **any**. (= any photographs)

■ **no + *noun* (no money / no job** etc.): **no . . . = not + any** *or* **not + a**
We use **no . . .** especially after **have/has (got)** and **there is/are**:
- He has got **no** money. (= He has**n't** got **any** money.)
- There are **no** buses after 11.30. (= There are**n't any** buses after 11.30.)
- It's a nice house but there's **no** garden. (= It's a nice house but there is**n't a** garden.)

■ Remember: *negative verb* + **any**   *positive verb* + **no**
- I **haven't** got **any** friends. *or* **I've** got **no** friends.
  (*but not* 'I haven't got no friends.')
- There **aren't any** good hotels in this town. *or* There **are no** good hotels in this town.

■ **no** and **none**
Use **no** + *noun* (**no money / no friends / no sugar** etc.):
- I can't wait. I've got **no time**.
- There is **no sugar** in your coffee.

Use **none** *alone* (*without a noun*):
- 'How much time have we got?'   '**None** (= no time). We must go now.'
- 'How many mistakes did you make?'   '**None**.' (= no mistakes)

■ **none** and **no-one**
none = **0** (zero). **None** is an answer for **How much? / How many?** (*things or people*):
- '**How much** money have you got?'   '**None**.' (= no money)
- '**How many** people did you meet?'   '**None**.' (= no people)

no-one = **nobody** (▶ Unit 72).   **No-one** is an answer for **Who?**:
- '**Who** did you meet?'   '**No-one**.' (= nobody)

UNIT 71   Exercises

71.1 Write these sentences again with **no**.

1 He hasn't got any money.   *He's got no money.*
2 There aren't any pictures on the walls.   There are ....
3 Carol hasn't got any free time.   Carol ....
4 There isn't a restaurant in this hotel.   ....

Write these sentences again with **any**.

5 He's got no money.   *He hasn't got any money.*
6 There's no oil in the tank.   There ....
7 I've got no stamps.   I ....
8 Tom's got no brothers or sisters.   ....

71.2 Put in **no** or **any**.

1 There aren't *any* good hotels here.
2 There are *no* buses today.
3 I didn't write .... letters last night.
4 There are .... shops in this part of the town.
5 She can't speak .... foreign languages.
6 Don't buy .... food. We don't need ....
7 My brother is married but he's got .... children.
8 I'm afraid there's .... coffee. Would you like some tea?
9 'Look at those birds!'   'Birds? Where? I can't see .... birds.'
10 The man asked me for money but I didn't give him ....

71.3 Complete the sentences. Use **any** or **no** + one of these words:

**cigarettes   difference   film   friends   furniture   money   photographs
questions   ~~work~~   swimming-pool**

1 I'm not going to do ...*any work*............ this evening.
2 I didn't smoke .... yesterday.
3 They want to go on holiday but they've got ....
4 It's a nice hotel but there's ....
5 I'm not going to answer ....
6 He's always alone. He's got ....
7 There is .... between these two machines. They are the same.
8 I can't take .... There's .... in the camera.
9 There wasn't .... in the room. It was completely empty.

71.4 Give short answers (one or two words) to these questions. Use **none** where necessary.

1 How many letters have you written today?   *Two/ A lot / None.*
2 How many sisters have you got?   ....
3 How much coffee did you drink yesterday?   ....
4 How many photographs have you taken today?   ....
5 How many legs has a snake got?   ....

UNIT 72   not + anybody/anyone/anything
nobody/no-one/nothing

not + anybody/anyone
nobody/no-one
(for people)

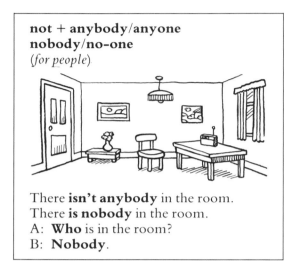

There **isn't anybody** in the room.
There **is nobody** in the room.
A: **Who** is in the room?
B: **Nobody**.

not + anything
nothing
(for things)

There **isn't anything** in the bag.
There **is nothing** in the bag.
A: **What**'s in the bag?
B: **Nothing**.

any**body** = any**one**   no**body** = no-**one** (**-body** and **-one** are the same):
   – I don't know **anybody** (*or* **anyone**).
   – There is **no-one** (*or* **nobody**) here.

> **not (n't) + anybody/anyone/anything**

   – Please do**n't** tell **anybody** (*or* **anyone**).
   – Jack has a bad memory. He ca**n't** remember **anything**.

> **nobody** = **not** + **anybody**
> **no-one** = **not** + **anyone**   **nothing** = **not** + **anything**

   – I'm lonely. I've got **nobody** to talk to. (= I have**n't** got **anybody**)
   – The house is empty. There is **no-one** in it. (= there is**n't anyone**)
   – She said **nothing**. (= She did**n't** say **anything**.)

You can use **nobody/no-one/nothing** at the beginning of a sentence or alone (without other words):
   – The house is empty. **Nobody** lives there. (*not* 'Anybody lives there.')
   – **Nobody** is perfect.
   – 'Who did you speak to?'   '**No-one**.'
   – 'What did you say?'   '**Nothing**.' (*not* 'Anything.')

■ Remember: *negative verb* + **anybody/anyone/anything**
            positive verb + **nobody/no-one/nothing**
   – He does**n't** understand **anything**. (*not* 'He doesn't understand nothing.')
   – Do**n't** tell **anybody**. (*not* 'Don't tell nobody.')
   – There **is nothing** to do in this town. (*not* 'There isn't nothing to do.')

144

UNIT 72   Exercises

72.1 Write these sentences again with **nobody/no-one/nothing**.

1 There isn't anything in the bag.   *There's nothing in the bag.*
2 There isn't anybody in the office.   There's ....
3 I haven't got anything to do.   I ....
4 There isn't anything on TV tonight.   ....
5 Jack hasn't got anyone to help him.   ....
6 We didn't find anything.   ....

72.2 Write these sentences again with **anybody/anyone/anything**.

1 There is nothing in the bag.   *There isn't anything in the bag.*
2 I've got nothing to read.   I haven't got ....
3 There's nobody in the bathroom.   ....
4 We've got nothing to eat.   ....
5 There was no-one on the bus.   ....
6 She heard nothing.   ....

72.3 Answer these questions with **nobody/no-one/nothing**.

1 What did you say? *Nothing*.............   5 Who knows the answer? ....
2 Who saw you? *Nobody*...............   6 What did you buy? ....
3 What do you want? ....   7 What happened? ....
4 Who did you meet? ....   8 Who was late? ....

Now answer the same questions with full sentences.
Use **nobody/no-one/nothing** or **anybody/anyone/anything**.

1a *I did'nt say anything*...............   5a .... the answer.
2a *Nobody saw me.*...............   6a I ....
3a I don't ....   7a ....
4a I didn't ....   8a ....

72.4 Complete the sentences with **nobody/no-one/nothing/anybody/anyone/anything**.

1 I went out of the house. ......*Nobody*............... saw me.
2 Jack has a bad memory. He can't remember ..*anything*...............
3 Be quiet! Don't say ....
4 I didn't know about the meeting. .... told me.
5 'What did you have to eat?' '.................................. I wasn't hungry.'
6 'What did you say?' 'I didn't say ....'
7 George has gone away. .... knows where he is. He didn't tell
   .... where he was going.
8 'What are you doing this evening?' '.................................. Why?'
9 I don't know .... about car engines.
10 'How much does it cost to visit the museum?' '...................................... It's free.'
11 She was sitting alone. She wasn't with ....
12 I heard a knock on the door but when I opened it there was .... outside.

145

UNIT 73 some-/any-/no- + -body/-one/-thing/-where

Somebody (or someone) has broken the window.

somebody/someone = a person but we don't know who

There is something in her mouth.

something = a thing but we don't know what

Tom lives somewhere near London.

somewhere = in a place or to a place but we don't know where

	people (-body or -one★)	things (-thing)	places (-where)
some- any- no-	somebody or someone anybody or anyone nobody or no-one	something anything nothing	somewhere anywhere nowhere

★ -body and -one are the same: somebody = someone, nobody = no-one etc.

somebody someone something somewhere	– There is somebody (or someone) in the garden. – She said something but I didn't understand her. – They live somewhere in the south of England.

in questions   (▶ Unit 70)
– Is there anybody (or anyone) in the garden?
– Are you doing anything this evening?
– Did you go anywhere interesting for your holidays?

anybody anyone anything anywhere	*in negatives* (not + any-) (▶ Units 70 and 72) – There isn't anybody (or anyone) in the garden. – It's dark. I can't see anything. – I'm staying here. I'm not going anywhere.

nobody no-one nothing nowhere	– There is nobody (or no-one) in the garden. – 'What did you say?' 'Nothing.' – I don't like this town. There is nowhere to go.

■ You can use something/anybody/nowhere etc. + to . . . :
  – I'm hungry. I want something to eat. (= something that I can eat)
  – He hasn't got anybody to talk to. (= anybody that he can talk to)
  – There's nowhere to go in this town. (= nowhere where people can go)

UNIT 73   Exercises

73.1 Put in **somebody** (or **someone**) / **something** / **somewhere**.

1   She said ..*something*................   What did she say?
2   I've lost ....   What have you lost?
3   They went ....   Where did they go?
4   I'm going to telephone ....   Who are you going to telephone?

Put in **nobody** (or **no-one**) / **nothing** / **nowhere**.

5   What did you say?   *Nothing*.........................
6   Where are you going?   ....
7   What do you want?   ....
8   Who are you looking for?   ....

Now answer the same questions with full sentences. Use **not** + **anybody** (or **anyone**) / **anything** /
anywhere.

5a *I didn't say anything*..........................   7a I ....
6a I'm not going ....   8a I ....

73.2 Put in **somebody/nothing/anywhere** etc.

1   It's dark. I can't see ..*anything*................
2   Tom lives *somewhere*............... near London.
3   Do you know .... about computers?
4   'Listen!'   'What? I can't hear ....'
5   'What are you doing here?'   'I'm waiting for ....'
6   'What's wrong?'   'I've got .... in my eye.'
7   'Did .... see you?'   'No, ...'
8   They weren't hungry, so they didn't eat ....
9   'What is going to happen?'   'I don't know. .... knows.'
10 'Do you know .... in London?'   'Yes, I've got a few friends there.'
11 'What's in that cupboard?'   '................................. It's empty.'
12 I'm looking for my lighter. I can't find it ....

73.3 Complete the sentences. Use a word from the first box + **to** + a word from the second box.
(You can use a word more than once.)

something anything nothing	to	do drink eat ~~go~~
somewhere anywhere nowhere		play read sit stay

1   We don't go out very much because there's ..*nowhere to go*.............................
2   There isn't any food in the house. We haven't got ....
3   I'm bored. I've got ....
4   'Why are you standing?'   'Because there isn't ....'
5   'Would you like ....?'   'Yes, please – a glass of orange juice.'
6   Children need ....
7   I want ....   I'm going to buy a magazine.
8   All the hotels were full. There was ....

147

UNIT 74   every   everybody/everything etc.

■ **every**

Every house in the street is the same.

(**every house** in the street = **all the houses** in the street)

Use **every** + *singular noun* (**every house** / **every country** / **every time** etc.):
- Alice has been to **every country** in Europe. (*not* 'every countries')
- **Every summer** we have a holiday by the sea.
- She looks different **every time** I see her.

Use a *singular verb* (**is/was/has** etc.) after **every** . . . :
- **Every house** in the street **is** the same. (*not* 'Every house . . . are')
- **Every country has** a national flag. (*not* 'Every country have')

Compare **every** and **all**:
- **Every student** in the class passed the examination.
  All the student**s** in the class passed the examination.
- **Every country has** a national flag.
  All countries have a national flag.

■ **every** }
  all }   **day/morning/evening/night/summer** etc.

every day = on all days:
- A: How often do you read a newspaper?
  B: **Every day**.
- Bill watches TV **every evening**.
  (= on all evenings of the week)

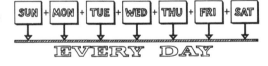

all day = the complete day from beginning to end:
- The weather was bad yesterday. It rained **all day**.
- I was tired after work yesterday, so I watched TV **all evening**. (= the complete evening)

■ **everybody** (*or* **everyone**)/**everything**/**everywhere**

everybody/everyone (*people*) **everything** (*things*) **everywhere** (*places*)	- **Everybody** (*or* **Everyone**) needs friends. (= all people need friends) - Have you got **everything** you need? (= all the things you need) - I've lost my watch. I've looked **everywhere** for it. (= I've looked in all places)

Use a *singular verb* after **everybody/everyone/everything**:
- **Everybody has** problems. (*not* 'Everybody have')

UNIT 74   Exercises

74.1 Complete the sentences. Use **every** + one of these words:

day   room   ~~student~~   time   word

1 ..*Every student*..... in the class passed the examination.
2 My job is very boring. .... is the same.
3 .... in the hotel has a private bathroom.
4 Kay is a good tennis player. When we play, she wins ....
5 'Did you understand what she said?'   'Yes, ...'

74.2 Put in **every** or **all**.

1 Yesterday it rained ...*all*... day.
2 Bill watches TV *every*. evening.
3 Barbara gets up at 6.30 .... morning.
4 I was ill yesterday, so I stayed in bed .... day.
5 I buy a newspaper .... day but I don't always read it.
6 'How often do you go skiing?'   '........... year, usually in March.'
7 'Were you at home at 10 o'clock yesterday?'   'Yes, I was at home .... morning. I went out after lunch.'
8 The weather was nice last Sunday, so we sat in the garden .... afternoon.
9 We didn't have a very good holiday. We went to the seaside for ten days and it rained .... day.
10 My sister likes cars. She buys a new one .... year.
11 I saw Jack at the party but he wasn't very friendly. He didn't speak to me .... evening.
12 They go away on holiday for two or three weeks .... summer.

74.3 Put in **everybody** (or **everyone**) / **everything** / **everywhere**.

1 ..*Everybody*...... needs friends.
2 Joy knows .... about computers.
3 I like the people here.   .... is very friendly.
4 It's a nice hotel. It's comfortable and .... is clean.
5 Ken never uses his car. He goes .... by motor-bike.
6 Let's have dinner.   .... is hungry.
7 Their house is full of books. There are books ....
8 You're right.   .... you say is true.

74.4 Complete the answers to these questions. Use **everybody**.

1	Do you know George?	Yes, ...*everybody knows*............... George.
2	Are you tired today?	Yes,.. .... today.
3	Do you like Mary?	Yes, ...
4	Are you going to the party?	Yes, ...
5	Have you seen the film?	Yes, ...
6	Were you surprised?	Yes, ...

UNIT 75   all   most   some   no/none   any

all   most   some   no / none / not + any   any

■ **all/most/some/no/any** + *noun* (**all cities / most people** etc.)

all most some no any	~~of~~	cities people music buses

– **All** big **cities** have the same problems.
– **Most people** like Jack.
– I like **some classical music** but not all.
– There are **no buses** on Sundays.
or There are**n't any buses** on Sundays.

Don't use **of** in these sentences:
     – **Most children** like playing. (*not* 'Most of children')
     – **Some birds** cannot fly. (*not* 'Some of birds')

■ **most of the . . . / some of my . . . / none of these . . .** etc.

most some none any	of	the . . . this/that . . . these/those . . . my/your . . . etc.

– **Most of my friends** live in London.
– **Some of this money** is yours.
– Have you read **any of these books**?
– **None of the students** passed the examination.
– I don't know **any of those people**.

■ Remember: **most children**   *but*   **most of the** children
                some people   *but*   **some of these** people
                no friends   *but*   **none of my** friends

Compare:
     – **Most children** like playing. (= most children in general)
but   **Most of the children** at this school are under 11 years old.

We usually say **all ~~of~~ the . . . / all ~~of~~ my . . .** etc. (*without* **of**):
     – **All the students** failed the exam.
     – She has lived in London **all her life**.

■ **all of it / most of them / some of us** etc.

all most some none any	of	it them us you

– You can have **some of this cake** but not **all of it**.
– A: Do you know those people?
   B: **Most of them**, but not **all of them**.
– **Some of us** are going out tonight. Would you like to come with us?
– He's got a lot of books but he has**n't** read **any of them**.

some/any ▶ Unit 70   **no/none** ▶ Unit 71

UNIT 75   Exercises

75.1 Complete the sentences. Use the word in brackets (**some/most** etc.). Sometimes you need **of** (**some of / most of** etc.).

1 Most........ people like Jack.   (most)
2 Some of. this money is yours.   (some)
3 .... people are stupid.   (some)
4 .... the shops in the city centre close at 5.30.   (most)
5 You can change money in .... banks.   (most)
6 I don't like .... the pictures in the living-room.   (any)
7 He's lost .... his money.   (all)
8 .... my friends are married.   (none)
9 Do you know .... the people in this photograph?   (any)
10 .... birds can fly.   (most)
11 I enjoyed .... the film but I didn't like the ending.   (most)
12 .... sports are very dangerous.   (some)
13 We can't find anywhere to stay. .... the hotels are full.   (all)
14 You must have .... this cheese. It's delicious.   (some)
15 The weather was bad when we were on holiday. It rained .... the time.   (most)

75.2 Look at the pictures and answer the questions. Use **all/most/some/none of them**.

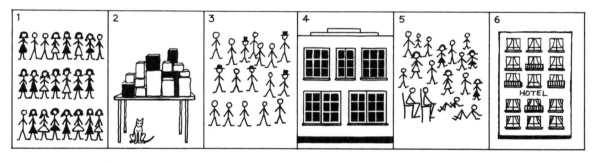

1 How many of the people are women?   Most of them.
2 How many of the boxes are on the table?
3 How many of the men are wearing hats?
4 How many of the windows are open?
5 How many of the people are standing?
6 How many of the hotel rooms have a balcony?

75.3 Answer these questions. Use the word in brackets (**all/most/some/none**) + **of it / of them**.

1 How much of that book did you read?   (some)   Some of it.
2 Are your friends going to the party?   (most)
3 How many of those books have you read?   (all)
4 How much of this money do you want?   (all)
5 Were the questions in the test easy?   (most)
6 Are the shops open tomorrow?   (some)
7 How many of those people do you know?   (none)
8 Did you understand the conversation?   (most)
9 Have you seen these photographs?   (some)

UNIT 76 both either neither

■ We use **both/either/neither** to talk about *two* things or people:

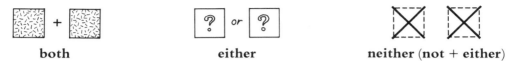

| both | either | neither (not + either) |

- Rosemary has two children. **Both** are married. (= both children)
- A: Do you like classical music or pop music?
  B: **Both**. (= classical *and* pop)
- Would you like tea or coffee? You can have **either**. (= tea *or* coffee)
- A: Do you want to go to the cinema or the theatre?
  B: **Neither**. I want to stay at home. (**neither** = *not* the cinema *or* the theatre)

■ **both/either/neither** + *noun*:

both + *plural*	**both** **windows/books/children** etc.
either **neither** + *singular*	**either** **window/book/child** etc. **neither** **window/book/child** etc.

- Ann has got two sisters and a brother. **Both sisters are** married.
- Last year I went to Paris and Rome. I liked **both cities** very much.
- I read two books but **neither book was** very interesting.
- There are two ways from here to the station. You can go **either way**.

■ **both/either/neither of . . .** :

both★ **either** **neither**	**of**	the . . . those/these . . . my/your/Tom's etc. . . .

- I like **both (of) those pictures**.
- **Both (of) Ann's sisters are** married.
- I have**n't** read **either of these books**.
- **Neither of my parents is** English.

★ You can say **both the . . . / both those . . . / both my . . .** etc. (*without* of):
both of those pictures *or* **both** those pictures

■ **both of them / neither of us** etc.

both **either** **neither**	**of**	**them** **us** **you**

- Ann has got two sisters. **Both of them are** married.
- Tom and I didn't eat anything. **Neither of us was** hungry.
- Who are those two people? I don't know **either of them**.

UNIT 76   Exercises

76.1 Put in **both/either/neither**.

1 Ann has got two sisters. ...*Both*... sisters are married.
2 There were two pictures on the wall. I didn't like .*either*.. of them.
3 It was a very good football match. .... teams played well.
4 It wasn't a good football match. .... team played well.
5 'Is your friend English or American?' '................ She's Australian.'
6 We went away for two days but the weather wasn't very good. It rained on .... days.
7 'I bought two newspapers. Which one do you want?' '................ It doesn't matter which one.'
8 I invited Jack and Jill to my party but .... of them came.
9 'Do you go to work by car or by bus?' '................ I always walk.'
10 'Which jacket do you prefer, this one or that one?' 'I don't like .... of them.'
11 'Do you work or are you a student?' '................ I've got a job but I study too.'
12 Ann and I didn't know the time because .... of us had a watch.

76.2 Write sentences for the pictures. Use **Both ...** and **Neither ...**

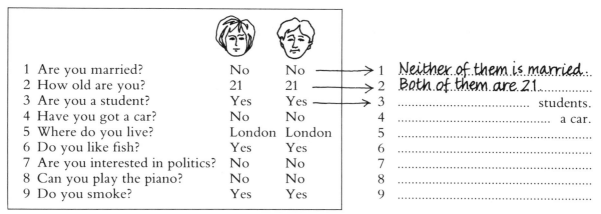

1 .*Both cups are empty.*................
2 .... are open.
3 .... wearing a hat.
4 .... cameras.
5 .... to the airport.
6 .... is right.

76.3 A man and a woman answered some questions. Their answers to all the questions were the same. Write sentences with **Both/Neither of them ...**

1 Are you married?	No	No	→ 1 *Neither of them is married.*
2 How old are you?	21	21	→ 2 *Both of them are 21*
3 Are you a student?	Yes	Yes	→ 3 .... students.
4 Have you got a car?	No	No	4 .... a car.
5 Where do you live?	London	London	5 ....
6 Do you like fish?	Yes	Yes	6 ....
7 Are you interested in politics?	No	No	7 ....
8 Can you play the piano?	No	No	8 ....
9 Do you smoke?	Yes	Yes	9 ....

153

UNIT 77   a lot   much   many

a lot of money
much money

a lot of books
many books

much + *uncountable noun* (▶ Unit 61): **much money** **much food** **much time** **much coffee**	**many** + *plural noun*: **many** books **many** shops **many** people **many** questions

a lot of + *uncountable or plural noun*:
a lot of food   **a lot of coffee**   **a lot of people**   **a lot of shops**

■ **much/many** are more usual in *questions* and *negative sentences*:

– Do you drink **much coffee?**
– **How much money** have you got?
– She has**n't** got **much money**.
– A: Have you got any **money**?
   B: I've got some but **not much**.
– Diana spoke to me but she did**n't**
   say **much**.
	– Do you know **many people**?
	– **How many photographs** did you take?
	– He has**n't** got **many friends**.
	– A: Did you take any **photographs**?
	   B: I took some but **not many**.

■ **a lot (of)** is more usual in *positive sentences*:
    – I **drink a lot of** coffee.
    – They **haven't** got **much** money but they**'ve** got **a lot of** friends.
    – There **aren't many** hotels in the town but there **are a lot of** restaurants.

You can use **a lot** without a noun. Compare:
    – He ate **a lot of food**. (**a lot of** + *noun*)
  but   He ate **a lot**. (*not* 'a lot **of**')

Note that we say:
    – There **is** a lot of **food/money/coffee** etc. (*singular verb*)
  but   There **are** a lot of tree**s**/shop**s**/**people** etc. (*plural verb*)
    – A lot of **people speak** English. (*not* 'A lot of people speaks')

■ Sometimes **much** or **a lot** = often:
    – 'Do you watch TV **much**?'   'No, **not much**.' (= not often)
    – We like films, so we go to the cinema **a lot**.

UNIT 77   Exercises

77.1 Answer the questions with **I've got some but not much/many**.

1	Have you got any money?
2	Have you got any coffee?
3	Have you got any books?
4	Have you got any cigarettes?
5	Have you got any cheese?
6	Have you got any friends?

I've got some but not much.
I've got some but ....
....
....
....
....

77.2 Write questions with **How much ... ?** or **How many ... ?**

1	I took some photographs.
2	I bought some stamps.
3	I lost some money.
4	I drank some water.
5	I made some mistakes.
6	I wrote some letters.
7	I bought some food.
8	I invited some people.

How many photographs did you take .... ?
How .... did you buy?
.... ?
.... ?
.... ?
.... ?
.... ?
.... ?

77.3 Put in **a lot / a lot of / much / many**.

1 Do you drink .... *much* ...... tea?
2 I like reading. I've got ...... *a lot of* ..... books.
3 There isn't .... milk in the fridge.
4 It costs .... money to travel round the world.
5 Please be quick! I haven't got .... time.
6 How .... foreign languages can you speak?
7 They didn't ask me .... questions.
8 There was .... food at the party but I didn't eat ....
9 We saw .... interesting things in the museum.
10 George knows .... about economics.
11 We went on a cheap holiday. It didn't cost ....
12 'Did you enjoy the party?'   'No, not ....'
13 Most of the town is modern – there aren't .... old buildings.
14 Most people in the town have jobs – there isn't .... unemployment.

77.4 Write the questions and answers. Use **much** and **a lot**.

1 (go to the cinema)	Do you go to the cinema much .... ?	No, not much.
2 (watch TV)	Do you watch TV much .... ?	Yes, a lot.
3 (go swimming)	.... go swimming .... ?	No, ...
4 (play tennis)	Do .... ?	Yes, ...
5 (travel)	.... ?	Yes, ...
6 (use the phone)	.... ?	No, ...

UNIT 78   (a) little   (a) few

a little water

a few books

(a) little + *uncountable noun:*

(a) little water	**(a) little** money
(a) little time	**(a) little** soup

(a) few + *plural noun:*

(a) few books	**(a) few** questions
(a) few people	**(a) few** days

---

a little = some but not much:

- She didn't eat anything but she drank **a little water**.
- I speak **a little Spanish**. (= some Spanish but not much)
- A: Can you speak **Spanish**?
  B: **A little**.

---

a few = some but not many:

- Last night I wrote **a few letters**.
- We're going away for **a few days**.
- I speak **a few words** of Spanish.

- A: Have you got any **cigarettes**?
  B: **A few**. Do you want one?

✗little (*without* **a**) = nearly no . . . *or* nearly nothing:

- There was **little food** in the fridge. It was nearly empty.

You can say **very little**:
- She's very thin because she eats **very little**. (= nearly nothing)

✗few (*without* **a**) = nearly no . . . :

- There were **few** people in the park. It was nearly empty.

You can say **very few**:
- Her English is very good. She makes **very few mistakes**.

---

little and **a little**:

a little is a *positive* idea:
- They have **a little money** so they're not poor. (= some but not much money)

✗little is a *negative* idea:
- They have **little money**. They are very poor. (= nearly no money)

---

few and **a few**:

a few is a *positive* idea:
- I've got **a few friends**, so I'm not lonely. (= some but not many friends)

✗few is a *negative* idea:
- I'm sad and lonely. I've got **few friends**. (= nearly no friends)

UNIT 78 Exercises

78.1 Answer the questions with **a little** or **a few**.

1 Have you got any money?	.A little....	5 Have we got any petrol?	....
2 Have you got any stamps?	....	6 Does he speak English?	....
3 Do you want any sugar?	....	7 Do you know many people?	....
4 Did he ask any questions?	....	8 Would you like some soup?	....

78.2 Put in **a little** or **a few** + one of these words:

air   chairs   days   friends   houses   ~~letters~~   milk   Russian
times

1 Yesterday evening I wrote .....*a few letters*............ to my family and friends.
2 Can I have .... in my coffee, please?
3 'When did John go away?'   '.. ago.'
4 'Do you speak any foreign languages?'   'Yes, Italian and ....,'
5 'Are you going out alone?'   'No, I'm going with ....,'
6 'Have you ever been to Rome?'   'Oh, yes. ....,'
7 I live in a very small village. There is a church, a shop and ....
   – that's all.
8 I'm going out for a walk. I need .... fresh ....
9 There wasn't much furniture in the room – just a table and ....

78.3 Complete the sentences. Use **very little** / **very few** + one of these words:

coffee   hotels   ~~mistakes~~   rain   tables   time

1 Her English is very good. She makes *very few mistakes.*................
2 I drink ....   I don't like it.
3 In summer the weather is very dry. There is ....
4 It's difficult to find a place to stay in this town. There are ....
5 We must hurry. We've got ....
6 It's a small restaurant. There are ....

78.4 Put in **little** or **a little** / **few** or **a few**.

1 There was ....*little*........................ food in the fridge. It was nearly empty.
2 'When did you see Sarah?'   '.. days ago.'
3 He's very lazy. He does .... work.
4 They're not rich but they've got .... money – enough to live.
5 Last night I went to a restaurant with .... friends.
6 The TV service is not very good. There are.. good programmes.
7 I can't decide now – I need .... time to think about it.
8 Nearly everybody has a job. There is .... unemployment.
9 He's not well-known.   .... people have heard of him.

UNIT 79   big/tired/beautiful etc. (*adjectives*)

■ *adjective + noun* (**nice day** / **blue eyes** etc.):

	adjective + noun
It's a **nice**	**day** today.
Ann has got **blue**	**eyes**.
There's a very **old**	**church** in this village.
Do you like **Italian**	**food**?
I don't speak any **foreign**	**languages**.
There are some **beautiful yellow**	**flowers** in the garden.

The adjective is *before* the noun:
- They live in a **modern house**. (*not* 'a house modern')

The endings of adjectives do not change:
a **different place**   **different** place**s** (*not* 'differents')

■ **be** (**am/is/are/was/were** etc.) + *adjective*:

- The weather **is nice** today.
- Those flowers **are** very **beautiful**.
- A: Can you close the window, please?
  B: Why? **Are** you **cold**?
- The film **wasn't** very **good**. It **was boring.**
- Please **be quiet**. I'm reading.

get + *adjective* ▶ Unit 51

■ **look/feel/smell/taste/sound** + *adjective*:

- 'You **look tired**.'   'Yes, I **feel tired** too.'
- George told me about his new job. It **sounds interesting**.
- Don't cook that meat. It doesn't **smell good**.

Compare:

He	is feels looks	tired.

They	are look sound	American.

It	is smells tastes	good.

UNIT 79 Exercises

79.1 The words in the box are adjectives (**black/foreign** etc.) or nouns (**air/job** etc.). Use an adjective and a noun to complete each sentence.

air	dangerous	fresh	interesting	~~languages~~	person	serious
black	expensive	holiday	job	long	photograph	sharp
clouds	~~foreign~~	hotels	knife	old	problem	

1 Jack doesn't speak any ..foreign languages...................
2 Look at those .... in the sky! It's going to rain.
3 She works very hard and she's very tired. She needs a ....
4 I enjoy talking to her. She's an ....
5 Fire-fighting is a ....
6 Can you open the window? We need some ....
7 This is an .... of Tom – he looks very different now.
8 I've got a .... I hope you can help me.
9 I need a .... to cut these onions.
10 They've got a lot of money – they always stay at ....

79.2 Write sentences for the pictures. Use:

look(s)	~~sound(s)~~		
feel(s)	smell(s)	taste(s)	

+

ill	nice	surprised
awful	new	~~happy~~

1 You .Sound happy.......   2 It ....   3 I ....

4 You ....   5 They ....   6 It ....

79.3 In these conversations you don't agree with Alex. Use the word in brackets ( ).

1	You sound happy.	Do I? (feel) ..I don't feel happy...............
2	He's American.	Is he? (sound) He doesn't ....
3	She's very rich.	Is she? (look) She ....
4	You look cold.	Do I? (feel) I ....
5	I'm English.	Are you? (sound) You ....
6	They are very friendly.	Are they? (look) They ....
7	Your meal looks good.	Does it? (taste) It ....

159

UNIT 80 quickly/badly/suddenly etc. (*adverbs*)

He ate his dinner very **quickly**.   **Suddenly** the shelf fell down.

Quickly and **suddenly** are *adverbs*.

---

adjective + **–ly** → *adverb*:

adjective	quick	bad	sudden	careful	heavy
adverb	quick**ly**	bad**ly**	sudden**ly**	careful**ly**	heav**ily** etc.

Spelling ▶ Appendix 4(4.2): eas**y** → eas**ily**   heav**y** → heav**ily**

Adverbs tell you how something happens or how somebody does something:

- The train **stopped suddenly**.
- I **opened** the door **slowly**.
- Please **listen carefully**.
- I **understand** you **perfectly**.

It's **raining heavily**.

Compare: *adjective* (▶ Unit 79) *adverb*

– Sue **is** very **quiet**.	*but*	Sue **speaks** very **quietly**. (*not* 'speaks very quiet')
– **Be careful!**		**Listen carefully!** (*not* 'listen careful')
– It was **a bad game**.		Our team **played badly**.

---

fast   hard   late   early   These words are adjectives *and* adverbs:

- Ben is **a fast runner**.   Ben can **run fast**. (*not* 'fastly')
- Her job **is** very **hard**.   She **works** very **hard**. (*not* 'hardly')
- The bus **was late/early**.   I **went** to bed **late/early**.

good (*adjective*) → **well** (*adverb*):

- Her English **is** very **good**.   She **speaks** English very **well**. (*not* 'speaks English very good')
- It was **a good game**.   Our team **played well**.

But **well** is also an *adjective* (= not ill, in good health):

- 'How are you?'   'I'**m** very **well**, thank you. And you?'

160

UNIT 80   Exercises

80.1 Look at the pictures and complete the sentences with one of these adverbs:

badly   **dangerously**   ~~heavily~~   **fast**   **angrily**   **quietly**

1 It's raining ......*heavily*...............................
2 He sings very ....
3 They came in ....

4 She shouted at me ....
5 He was driving ....
6 She can run very ....

80.2 Choose a verb + adverb from the box to complete these sentences.

come	explain	know	~~listen~~			carefully	clearly	easily	well
sleep	think	win	work	+		carefully	quickly	hard	well

1 I'm going to say something very important, so please ......*listen*....... to me ..*carefully*...
2 John! I need your help. .... !
3 I've met him but I don't .... him very ....
4 They .... At the end of the day they're always tired.
5 I'm tired this morning. I didn't .... last night.
6 You're a much better tennis player than me. When we play, you always ....
7 .... before you answer the question.
8 Our teacher isn't very good. He doesn't .... things very ....

80.3 Choose the right word.

1 I opened the door ~~slow~~/slowly. (<u>slowly</u> is *right*)
2 Why are you <u>angry/angrily</u>? I haven't done anything.
3 Bill is a <u>careful/carefully</u> driver. He drives <u>careful/carefully</u>.
4 Can you please repeat that <u>slow/slowly</u>?
5 Come on, George! Why are you always so <u>slow/slowly</u>?
6 The party was very <u>good/well</u>. I enjoyed it very much.
7 Tom didn't do very <u>good/well</u> in his examination.
8 Jane is studying <u>hard/hardly</u> for her examinations.
9 'Where's Diane?' 'She was here, but she left <u>sudden/suddenly</u>.'
10 I met them a long time ago, so I don't remember them very <u>good/well</u>.
11 My brother isn't very <u>good/well</u> at the moment.
12 Don't eat your dinner so <u>quick/quickly</u>. It's not good for you.
13 Those oranges look <u>nice/nicely</u>. Can I have one?
14 I don't want to work for that company. They pay their workers very <u>bad/badly</u>.
15 Please be <u>quiet/quietly</u>. I'm reading.

UNIT 81   old/older   expensive/more expensive

old   **older**   heavy   **heavier**   expensive   **more expensive**

Older / heavier / more expensive are *comparative* forms.
The comparative form is **–er** (**older**) *or* **more . . .** (**more expensive**).

short adjectives (1 syllable) **old/cheap/nice** etc. → **–er**

---

old → older	**slow** → slower	**cheap** → cheaper
nice → nicer	**late** → later	**big** → bigger

Spelling ▶ Appendix 4(4.4): big → bi**gg**er   hot → ho**tt**er   thin → thi**nn**er

– Rome is **old** but Athens is **older**. (*not* 'more old')
– Is it **cheaper** to go by car or by train? (*not* 'more cheap')
– Sue wants to buy a **bigger** car.
– This coat is okay but I think the other one is **nicer**.

but **good/well** → **better**   **bad** → **worse**   **far** → **further**
– The weather wasn't very **good** yesterday but it's **better** today.
– Which is **worse** – a headache or toothache?
– 'Do you feel **better** today?'   'No, I feel **worse**.'
– 'How **far** is the station? A mile?'   'No, **further**. About two miles.'

–y *adjectives* (2 syllables) **easy/heavy** etc. → **–ier**

---

eas**y** → eas**ier**   heav**y** → heav**ier**   earl**y** → earl**ier**
– Don't send a letter. It's **easier** to phone me. (*not* 'more easy')
– The bag is **heavy** but the suitcase is **heavier**.

---

long adjectives (2/3/4 syllables) **modern** (= MOD-ERN) / **expensive** (= EX-PENS-IVE) etc.
→ **more . . .**

---

modern → **more modern**	**polite** → **more polite**	**tired** → **more tired**
expensive → **more expensive**	**interesting** → **more interesting**	

– I don't like this house. I prefer **more modern** houses. (*not* 'moderner')
– Don't talk about your job. Let's talk about something **more interesting**.
– Is it **more expensive** to go by car or by train?

▶ Unit 82   **older than . . .**   **more expensive than . . .**

UNIT 81   Exercises

81.1 Look at the pictures and write the comparative (**older / more modern** etc.).

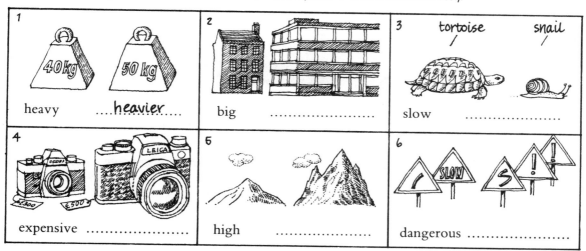

1 40kg 50kg heavy ....*heavier*....	2 big	3 tortoise / snail / slow ....
4 expensive	5 high	6 dangerous ....

81.2 Write the comparative (**older / more modern** etc.).

1 old ....*older*.............................
2 strong ....
3 happy ....
4 careful ....
5 important ....
6 bad ....

7 difficult ....
8 large ....
9 far ....
10 serious ....
11 crowded ....
12 pretty ....

81.3 Write the opposite.

1 younger .....*older*.............   3 cheaper ....   5 nearer ....
2 colder ....   4 better ....   6 easier ....

81.4 Complete the sentences. Use a comparative.

1 Sue's car isn't very big. She wants a *bigger*................ car.
2 This house isn't very modern. I prefer .*more modern*..... houses.
3 You're not very tall. Your brother is ....
4 Bill doesn't work very hard. I work ....
5 My chair isn't very comfortable. Yours is ....
6 Jill's idea wasn't very good. My idea was ....
7 These flowers aren't very nice. The blue ones are ....
8 My case isn't very heavy. Your case is ....
9 I'm not very interested in art. I'm .... in history.
10 It isn't very warm today. It was .... yesterday.
11 These tomatoes don't taste very good. The other ones tasted ....
12 Britain isn't very big. France is ....
13 London isn't very beautiful. Paris is ....
14 This knife isn't very sharp. Have you got a .... one?
15 People today aren't very polite. In the past they were ....

UNIT 82 older than ... more expensive than ...

▶ Unit 81   **old/older**   **expensive / more expensive**

She's **taller than** him.   The Europa Hotel is **more expensive than** the Grand.

■ We use **than** after *comparatives* (**older than ...   more expensive than ...** etc.):
- Athens is **older than** Rome.
- Are oranges **more expensive than** apples?
- It's **easier** to phone **than** to write a letter.
- 'How are you today?'   'Not bad. **Better than** yesterday.'
- Last night the restaurant was **more crowded than** usual.

■ We say ... than **me** / than **him** / than **her** / than **us** / than **them**:
- I can run faster **than him**. *or* I can run faster **than he can**.
- You are a better singer **than me**. *or* You are a better singer **than I am**.
- I got up **earlier than her**. *or* I got up earlier **than she did**.

■ **more/less than ...**
- A: How much did your shoes cost? £25?
  B: No, **more than** that. (= **more than** £25)
- The film was very short – **less than** an hour.
- They've got **more money than they need**.
- You go out **more than me**. (= more often than me)

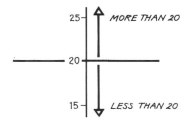

■ **a bit** / **much** + **older** / **more expensive** etc.

   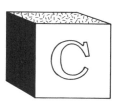

Box A is **a bit bigger** than Box B.

a bit much	bigger older better more difficult more expensive	than ...

Box C is **much bigger** than Box D.
- Canada is **much bigger** than France.
- Jill is **a bit older** than Gary – she's 25 and he's 24½.
- A car is **much more expensive** than a motor-bike.

164

UNIT 82   Exercises

82.1 Write sentences about Liz and Ben. Use **than**.

1 I'm 26.	1 I'm 24.
2 I'm not a very good swimmer.	2 I'm a very good swimmer.
3 I'm 1 metre 68 tall.	3 I'm 1 metre 66 tall.
4 I start work at 8 o'clock.	4 I start work at 8.30.
5 I don't work very hard.	5 I work very hard.
6 I haven't got much money.	6 I've got a lot of money.
7 I'm a very good driver.	7 I'm not a very good driver.
8 I'm not very friendly.	8 I'm very friendly.
9 I'm not a very good dancer.	9 I'm a good dancer.
10 I'm very intelligent.	10 I'm not very intelligent.
11 I speak French very well.	11 I don't speak French very well.
12 I don't go to the cinema very much.	12 I go to the cinema a lot.

LIZ   BEN

1 *Liz is older than Ben.*
2 *Ben is a better swimmer than Liz*
3 Liz is taller ....
4 Liz starts .... Ben.
5 Ben .... Liz.
6 Ben has got ....

7 Liz is a ....
8 Ben ....
9 Ben ....
10 Liz ....
11 Liz ....
12 Ben ....

82.2 Complete the sentences. Use **than**.

1 He isn't very tall. You*'re taller than him. (OR: ...... than he is)* ....
2 She isn't very old. You're ....
3 I don't work very hard. You work ....
4 He doesn't smoke very much. You ....
5 I'm not a very good cook. You ....
6 We don't know many people. You ....
7 They haven't got much money. You've got ....
8 I can't run very fast. You can ....
9 She hasn't been here very long. You ....
10 I didn't get up very early. You ....
11 He isn't very interesting. You ....

82.3 Complete the sentences with **a bit** or **much** + a comparative (**older/better** etc.).

1 Jill is 25. Gary is 24½. *Jill is a bit older than Gary.* ....
2 Jack's mother is 54. His father is 68. Jack's mother ....
3 My camera cost £100. Yours cost £96. My camera ....
4 Yesterday I felt terrible. Today I feel okay.
   I feel ....
5 Today the temperature is 12 degrees. Yesterday it was ten degrees.
   It's .... today .... yesterday.
6 Ann is a fantastic tennis player. I'm not very good.
   Ann ....

165

UNIT 83   not as ... as

She's old but she's **not as old as** he is.

Box A is**n't as big as** Box B.

■ **not as ... as ... :**
- Rome is **not as old as** Athens. (= Athens is **older**)
- The Grand Hotel is**n't as expensive as** the Europa. (= the Europa is **more expensive**)
- I do**n't** play tennis **as often as** you. (= you play **more often**)
- The weather is better than yesterday. It is**n't as cold**. (= as cold **as yesterday**)

■ **not as much as ... / not as many as ...** (much/many ▶ Unit 77):
- I have**n't** got **as much money as** you. (= you've got **more money**)
- I do**n't** know **as many people as** you. (= you know **more people**)
- I do**n't** go out **as much as** you. (= you go out **more**)

Compare **not as ... as** and **than**:
- Rome is **not as old as** Athens.
  Athens is **older than** Rome. (*not* 'older as Rome')

- Tennis is**n't as popular as** football.
  Football is **more popular than** tennis.

- I do**n't** go out **as much as** you.
  You go out **more than** me.

■ We say ... as **me** / as **him** / as **her** etc.:
- She's not as old **as him.**   *or*   She's not as old **as he is.**
- You haven't got as much money **as me.**   *or*   You haven't got as much money **as I have**.

■ Note that we say **the same as ... :**
- My hair is **the same colour as** yours. (*not* 'the same like')
- I arrived at **the same time as** Tom.

UNIT 83 Exercises

83.1 Look at the pictures and write sentences about A, B and C.

1 A *is bigger than C but not as big as B.*
2 A is .... B but not .... C.
3 C is .... A but ....
4 A is .... but ....
5 B has got ....
6 C works ....

83.2 Write sentences with **as ... as ...**

1 Athens is older than Rome.   Rome *isn't as old as Athens.*..............................
2 My room is bigger than yours.   Your room isn't ....
3 You got up earlier than me.   I didn't ....
4 We played better than them.   They didn't ....
5 I've been here longer than you.   You haven't ....

83.3 Put in **as** or **than**.

1 Athens is older *than* Rome.
2 I don't watch TV as much .... you.
3 You eat more .... me.
4 I feel better .... I felt yesterday.

5 Jim isn't as clever .... he thinks.
6 Belgium is smaller .... Switzerland.
7 Brazil isn't as big .... Canada.
8 I can't wait longer .... an hour.

83.4 Read about the three people and complete the sentences with **the same ... as ...**   Use the word in brackets ( ).

JULIA
I'm 22.
I live in Hill street.
I got up at 7.15.
I haven't got a car.

ANDREW
I'm 24.
I live in Baker Street.
I got up at 7.15.
My car is green.

CAROLINE
I'm 24.
I live in Hill street.
I got up at 7.45.
My car is green.

1 (age)   *Andrew is the same age as Caroline.*..................................
2 (street)   Julia lives .... Caroline.
3 (time)   Julia got up ....
4 (colour)   Andrew's ....

UNIT 84   the oldest   the most expensive

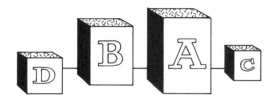

HOTEL PRICES IN KINTON			
(per person, per night)			
Europa Hotel	£90	Grosvenor	£55
Grand Hotel	£80.50	Bennett's	£53
Royal	£78	Carlton	£50
Astoria	£60	Star	£45
Palace	£60	Station	£40

Box A is **bigger than** box B.

Box A is **bigger than** all the other boxes.
Box A is **the biggest** box.

The Europa Hotel is **more expensive than** the Grand.

The Europa Hotel is **more expensive than** all the other hotels in the town.
The Europa Hotel is **the most expensive** hotel in the town.

Big**ger** / old**er** / **more** expensive etc. are *comparative* forms   (▶ Unit 81).
Big**gest** / old**est** / **most** expensive etc. are *superlative* forms.

■ The superlative form is **-est** (old**est**) *or* **most** . . . (**most expensive**):

---

short adjectives (**old/cheap/nice** etc.) → **the -est**:

old → **the** old**est**   cheap → **the** cheap**est**   nice → **the** nic**est**
but   **good → the best   bad → the worst**
Spelling   ▶ Appendix 4(4.4):   big → **the** bi**gg**est   hot → **the** ho**tt**est

---

-y *adjectives* (**easy/heavy** etc.) → **the -iest**:

eas**y** → **the** eas**iest**   heav**y** → **the** heav**iest**   prett**y** → **the** prett**iest**

---

long adjectives (**modern/expensive/interesting** etc.) → **the most** . . .

modern → the most modern   **interesting → the most interesting**

■ Don't forget **the**. We say: **the** oldest . . . / **the** most expensive . . . etc.:
  – The church is very old. It's **the oldest** building in the town.
    (= it is old**er than** all the other buildings)
  – What is **the longest** river in the world?
  – Money is important but it isn't **the most important** thing in life.
  – Excuse me, where is **the nearest** bank?

■ You can use **the oldest** / **the best** / **the most expensive** etc. *without* a noun:
  – Ken is a good tennis player. I think he is **the best** in the club.
    (**the best** = the best player)

■ You can use the superlative + **I've ever** . . . / **you've ever** . . . (▶ Unit 16):
  – It was a very bad film – **the worst** film **I've ever** seen.
  – What is **the most unusual** thing **you've ever done**?

84.1 Write sentences with comparatives (**older** etc.) and superlatives (**the oldest** etc.).

1

(**big/small**)
(A/D) A is bigger than D.
(A)   A is the biggest.
(B)   B is the smallest.

2

(**long/short**)
(C/A) C is .... A.
(D)   D is ....
(B)   B ....

3

(**young/old**)
(D/C) D ....
(B)   B ....
(C)   ....

4

(**expensive/cheap**)
(D/A) ....
(C)   ....
(A)   ....

5
RESTAURANT A	excellent
RESTAURANT B	not bad
RESTAURANT C	good but not wonderful
RESTAURANT D	awful

(**good/bad**)
(A/C) ....
(A)   ....
(D)   ....

84.2 Write sentences with a superlative (**the longest** etc.).

Sydney Brazil	large	country planet	the USA the solar system
Everest Jupiter	long	~~city~~ state	Africa South America
Alaska the Nile	high	river mountain	the world ~~Australia~~

1 Sydney is the largest city in Australia.
2 Everest ....
3 ....
4 ....
5 ....
6 ....

84.3 Complete the sentences. Use a superlative (**the oldest** etc.).

1 This building is very old. It's *the oldest building* .... in the town.
2 It was a very happy day. It was .... of my life.
3 It's a very good film. It's .... I've ever seen.
4 She's a very popular singer. She's .... in our country.
5 It was a very bad mistake. It was .... I've ever made.
6 It's a very pretty village. It's .... I've ever seen.
7 It was a very cold day. It was .... of the year.
8 He's a very interesting person. He's .... I've ever met.

UNIT 85   enough

Alice wants to buy a sandwich.

A sandwich is 80 pence.
Alice has got only 60 pence.

So she can't buy a sandwich because she hasn't got **enough** money.

■ **(not) enough** + *noun* (**enough money / enough houses** etc.):
- A: Is there **enough sugar** in your coffee?
  B: Yes, thank you.
- We wanted to play football but we didn't have **enough players**.
- Why don't you buy a car? You've got **enough money**. (*not* 'money enough')

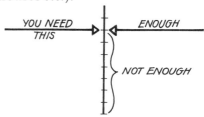

■ **(not) enough** *without a noun*:
- I've got some money, but **not enough** to buy a car. (= I need more money to buy a car.)
- 'Would you like some more to eat?' 'No, thanks, I've had **enough**.'
- You are always at home. You don't go out **enough**.

■ *adjective* + **enough** (**good enough / warm enough** etc.):

He isn't
tall enough
(to reach
the shelf).

- A: Shall we go swimming?
  B: No, it's not **warm enough**. (*not* 'enough warm')
- Can you hear the radio? Is it **loud enough** for you?
- Don't buy that coat. It's nice but it isn't **long enough**. (= it's too short)

■ Remember
  enough + *noun*:   **enough** money   **enough** time   **enough** people
  but *adjective* + **enough**:   good **enough**   old **enough**   loud **enough**

■ We say | **enough** | **for** somebody/something | **to do** something |

- This pullover isn't big **enough for me**.
- I haven't got **enough** money **for a car**.

but I haven't got **enough** money **to buy** a car. (*not* 'for buy a car')
- Is your English good **enough to have** a conversation?
- There weren't **enough chairs for everybody to sit** down.

UNIT 85 Exercises

85.1 Look at the pictures and complete the sentences. Use **enough** + one of these words:

big   chairs   long   ~~money~~   paint   strong   ~~tall~~   wind

1 *She hasn't got enough money.*
2 *He isn't tall enough.*
3 She hasn't got ....
4 The car isn't ....
5 His legs aren't ....
6 There aren't ....
7 There isn't ....
8 He isn't ....

85.2 Complete the sentences. Use **enough** + one of these words:

big   clothes   eat   fruit   ~~loud~~   old   practise   ~~sugar~~   time   tired

1 'Is there ...*enough sugar*........ in your coffee?' 'Yes, thank you.'
2 Can you hear the radio? Is it ...*loud enough*.......... for you?
3 He can leave school if he wants to – he's ....
4 Did you have .... to answer all the questions in the exam?
5 This house isn't .... for a large family.
6 She's very thin. She doesn't ....
7 You don't eat .... You should eat more – it's good for you.
8 It's late but I don't want to go to bed now. I'm not ....
9 He's got .... He doesn't need any new ones.
10 She's not a very good tennis player because she doesn't ....

85.3 Complete the sentences. Use **enough** + one of these words + **to** ...:

bread   ~~money~~   money   old   warm   well

1 I'm not going to buy a car. I haven't got *enough money to buy a car.*
2 They're not getting married. They're not .... married.
3 Don't sit in the garden. It isn't .... the garden.
4 We can't make sandwiches. We haven't got ....
5 They didn't go on holiday. They didn't have ....
6 Don't go to work today. You aren't ....

171

UNIT 86   too

There is **too much sugar** in it.

The shoes are **too big** for him.

■ **too much / too many** = more than you want, more than is good:
   – I don't like the weather here. There is **too much rain**. (= more rain than is good)
   – Let's go to another restaurant. There are **too many people** here.
   – She studies all the time. I think she studies **too much**.

much/many ▶ Unit 77

■ **too** + *adjective* (**too big / too loud** etc.):
   – Please turn the radio down. It's
     too loud. (= louder than I want)
   – I can't work. I'm **too tired**.

■ **too** and **not enough**   (enough ▶ Unit 85):

– There's **too much sugar** in my coffee. (= more sugar than I want)	– There's **not enough sugar** in my coffee. (= I want more sugar)
– I don't feel very well. I **ate too much**.	– You're very thin. You **don't eat enough**.
– The radio is **too loud**. Can you turn it down, please?	– The radio is**n't loud enough**. Can you turn it up, please?
– The hat is **too big** for her.	– The hat is**n't big enough** for her. (= it's **too small** for her)

■ We say: **too . . . for** somebody/something **to do** something:
   – These shoes are **too** big **for me**.
   – It's a small house – **too** small **for a large family**.
but
   – It's **too cold to go** out. (*not* 'for go out')
   – I'm **too** tired **to work**.
   – She speaks **too** fast **for me to understand** her.

172

UNIT 86　Exercises

86.1 Look at the pictures and complete the sentences. Use **too** + one of these words:

big　　crowded　　fast　　high　　hot　　~~loud~~

1　The radio is　.*too loud*..........................
2　The net is　...
3　It's　..
4　She's driving　...
5　The ball is　...
6　The restaurant is　...

86.2 Complete the sentences. Use **too much / too many** or **enough**.

1　You're very thin. You don't eat　..*enough*........
2　I don't like the weather here. There's　..*too much*..... rain.
3　I can't wait for them. I haven't got　........................ time.
4　'Did you have　........................ to eat?'　'Yes, thank you.'
5　You drink　........................ coffee. It's not good for you.
6　You don't eat　........................ fruit. You should eat more.
7　There was nowhere to sit on the beach. There were　........................ people.

86.3 Complete the sentences. Use **too** or **enough** + one of these words:

big　　busy　　expensive　　far　　~~loud~~　　~~loud~~　　sharp　　warm

1　Please turn the radio down.　It　*'s too loud*...
2　Can you turn up the radio, please?　It　*isn't loud enough*..
3　I don't want to walk home.　It's　..
4　Don't buy anything in that shop.　It　...
5　You can't put all your things in this bag.　It　...
6　We didn't go to the beach.　It　...
7　I can't talk to you now.　I　...
8　I can't cut anything with this knife.　It　..

86.4 Complete the sentences. Use **too** (+ adjective) **to (do something)**.

1　I'm not going out.　(cold)　It's　..*too cold to go out*...
2　I'm not going to bed.　(early)　It's too early　...
3　Don't wear a coat.　(warm)　It's too　...
4　They're not getting married.　(young)　They're　...
5　Nobody goes out at night.　(dangerous)　It's　...
6　Don't phone Ann now.　(late)　It's　..
7　They didn't say anything.　(surprised)　They were　...

173

UNIT 87　*word order (1)*

■ *verb + object*

Jill	**reads**	**a newspaper**	every day.
subject	verb	object	

subject　　object

The *verb* (**reads**) and the *object* (**a newspaper**) are usually together:

　　　– Jill **reads a newspaper** every day.

　　　(*not* 'Jill **reads** every day **a newspaper**.')

subject	verb	+ object	
You	**speak**	**English**	very well.
I	**watched**	**television**	all evening.
We	**invited**	**a lot of people**	to the party.
My brother	**phoned**	**the police**	immediately.

　　　– I **like Italian food** very much. (*not* 'I like very much Italian food.')
　　　– Ann **borrowed some money** from the bank. (*not* 'Ann borrowed from the bank some money.')
　　　– I **opened the door** very quietly. (*not* 'I opened very quietly the door.')
　　　– George usually **wears a black hat**. (*not* 'George wears usually a black hat.')
　　　– Why do you always **make the same mistake**? (*not* 'Why do you make always the same mistake?')

■ *place* and *time*

	place (where?)	time (when? how long? how often?)
George walks	**to work**	**every morning**.
We arrived	**at the airport**	**at 7 o'clock**.
Are you going	**to the party**	**tonight**?
They've lived	**in the same house**	**for 20 years**.
I usually go	**to bed**	**early**.

place is usually before *time*:

　　　– They go **to school every day**. (*not* 'They go every day to school.')
　　　– I went **to the bank yesterday afternoon**. (*not* 'I went yesterday afternoon to the bank.')
　　　– Jack's brother has been **in hospital since June**. (*not* '. . . since June in hospital.')

UNIT 87 Exercises

87.1 Put the words in the right order.

1 (a newspaper / reads / every day / Jill) *Jill reads a newspaper every day.*
2 (football / don't like / very much / I) I ....
3 (lost / I / my watch / last week) ....
4 (Tom / the letter / slowly / read) ....
5 (London / do you know / very well?) ....?
6 (ate / we / very quickly / our dinner) ....
7 (did you buy / in England / that jacket?) ....?
8 (I / very well / French / don't speak) ....
9 (crossed / the street / they / carefully) ....
10 (from my brother / borrowed / £50 / I) ....
11 (we / enjoyed / very much / the party) ....
12 (passed / Ann / easily / the examination) ....
13 (every day / do / the same thing / we) ....
14 (I / this picture / don't like / very much) ....
15 (in her bag / the money / put / the woman) ....
16 (did you watch / on television / the news?) ....?
17 (my plan / carefully / I / explained) ....
18 (she / smokes / every day / ten cigarettes) ....
19 (a lot of housework / did / I / yesterday) ....
20 (we / at the concert / some friends / met) ....
21 (you / the same clothes / wear / every day) ....
22 (I / want to speak / fluently / English) ....

87.2 Put the words in the right order.

1 (to work / every morning / walks / George) *George walks to work every morning.*
2 (at the party / we / early / arrived) We ....
3 (didn't go / yesterday / I / to work) I ....
4 (to work / tomorrow / are you going?) ....?
5 (they / since 1984 / here / have lived) ....
6 (will you be / this evening / at home?) ....?
7 (next week / they / to London / are going) ....
8 (to the cinema / last night / did you go?) ....?
9 (on Monday / here / will they be?) ....?
10 (goes / every year / to Italy / Jill) ....
11 (in London / Alice / in 1951 / was born) ....
12 (I / in bed / this morning / my breakfast / had)

....

13 (in October / Barbara / to university / is going)

....

14 (many times / my parents / have been / to the United States)

....

15 (a beautiful bird / this morning / I / in the garden / saw)

....

16 (my umbrella / last night / I think I left / in the restaurant)

....

UNIT 88   *word order (2)*

always	usually	often	sometimes	rarely/seldom	never	ever
also	just	still	already	both	all	

These words (**always/usually** etc.) are often with the verb in the middle of a sentence:
- My brother **never speaks** to me.
- She**'s always** late.
- Do you **often eat** in restaurants?
- I **sometimes eat** too much. (*or* **Sometimes** I eat too much.)
- I don't want to go to the cinema. I**'ve already seen** the film.
- I've got three sisters. They**'re all** married.

■ **always/never** etc. go *before* the verb:

	verb
always	**go**
often +	**play**
never	**feel**
etc.	etc.

- I **always go** to work by car. (*not* 'I go always')
- Ann **often plays** tennis.
- I **sometimes feel** sad.
- They **usually have** dinner at 7 o'clock.
- We **rarely** (*or* **seldom**) **watch** television.
- Tom is a good footballer. He **also plays** tennis and volleyball. (*not* 'He plays also tennis . . .')
- I've got three sisters. They **all live** in London.

■ *but* **always/never** etc. go *after* **am/is/are/was/were**:

am	
is	**always**
are +	**often**
was	**never**
were	etc.

- I **am never** ill. (*not* 'I never am ill.')
- They **are usually** at home in the evenings.
- In winter it **is often** very cold here.
- When I was a child, I **was always** late for school.
- 'Where's George?'   'He**'s still** in bed.'
- I've got two brothers. They**'re both** doctors.

■ **always/never** etc. go *between* two verbs (**have . . . been / can . . . find** etc.):

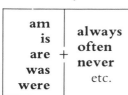

verb 1		*verb 2*
will		**go**
can	**always**	**find**
do	**often**	**remember**
etc.	**never**	etc.
have	etc.	**gone**
has		**been**
		etc.

- I **will always remember** you.
- It **doesn't often rain** here.
- **Do** you **usually go** home by car?
- I **can never find** my keys.
- **Have** you **ever been** to Rome?
- A: Where's Linda?
  B: She**'s just gone** out. (she**'s** = she **has**)
- A: Where are your friends?
  B: They**'ve all gone** to the cinema.

all ▶ Unit 75   **both** ▶ Unit 76   **still** ▶ Unit 89

UNIT 88 Exercises

88.1 Look at Sam's answers to the questions and write sentences with **often/never** etc.

SAM

1	Do you ever play tennis?	Yes, often.	Sam often plays tennis.
2	Do you ever smoke?	Yes, sometimes.	He ....
3	Are you ever ill?	Yes, often.	He ....
4	Do you eat fish?	No, never.	....
5	Are you ever late for work?	Yes, always.	....
6	Do you ever write letters?	Very rarely.	He .... letters.

88.2 Write these sentences again with the words in brackets ( ).

1 My brother speaks to me. (never) My brother never speaks to me. ....
2 Susan is polite. (always) Susan ....
3 I finish work at half past five. (usually) I ....
4 Jill has started a new job. (just) Jill ....
5 I go to bed before midnight. (rarely) ....
6 The bus isn't late. (usually) ....
7 I don't eat meat. (often) ....
8 I will forget what you said. (never) ....
9 Have you broken your leg? (ever) ....
10 Do you work in the same place? (still) ....
11 They stay in the same hotel. (always) ....
12 Diane doesn't work on Saturdays. (usually) ....
13 I can remember his name. (never) ....
14 What do you have for breakfast? (usually) ....
15 When I arrived, Jan was there. (already) When I arrived, ...

88.3 Write sentences with **also**. Use the words in brackets ( ).

1 Do you play football? (tennis) Yes, and I also play tennis. ....
2 Do you speak Italian? (French) Yes, and I ....
3 Are you tired? (hungry) Yes, and ....
4 Have you been to England? (Ireland) Yes, ...
5 Did you buy any clothes? (some books) ....

88.4 Write sentences with **both** and **all**.

I live in London.	I live in London.
I like football.	I like football.
I'm a student.	I'm a student.
I've got a car.	I've got a car.

I'm married, I was born in England, I live in New York.

1 They both live in London. ....
2 They .... football.
3 .... students.
4 .... cars.

5 They .... married.
6 They .... England.
7 ....

UNIT 89   still   yet

■ **still**

An hour ago it was raining.   It is **still** raining now.

still = something is the same as before:
- A: Does your daughter work?
  B: No, she's **still** at school. (= she was at school before and she's at school now)
- I had a lot to eat but I'm **still** hungry.
- 'Did you sell your car?'   'No, I've **still** got it.'
- 'Do you **still** live in Paris?'   'No, I live in London now.'

■ **yet**

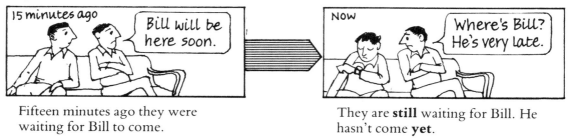

Fifteen minutes ago they were   They are **still** waiting for Bill. He
waiting for Bill to come.   hasn't come **yet**.

Yet = until now.
We use **yet** in *negative sentences* (**He hasn't come yet.**) and in *questions* (**Has he come yet**?)
Yet is usually at the end of a sentence:
- 'Where's Tom?'   'He **isn't** here **yet**.' (= He will be here but until now he hasn't come.)
- 'What are you doing this evening?'   'I **don't** know **yet**.' (= I will know later but I don't know at the moment.)
- 'Are you ready to go **yet**?'   '**Not yet**. Wait a moment.' (= I will be ready but I'm not ready at the moment.)

We often use the *present perfect* (**I have done**   ▶ Units 15–16) + **yet**:
- 'What's in the newspaper today?'   'I don't know. I **haven't read** it **yet**.' (= I'm going to read it but I haven't read it until now.)
- '**Has** it **stopped** raining **yet**?'   'No, it's still raining.'

■ Compare **yet** and **still**:
- She hasn't gone **yet**. = She's **still** here. (*not* 'She is yet here.')
- I haven't finished eating **yet**. = I'm **still** eating.

178

UNIT 89 Exercises

89.1 You meet Carol. The last time you saw her was two years ago. You ask her some questions with **still**.

Carol – two years ago

1 I play the piano.	2 I smoke.
4 I go to the cinema a lot.	3 I'm a student.
5 I've got a motor-bike.	6 I play tennis.

1 Do you still play the piano .... ?
2 Do you .... ?
3 Are .... ?
4 .... ?
5 .... ?
6 .... ?

89.2 Write questions with **yet**.

1 It was raining ten minutes ago. Perhaps it has stopped now.
   You ask: .Has it stopped raining yet... ?
2 You are waiting for Ann to arrive. She wasn't here half an hour ago. Perhaps she is here
   now.   *You ask:* .... Ann .... ?
3 You are waiting for me to finish reading the newspaper. Perhaps I have finished now.
   You ask: .... you .... ?
4 We are going out together. You are waiting for me to get ready. Perhaps I am ready
   now.   *You ask:* .... ?
5 Tom can't decide where to go on holiday. Perhaps he has decided now.
   You ask: .... ?

89.3 Write three sentences for each situation. Look at the example carefully.

before   *now*

1   (*before*) It was raining..
    (*still*)   It is still raining....................................
    (*yet*)   It hasn't stopped raining yet...................

2   (*before*) They were ....
    (*still*)   .... still ....
    (*yet*)   The bus ....

3   (*before*) He was ....
    (*still*)   .... a job.
    (*yet*)   .... yet.

4   (*before*) She ....
    (*still*)   ....
    (*yet*)   ....

5   (*before*) They ....
    (*still*)   ....
    (*yet*)   ....

UNIT 90   Give me that book!   Give it to me!

| give | lend | pass | send | show |

After these verbs (**give**, **lend** etc.) there are two possible structures:

(give) something to somebody

> – I gave **the money to Jack**.

or **(give) somebody something**

> – I gave **Jack the money**.

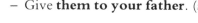

■ **(give) something to somebody**
> – That book is mine. **Give it to me**!
> – This is your father's key. Can you **give it to him**?
> – I **lent my car to a friend of mine**.
> – 'Have you seen these photographs?'   'Yes, you **showed them to us**.'

		(**something**)	to (**somebody**)
Can you	**give**	this key	**to** your father?
Can you	**give**	it	**to** him?
I	**lent**	my car	**to** a friend of mine.
You	**showed**	them	**to** us.

■ **(give) somebody something**
> – Give **me that book**! It's mine. (*not* 'Give to me that book!')
> – Tom gave **his mother some flowers**. (*not* 'Tom gave to his mother some flowers.')

		(**somebody**)	(**something**)
Tom	**gave**	his mother	some flowers.
Don't forget to	**send**	Jill	a birthday card.
Can you	**pass**	me	the salt, please?
If you see Jack, can you	**give**	him	this letter?
How much money did you	**lend**	them?	

Compare:
> – I gave **the book to Pat**.
> *but*   I gave **Pat the book**. (*not* 'I gave to Pat the book.')

We prefer the first structure (**give something to somebody**) when the *thing* is **it** or **them**:
> – I gave **it to her**. (*not usually* 'I gave her it.')
> – Give **them to your father**. (*not usually* 'Give your father them.')

UNIT 90   Exercises

90.1 Mark had some things that he didn't want – an armchair, a TV set, some books, some cassettes, a radio and a lamp. He gave these things to different people. Look at the pictures and write a sentence for each thing.

1 → his brother	2 → Jack	3 → his sister	4 → a friend	5 → his cousin	6 → Sarah

1 He gave the armchair to his brother......   4 ....

2 He gave ....   5 ....

3 He ....   6 ....

90.2 You wanted to give presents to your friends. You thought about it and and you decided to give them the things in the pictures. Write a sentence for each person.

1 George	2 Alice	3 Mark	4 Diane	5 Kevin	6 Mary

1 I gave George a tennis-racket...........   4 ....

2 I gave Alice ....   5 ....

3 I ....   6 ....

90.3 Write questions beginning **Can you ... ?** Use the verb in brackets (   ).

1 (you want the salt)	(pass)	Can you pass me the salt.......................... ?
2 (you need an umbrella)	(lend)	Can you lend .... ?
3 (you want your coat)	(give)	Can you .... my .... ?
4 (Mary needs a bicycle)	(lend)	Can .... Mary ....?
5 (Tom wants some information)	(send)	.... ?
6 (you want to see the letter)	(show)	.... me .... ?
7 (they need £100)	(lend)	.... ?

90.4 Write questions beginning **Can you give ... ?**

1	Do you want the book?	Yes, can you give it to me, please.............. ?
2	Do you want this key?	Yes, can you .... , please?
3	Do you want these keys?	Yes, can .... ?
4	Do you want this knife?	Yes, ... ?
5	Do you want this money?	Yes, ... ?
6	Do you want these letters?	Yes, ... ?

181

UNIT 91   at 10.30   on Monday   in April

■ **at**

at	8 o'clock 10.30 midnight etc.

– I start work **at 8 o'clock**.
– The shops close **at 5.30 p.m.**

■ **on**

on	Sunday(s)/Monday(s) etc. 25 April / 6 June etc. New Year's Day etc.

– Goodbye! See you **on Friday**.
– I don't work **on Sundays**.
– The concert is **on 22 November**.

■ **in**

APRIL

in	April/June etc. 1985/1750 etc. (the) summer/spring etc.

– I'm going on holiday **in October**.
– Jill left school **in 1984**.
– The garden is lovely **in spring**.

also

at the weekend	– Are you going away **at the weekend**?
at night	· I can't sleep **at night**.
at Christmas/Easter	· In Britain children get presents **at Christmas**. (*but* **on** Christmas **Day**)
at the end of . . .	– I'm going on holiday **at the end of October**.
at the moment	– Are you busy **at the moment**?

in the morning / in the afternoon / in the evening
     – I always feel good **in the morning**.
     – Do you often go out **in the evening**?

but

on Monday morning / on Tuesday afternoon / on Friday evening / on Saturday night etc.
     – I'm meeting Jill **on Monday morning**.
     – Are you doing anything **on Friday evening**?

■ **in five minutes / in a few days / in six weeks / in two years** etc.

now   in five minutes

– Hurry! The train leaves **in five minutes**.
  (= it leaves five minutes from now)
– Goodbye. I'll see you **in a few days**.
  (= a few days from now)

■ ~~at~~ ~~on~~ ~~in~~   We do *not* use **at/on/in** before:
this . . . (this morning / this week etc.)   **last . . . (last August / last week** etc.)
every . . . (every day / every week etc.)   **next . . . (next Monday / next week** etc.)

     – They're going on holiday **next Monday**. (*not* 'on next Monday')
     – **Last summer** we went to Scotland. (*not* 'In last summer')

UNIT 91   Exercises

91.1 Write **at/on/in**.

1 .on... 6 June
2 .at... 8 o'clock
3 .... Wednesday
4 .... 12.30 a.m.
5 1977
6 .... September
7 .... 24 September
8 .... Friday
9 1984
10 .... half past two
11 .... Christmas Day
12 .... winter

13 .in... the evening
14 .... the morning
15 .... Monday morning
16 .... Saturday night
17 .... night
18 .... Christmas
19 .... the weekend
20 .... Tuesday afternoon
21 .... the end of my holiday

91.2 Write **at/on/in**.

1 Goodbye! See you .on.. Friday.
2 Where were you .... 28 February?
3 I got up .... 8 o'clock this morning.
4 I like getting up early .... the morning.
5 My sister got married .... May.
6 Diane and I first met .... 1979.
7 Did you go out .... Friday?
8 Did you go out .... Friday evening?
9 Do you often go out .... the evening?
10 Let's meet .... 7.30 tomorrow evening.
11 I'm starting my new job .... 3 June.
12 We often go to the beach .... summer.
13 George isn't here .... the moment.
14 Julia's birthday is .... January.
15 Do you work .... Saturdays?
16 I will send you the money .... the end of this month.
17 .... autumn, the leaves fall from the trees.
18 The company started .... 1969.
19 I often go away .... the weekend.
20 I like looking at the stars in the sky .... night.

91.3 Write sentences with **in ...**

1
     now
     17.25   →   17.30

It's 17.25 now. The train leaves at 17.30.
..The train leaves in five minutes................................

2
     MONDAY → THURSDAY

It's Monday today. I'll phone you on Thursday.
I'll .... days.

3
     14 JUNE → 28 JUNE

It's 14 June today. My exam is on 28 June.
My ....

4

It's 3 o'clock now. Tom will be here at 3.30.
Tom ....

91.4 Write **at/on/in** if necessary. (Sometimes there is no preposition.)

1 I'm leaving .on.. Saturday.
2 I'm leaving ..—.. next Saturday.
3 I always feel tired .... the evening.
4 Will you be at home .... this evening?
5 We went to Scotland .... last summer.
6 What do you usually do .... the weekend?
7 She phones me .... every Sunday.
8 Can you play tennis .... next Sunday?
9 I'm afraid I can't come to the party .... Sunday.
10 We went to bed late .... last night.
11 I don't like going out alone .... night.
12 I won't be out very long. I'll be back .... ten minutes.

UNIT 92   from ... to   until   since   for

■ **from ... to ...:**

- We lived in Canada **from 1977 to 1985**.
- I work **from Monday to Friday**.

You can also say **from ... until ...:**

- We lived in Canada **from 1977 until 1985**.

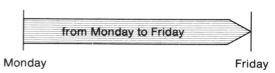

from Monday to Friday

Monday   Friday

■ **until** + *the end of a period*:

until Friday   until 1999   until 10.30   until I come back

- They're going away tomorrow. They'll be away **until Friday**.
- I went to bed early last night but I wasn't tired. I read a book **until 3 a.m.**
- Wait here **until I come back**.

You can also say **till** (= **until**):

- Wait here **till I come back**.

Compare:

- '**How long** will you be away?' '**Until** (*or* **till**) Monday.'
- '**When** are you coming back?' '**On** Monday.'

until Friday

Friday

■ **since** + *the beginning of a period (from the past to now)*:

since Monday   since 1958   since 2 o'clock   since I arrived

We use **since** after the *present perfect* (**have been** / **have done** etc.):

- John is in hospital. He has been in hospital **since Sunday**. (= from Sunday to now)
- Mr and Mrs Kelly have been married **since 1958**. (= from 1958 to now)
- It has been raining **since I got up**.

since Sunday

Sunday   now

Compare:

- We lived in Canada **from** 1977 **to** 1985.
  We lived in Canada **until** 1985.
  Now we live in England. We came to England **in** 1985.
  We have lived in England **since** 1985. (= from 1985 until now)

Use **for** (*not* **since**) + *a period of time* (**three days** / **ten years** etc.):

- John has been in hospital **for three days**. (*not* 'since three days')

■ **for** + *a period of time*:

for three days   for ten years   for ten minutes   for a long time

- George stayed with us **for three days**.
- I'm going away **for a few weeks**.
- They've been married **for ten years**.

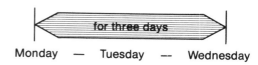

for three days

Monday — Tuesday — Wednesday

present perfect + **for** and **since** ▶ Units 17–18

UNIT 92   Exercises

92.1 Read the information about these people and complete the sentences. Use **from ... to** / **until** / **since**.

1 (Alex / Canada / 1977–85)   <u>Alex lived in Canada from 1977 to 1985.</u>
2 (Alex / Canada / → 1985)   Alex lived in Canada .... 1985.
3 (Alex / England / 1985 →)   Alex has lived in England .... 1985.
4 (Alice / France / → 1986)   Alice lived in ....
5 (Alice / Switzerland / 1986 →) Alice has lived in ....
6 (Carol / a hotel / 1985–88) Carol worked .... 1985 ....
7 (Carol / a restaurant / 1988 →) Carol has worked ....
8 (Gerry / a teacher / 1978–84) Gerry was a ....
9 (Gerry / a salesman / 1984 →) Gerry has been ....

Now write sentences with **for**.

10 (Alex / Canada)   <u>Alex lived in Canada for eight years.</u>
11 (Alex / England)   Alex has lived in England ....
12 (Alice / Switzerland)   Alice has lived ....
13 (Carol / a hotel)   Carol worked in ....
14 (Carol / a restaurant) Carol has worked ....
15 (Gerry / a teacher)   Gerry was ....
16 (Gerry / a salesman)   Gerry has been ....

92.2 Put in **until/since/for**.

1 Mr and Mrs Kelly have been married *since* 1958.
2 I was tired this morning. I stayed in bed .... 10 o'clock.
3 We waited .... half an hour, but they didn't come.
4 'How long have you been here?'   '........... half past eight.'
5 'How long did you stay at the party last night?'   '........... midnight.'
6 John and I are good friends. We have known each other .... ten years.
7 I'm tired. I'm going to lie down .... a few minutes.
8 Don't open the door of the train .... it stops.
9 I've lived in this house .... I was seven years old.
10 Jack has gone away. He'll be away .... next Wednesday.
11 Next week I'm going to Paris .... four days.
12 I usually finish work at 5.30, but sometimes I work .... 6 o'clock.
13 'How long have you known Ann?'   '........... we were at school together.'
14 Where have you been? I've been waiting for you .... 20 minutes.

185

UNIT 93   before   after   during   while

before · during · after

before the film   **during** the film   **after** the film

- **Before the examination** everybody was very nervous.
- I went to sleep **during the film**.
- We were tired **after our visit** to the museum.

before · while · after

before we played   **while** we were playing   **after** we played

- Don't forget to close the windows **before you go** out.
- I went to sleep **while I was watching** television.
- They went home **after they did** the shopping.

■ We use **during** + *noun* (during **the film**), **while** + *verb* (while I **was watching**):
- We didn't speak **during the meal**.
- *but*   We didn't speak **while we were eating**. (*not* 'during we were eating')

past continuous (**I was ·ing**)   ▶ Units 12–13

■ You can say **before –ing** and **after –ing**:

before –ing	after –ing
- I always have breakfast **before going** to work. (= before I go to work) - **Before** eat**ing** the apple, she washed it very carefully. (= before she ate the apple)	- I started work **after** read**ing** the newspaper. (= after I read the newspaper) - **After** do**ing** the shopping, they went home. (= after they did the shopping)

186

UNIT 93   Exercises

93.1 Complete the sentences. Use **before/during/after** + the best ending from the box.

before during after	+	the concert the course the end	~~the examination~~ lunch the night	they went to Australia you cross the road

1 Everybody was nervous *before the examination.*..
2 I usually have lunch at 1.30, and .... I go back to work.
3 The film was very boring. We left ....
4 Ann went to evening classes to learn Spanish. She learnt a lot ....
5 My aunt and uncle lived in London ....
6 Somebody broke a window .... Did you hear anything?
7 A: Are you going home .... ?
   B: No, we're going to a restaurant.
8 Always look both ways ....

93.2 Put in **during** or **while**.

1 We didn't speak ..*while*........ we were eating.
2 We didn't speak ..*during*..... the meal.
3 George telephoned .... you were out.
4 She wrote a lot of letters .... she was on holiday.
5 The students looked very bored .... the lesson.
6 I read the newspaper .... I was waiting for Jack.
7 I don't eat much .... the day, but I always have a big meal in the evening.
8 I fell out of bed .... I was asleep.

93.3 Complete these sentences with **before -ing ...**

1 She washed the apple. Then she ate it.
   She washed the apple before eating it..... or *Before eating the apple, she washed it.*....
2 Think carefully. Then answer the question.
   Think carefully before ....
3 Mary put on her glasses. Then she read the letter.
   Mary put on her glasses ....
4 The man took off his coat. Then he got into the car.
   Before .... his coat.

Write sentences with **after -ing ...**

5 We walked for three hours. We were very tired.
   We were very tired after ....
6 I ate too much chocolate. I felt sick.
   I felt ....
7 I read the book a second time. I understood it better.
   ....
8 John left school. Then he worked in a department store for two years.
   ....

UNIT 94   in   at   (*places*)

■ **in**

in a room   **in** a garden   **in** France   **in** the water
in a shop   **in** a park   **in** Rome   **in** the sea
in a box   **in** a town   **in** the city centre   **in** my coffee

    – 'Where's Tom?'   '**In the kitchen**. / **In the garden**. / **In London**.'
    – Milan is **in the north of Italy**.
    – I like swimming **in the sea**.
    – I live **in a town** but I want to live **in the country**.

also

> **in bed**   **in hospital / in prison**
> **in a street**   **in the sky**   **in the world**
> **in a newspaper / in a magazine / in a book**
> **in a photograph / in a picture**
> **in a car** (*but* **on** a bus / **on** a train / **on** a plane)
> **in the middle (of . . .)**

■ **at**

    **at** the top (of the page)

at the door   **at** the traffic lights   **at** the bus-stop   **at** the bottom

    – Why is that woman standing **at the door?**
    – Turn left **at the traffic lights**.
    – There's a man **at the bus stop**.
    – Please write your name **at the top of the page**.

also

> **at home / at work / at school**   **at university**
> **at the station / at the airport**   **at the end** (of the street)
> **at the hairdresser('s) / at the doctor('s) / at the dentist('s)** etc.
> **at Jane's** (house) / **at my sister's** (house)
> **at a concert / at a conference / at a party / at a football match** etc.

    – 'Where's Tom?'   '**At work**. / **At home**. / **At the doctor's**.'
    – Do you want me to meet you **at the airport**?
    – There weren't many people **at the party**.
    – My house is **at the end of the street**.

■ Often **in** *or* **at** is possible for a building (hotels, restaurants etc.):
    – We stayed **at a nice hotel**.   *or*   We stayed **in a nice hotel**.

UNIT 94   Exercises

94.1 Complete the sentences for the pictures. Use **in** or **at** + one of these:

the airport   **bed**   **a box**   **the end of the street**   ~~the garden~~   **hospital**
a party   **the sky**

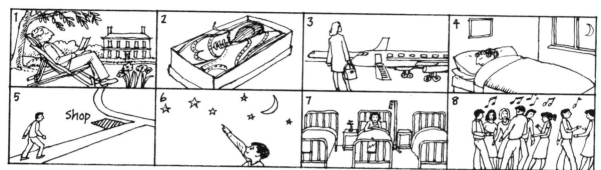

1 He's ..*in the garden*..................................
2 The shoes are ....
3 She's ....
4 He's ....

5 The shop is ....
6 The stars are ....
7 She's ....
8 They're ....

94.2 Complete the sentences. Use **in** + one of these:

this book   **that field**   ~~the kitchen~~   **this photograph**   **the river**   **my tea**

1 Pat is ..*in the kitchen*... . She's cooking the dinner.
2 Look at those beautiful horses ....
3 Don't swim .... The water is very dirty.
4 There's too much sugar .... I can't drink it.
5 How many pages are there .... ?
6 Who is the man .... ? Do you know him?

94.3 Write **in** or **at**.

1 'Where's Tina?' 'She's ..*at*. work.'
2 Why didn't the bus-driver stop .... the bus-stop?
3 Go straight on .... the roundabout and turn right .... the church.
4 There was a big table .... the middle of the room.
5 What is the longest river .... the world?
6 Were there many people .... the concert on Friday?
7 My brother is studying mathematics .... London University.
8 'Where does your sister live?' '........ Brussels.'
9 Did you read about the accident .... the newspaper?
10 Will you be .... home tomorrow afternoon?
11 Munich is a large city .... the south of Germany.
12 'Do you work?' 'No, I'm still .... school.'
13 George is coming by train. I'm going to meet him .... the station.
14 Charlie is .... hospital. He's going to have an operation tomorrow.
15 There was a list of names on the notice-board. My name was .... the bottom of the list.
16 I usually do my shopping .... the city centre.

UNIT 95   to   in   at   (*places*)

■ **to**

> **go/come/return/walk** etc. **to . . .**
>
>
>
> — We're **going to London** next week.
>
> — I want to **go to Italy**.
> — We **walked** from my house **to the city centre**.
> — What time do you **go to bed**?
>
> — He is **walking to the door**.
>
> — I **went to the airport** by car.
> — Tom didn't **go to work** yesterday.
> — I'm **going to a party** tonight.
> — Do you want to **go to university**?
> — You must **come to our house**.
>
> **go/come/walk** etc. ❌ **home**
> — I'm tired. I'm **going home**.
>   (*not* 'to home')
> — Did you **walk home**?

■ **in/at**   (▶ Unit 94)

> **be / stay / do something** etc. **in . . .**
>
>
>
> — Piccadilly Circus **is in London**.
>
> — My brother **lives in Italy**.
> — The best shops **are in the city centre**.
> — I like **reading in bed**.

> **be / stay / do something** etc. **at . . .**
>
>
>
> — He is **standing at the door**.
>
> — I met Ann **at the airport**.
> — Ann **wasn't at work** yesterday.
> — I **met** a lot of people **at the party**.
> — My sister **is at university**.
> — Ann **is at her sister's house**.
>
> **be/stay/do something** etc. **at home**
> — I'm not going out this evening.
>   I'm **staying at home**.
> — 'Where's Ann?'   '**At home**.'

■ **arrive in . . .** and **arrive at . . .**

> **arrive in** *a country or town* (**arrive in Italy** / **arrive in Paris** etc.):
>   — They **arrived in England** last week. (*not* 'arrived to England')
>
> **arrive at** other places (**arrive at the station** / **arrive at work** etc.):
>   — What time did they **arrive at the hotel**? (*not* 'arrive to the hotel')
>
> **arrive home** (*no preposition*):
>   — I was tired when I **arrived home**.
>
> **get to** (= arrive) ▶ Unit 51

UNIT 95   Exercises

95.1 Complete these sentences. Use **to** + one of these:

the bank   **bed**   **the cinema**   **a concert**   **France**   **hospital**   ~~work~~

1 Joy was ill yesterday, so she didn't go ..*to work*...
2 It's late and I'm tired. I think I'll go ....
3 We must go .... today. We haven't got any money.
4 'Are you going out this evening?'   'Yes, I'm going ....,'
5 I'd like to go .... I've never been there before.
6 We don't go .... very often but we watch a lot of films on TV.
7 After the accident three people were taken ....

95.2 Write **to** or **in**.

1 'Where's Jack?'   '..*In*.. bed.'
2 I'm going .... the shop to buy some milk.
3 Tom went .... the kitchen to make some coffee.
4 'Where's Tom?'   'He's .... the kitchen making some coffee.'
5 Would you like to go .... the theatre this evening?
6 I got a postcard from Sue this morning. She's on holiday .... Switzerland.
7 John lives .... a small village .... the south-west of England.
8 What time do you usually go .... bed?
9 Kevin's sister is very ill. She's .... hospital.
10 Excuse me, I must go .... the toilet.
11 The train left Brussels at 7 o'clock and arrived .... Paris at 9.30.
12 I was tired this morning. I stayed .... bed until 10 o'clock.
13 Next year we hope to go .... Canada to visit some friends.
14 Would you like to live .... another country?

95.3 Write **to** or **at** if necessary. (Sometimes there is no preposition.)

1 Joy didn't go ..*to*.. work yesterday.
2 Ann is ill. She has gone .... the doctor.
3 Are you going .... the party on Saturday evening?
4 I talked to some nice people .... the party.
5 'Where were you this morning?'   'I was .... work.'
6 'Do you usually walk .... work?'   'No, I go by bicycle.'
7 We had a good meal .... a restaurant and then we went back .... the hotel.
8 What time are you going .... home?
9 Will you be .... home this afternoon?
10 I went .... Mary's house but she wasn't .... home.
11 There were no taxis, so we walked .... home.
12 How often do you go .... the dentist?
13 What time do you usually arrive .... work in the morning?
14 It was very late when we arrived .... home.
15 The boy jumped into the river and swam .... the other side.
16 Would you like to study .... university?
17 There were 20,000 people .... the football match.
18 'Are your children here?'   'No, they're .... school.'

191

UNIT 96   on   under   behind etc. (*prepositions*)

■ on

on a table
on a plate
on the floor etc.

on a wall
on a door
on the ceiling etc.

on a bus
on a train
on a plane

on the ground floor
on the first floor etc.

— There are some books **on the shelf** and some pictures **on the wall**.
— I met Alice **on the bus**.
— The office is **on the first floor**. (*not* 'in the first floor')
— There are a lot of apples **on the tree**.

also **on a horse** / **on a bicycle** / **on a motor-bike**

■ under

under the table   **under** a tree

— The cat is **under** the table.
— The girl is standing **under** a tree.
— I'm wearing a jacket **under** my coat.

■ next to (*or* beside) / between / in front of / behind

A is **next to** B. *or* A is **beside** B.
B is **between** A and C.
D is **in front of** B.
E is **behind** B.

also
A is **on the left**.
C is **on the right**.
B is **in the middle** (*of the group*).

■ opposite

The supermarket is **opposite** the cinema.

■ above and below

A is **above** the line.

B is **below** the line.

The pictures are **above** the shelves.

The shelves are **below** the pictures.

UNIT 96 Exercises

96.1 Complete the sentences. Use **on** + one of these:

the beach   **a bicycle**   **his finger**   **this plant**   **the door**   ~~the wall~~

1 The pictures .on the wall............... look very nice.
2 When the weather is nice in summer, I like lying ....
3 The leaves .... are a beautiful colour.
4 Our house is number 45 – the number is ....
5 He was wearing a silver ring ....
6 It's difficult to carry a lot of things ....

96.2 Look at the pictures and complete the sentences with a preposition (**on/under** etc.).

1 The cat is ....under............... the table.
2 There is a tree .... the house.
3 My flat is .... a shop.
4 She is standing .... the piano.
5 His name is .... the door.

6 The town hall is .... the station.
7 The switch is .... the window.
8 The cupboard is .... the sink.
9 There are some shoes .... the bed.
10 In Britain, we drive .... the left.

96.3 Nine people live in a block of flats. Use the picture and complete the sentences with **on /
next to / between / above / below**.

1 Chris lives **between** Catherine and Paul.
2 Joe lives .... the ground floor.
3 Mary lives .... Steve and Bill.
4 Paul lives .... the first floor .... Chris.
5 Catherine lives .... Janet.
6 Chris lives .... Sandra and .... Mary.

96.4 Where are the people in the big picture?

1 Arthur is standing .on the left...............
2 Brian is sitting ....
3 Alice is sitting ....
4 Arthur is standing .... Barry.
5 Brian is sitting .... Albert.
6 Albert is standing .... Jane.

UNIT 97 up over through etc. (*prepositions*)

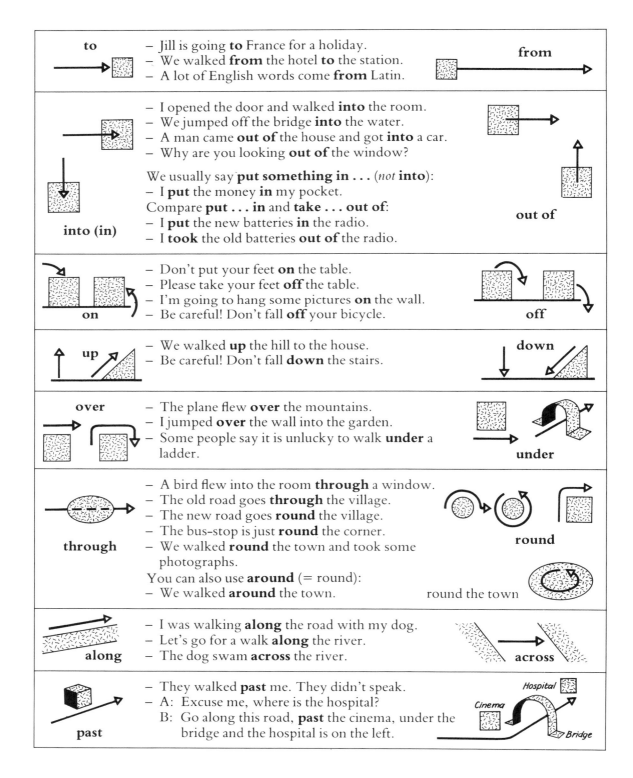

to	– Jill is going **to** France for a holiday. – We walked **from** the hotel **to** the station. – A lot of English words come **from** Latin.
into (in)	– I opened the door and walked **into** the room. – We jumped off the bridge **into** the water. – A man came **out of** the house and got **into** a car. – Why are you looking **out of** the window? We usually say **put something in . . .** (*not* **into**): – I **put** the money **in** my pocket. Compare **put . . . in** and **take . . . out of**: – I **put** the new batteries **in** the radio. – I **took** the old batteries **out of** the radio.
on	– Don't put your feet **on** the table. – Please take your feet **off** the table. – I'm going to hang some pictures **on** the wall. – Be careful! Don't fall **off** your bicycle.
up	– We walked **up** the hill to the house. – Be careful! Don't fall **down** the stairs.
over	– The plane flew **over** the mountains. – I jumped **over** the wall into the garden. – Some people say it is unlucky to walk **under** a ladder.
through	– A bird flew into the room **through** a window. – The old road goes **through** the village. – The new road goes **round** the village. – The bus-stop is just **round** the corner. – We walked **round** the town and took some photographs. You can also use **around** (= round): – We walked **around** the town.
along	– I was walking **along** the road with my dog. – Let's go for a walk **along** the river. – The dog swam **across** the river.
past	– They walked **past** me. They didn't speak. – A: Excuse me, where is the hospital? B: Go along this road, **past** the cinema, under the bridge and the hospital is on the left.

UNIT 97   Exercises

97.1 Somebody asks you the way to a place and you tell him/her which way to go. Look at the pictures and complete the sentences (**Go...**).

Excuse me, where is...?
Go...

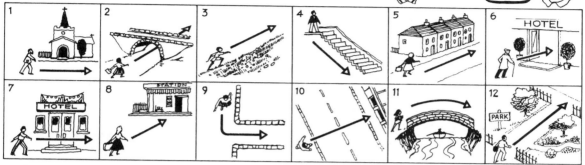

1 Go past the church.
2 Go .... the bridge.
3 Go .... the hill.
4 Go .... the stairs.

5 Go .... the street.
6 Go ....
7 ....
8 ....

9 ....
10 ....
11 ....
12 ....

97.2 Look at the pictures and complete the sentences with a preposition (**up/over** etc.).

1 The dog swam ...... across .... the river.
2 The book fell .... a shelf.
3 The plane flew .... the village.
4 He threw the book .... the window.

5 They drove .... the village.
6 A woman got .... a car.
7 A man walked .... the shop.
8 The Moon travels .... the Earth.

97.3 Put in a preposition (**up/off/through** etc.).

1 We jumped ..... off ..... the bridge ... into .... the water.
2 Do you know how to put a film .... this camera?
3 You can put your coat .... the back of the chair.
4 She took a key .... her bag and opened the door.
5 We didn't have a key, so we climbed .... a window .... the house.
6 I looked .... the window and watched the people in the street.
7 We walked .... the museum and saw a lot of interesting things.
8 In tennis, you have to hit the ball .... the net.
9 Don't forget to put a stamp .... the postcard before you post it.

UNIT 98 at by with/without about
(*prepositions*)

◼ at

at (the age of) 20 /at 90 kilometres an hour / at 100 degrees

- Sarah left school **at 16**. (*or* **. . . at the age of 16**.)
- He was driving **at 90 kilometres an hour**.
  (*or* He was **doing 90 kilometres an hour**.)
- Water boils **at 100 degrees celsius**.

◼ by

by = next to / beside   (▶ Unit 96):
- Our house is **by the sea**. (= next to the sea)
- John is standing **by the window**.

by the window

(go) **by car / by bus / by plane** (*or* **by air**) / **by bike** etc.
- Do you like travelling **by train**?
- Jane usually goes to work **by bike**.
but **on foot**:
- She goes to work **on foot**. (= She **walks** to work.)

by bus

on foot

a book **by . . .** / a painting **by . . .** / a piece of music **by . . .** etc.:
- Have you read any books **by George Orwell**?
- **Who** is that painting **by**? Picasso?

← (*the title*)
by
← (*the writer*)

by after the passive   (▶ Unit 20):
- I was bitten **by a dog**.

◼ with/without

- Did you stay at a hotel or **with friends**?
- Wait for me. Please don't go **without me**.
- Do you like your coffee **with** or **without milk**?

with milk   without milk

do something **with** something (= use something to do something):
- I **cut** the paper **with a pair of scissors**.
- She can't **read without glasses**. (= She needs glasses to read.)

a man with a beard / a woman with glasses / a house with a garden etc.
- Who is **that man with the beard**?
- I'd like to have **a house with a garden**.

a man with a beard

◼ about

talk/speak/think/hear/know about . . . etc.
- Some people **talk about their work** all the time.
- I don't **know** much **about cars**.

a book / a question / a programme about . . . etc.
- Did you see **the programme about computers** on TV last night?

UNIT 98 Exercises

98.1 Look at the pictures. Complete the sentences with a preposition (**at/by** etc.).

1 I cut the paper **with** a pair of scissors.
2 He's sitting .... the telephone.
3 Who is the woman .... short hair?
4 She's reading a book ....
   languages .... Vera P. Bull.
5 Sara usually goes to work .... car.

6 They are listening to some music .... Mozart.
7 Who is the man .... the sunglasses?
8 They're talking .... the weather.
9 The plant is .... the piano.
10 The plane is flying .... 600 miles an hour.

98.2 Complete the sentences with a preposition (**at/by/with** etc.).

1 Some people talk ..**about**.. their work all the time.
2 'How did you get here? .... bus?' 'No, ... foot.'
3 In Britain, children normally start school .... the age of five.
4 It's not easy to live .... money.
5 In tennis, you hit the ball .... a racket.
6 *Hamlet*, *Othello* and *Macbeth* are plays .... William Shakespeare.
7 'Do you know much .... economics?' 'Yes, I studied it at university.'
8 How long does it take from New York to Los Angeles .... plane?
9 'Which is your house?' 'The one .... the red door.'
10 These trains are very fast – they can travel .... very high speeds.
11 Did Val tell you .... her new job in a bookshop?
12 A: Have you heard the new record .... Calvin Swoon?
   B: Yes, it's great. I like his songs very much.
13 My grandmother died .... the age of 98.
14 Yesterday evening I went to a restaurant .... some friends of mine.
15 The door is locked. You can't get into the room .... a key.
16 Two men were arrested .... the police and taken to the police station.
17 Can you give me some information .... hotels in this town?
18 I like stories .... happy endings.
19 She doesn't use her car very often – she goes everywhere .... bicycle.
20 Would you like something to drink .... your meal?
21 Water freezes .... 0 degrees celsius.
22 In Britain it's expensive to travel .... train.

UNIT 99 afraid of   on holiday etc.
(word + preposition)

■ These words and prepositions (**at/in/of** etc.) usually go together:

afraid of ...	Are you **afraid of** dogs?
good at ... / **bad at** ...	Are you **good at** mathematics? She's very **bad at** writing letters.
interested in ...	George isn't **interested in** sport.
different from ...	Ann is very **different from** her sister.
sorry about (something)	**Sorry about** the noise last night. We had a party.
sorry for (doing something)	I'm **sorry for** shouting at you. (*or* **I'm sorry I shouted** . . .)
married to ...	She's **married to** an Italian. (= Her husband is Italian.)
fed up with ...	I'm **fed up with** my job. I want to do something different. (= I've had enough of my job – I want to change.)
nice/kind of somebody to do something	It was very **kind of** you to help us. Thank you very much.
(be) **nice / kind to** somebody	They were very **nice to** us. They helped us a lot.

■ **on** ...   Learn these expressions:

on holiday	Jane isn't at work. She's **on holiday.**
on television	We watched the news **on television**.
on the radio	We listened to the news **on the radio**.
on the (tele)phone	I spoke to Jack **on the phone** last night.
on fire	The house is **on fire**! Call the fire brigade.
on time (= not late)	'Was the train late?' 'No, it was **on time**.'

■ After a preposition, a verb ends in **-ing** (**at** do**ing** / **of** buy**ing** / **for** be**ing** etc.):

Are you good **at**	repair**ing**	things?
I'm fed up **with**	do**ing**	the same thing every day.
She went away **without**	say**ing**	goodbye. (= she didn't say goodbye)
I'm thinking **of**	buy**ing**	a new car.
I'm sorry **for**	be**ing**	late.

UNIT 99   Exercises

99.1 Look at the pictures and complete the sentences with a preposition (**at/of** etc.).

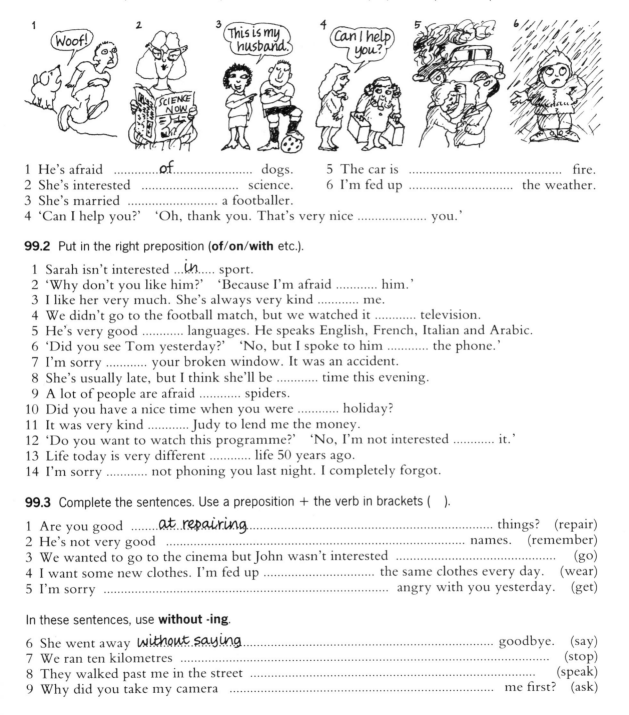

1 He's afraid ....*of*.................. dogs.
2 She's interested .... science.
3 She's married .... a footballer.
4 'Can I help you?' 'Oh, thank you. That's very nice .... you.'
5 The car is .... fire.
6 I'm fed up .... the weather.

99.2 Put in the right preposition (**of/on/with** etc.).

1 Sarah isn't interested ...*in*..... sport.
2 'Why don't you like him?' 'Because I'm afraid .... him.'
3 I like her very much. She's always very kind .... me.
4 We didn't go to the football match, but we watched it .... television.
5 He's very good .... languages. He speaks English, French, Italian and Arabic.
6 'Did you see Tom yesterday?' 'No, but I spoke to him .... the phone.'
7 I'm sorry .... your broken window. It was an accident.
8 She's usually late, but I think she'll be .... time this evening.
9 A lot of people are afraid .... spiders.
10 Did you have a nice time when you were .... holiday?
11 It was very kind .... Judy to lend me the money.
12 'Do you want to watch this programme?' 'No, I'm not interested .... it.'
13 Life today is very different .... life 50 years ago.
14 I'm sorry .... not phoning you last night. I completely forgot.

99.3 Complete the sentences. Use a preposition + the verb in brackets (   ).

1 Are you good ....*at repairing*... things? (repair)
2 He's not very good .... names. (remember)
3 We wanted to go to the cinema but John wasn't interested .... (go)
4 I want some new clothes. I'm fed up .... the same clothes every day. (wear)
5 I'm sorry .... angry with you yesterday. (get)

In these sentences, use **without -ing**.

6 She went away *without saying*.. goodbye. (say)
7 We ran ten kilometres .... (stop)
8 They walked past me in the street .... (speak)
9 Why did you take my camera .... me first? (ask)

UNIT 100   look at ...   listen to ... etc.
(verb + preposition)

These verbs and prepositions (**to/of/at** etc.) usually go together:

listen to ...   – **Listen to** this music. It's beautiful.

talk/speak to somebody (**about** something)
                                                 – Did you **talk to** Jack **about** your problem?
                                                 – (*on the phone*) Can I **speak to** Kay, please?

write (a letter) **to** somebody
                                                 – I never get letters. Nobody **writes to** me.
but (**tele**)**phone** somebody (*not* phone to ...):
                                                 – Can you **phone me** tomorrow? (*not* 'phone to me')

belong to ...   – Does this book **belong to** you? (= Is this your book?)

happen to ...   – I put my pen on the table five minutes ago and now
                                                   it isn't there. What's **happened to** it?

wait for ...   – Don't go yet. **Wait for** me.

thank somebody **for ...**   – **Thank you** very much **for** your help.

ask (somebody) **for ...** (= ask somebody to give you ...)
                                                 – A man stopped me and **asked me for** money.

think about/of ...   – He never **thinks about** (*or of*) other people.
                                                 – I'm **thinking of** (*or about*) buying a new car.

depend on ...   – A: Do you like eating in restaurants?
                                                   B: Sometimes, yes. It **depends on** the restaurant.

You can say **it depends what/where/how** (etc.) *with or without* **on**:
                                                 – A: Do you want to come out with us?
                                                   B: **It depends (on) where** you're going.

---

look at ...   – She's **looking at** her watch.
                                                 – **Look at** those flowers. They're beautiful.
                                                 – Why are you **looking at** me like that?

look for ... (= try to find)

   – He's lost his key. He's **looking for** it.
                                                 – I'm **looking for** Ann. Have you seen her?

look after ... (= take care of, keep safe)
       – Mary goes to work every day but she has a young child. When she is at work, a
         friend of hers **looks after** her child.
       – Don't lose this book. **Look after** it. (= Keep it safe.)

UNIT 100   Exercises

100.1 Look at the pictures and complete the sentences with a preposition (**to/for** etc.).

1 She's looking ...**at**.... her watch.
2 He's listening .... the radio.
3 They're waiting .... a taxi.

4 Bill is talking .... Jane.
5 They're looking .... the picture.
6 She's looking .... Tom.

100.2 Complete the sentences with a preposition (**to/for/about** etc.) if necessary.

1 Thank you very much ....**for**... your help.
2 This is not my bicycle. It belongs .... a friend of mine.
3 (*on the telephone*) Hello, can I speak .... Mr Davis, please?
4 (*on the telephone*) Thank you .... phoning. Goodbye!
5 What happened .... Mary last night? Why didn't she come to the party?
6 Jack's brother is thinking .... going to Australia next year.
7 We asked the waiter .... coffee but he brought us tea.
8 'Do you like going to museums?' 'It depends .... the museum.'
9 Please listen .... me. I have something very important to tell you.
10 We waited .... John until 2 o'clock but he didn't come.
11 'Are you writing a letter?' 'Yes, I'm writing .... Julia.'
12 Don't forget to telephone .... your mother this evening.
13 He's alone all day. He never talks .... anybody.
14 'Are you playing tennis this afternoon?' 'It depends .... the weather.'
15 Katherine is thinking .... changing her job.
16 I looked .... the newspaper but I didn't read it carefully.
17 When you are ill, you need somebody to look .... you.
18 Excuse me, I'm looking .... Hill Street. Can you tell me where it is?
19 Goodbye! Have a nice holiday and look .... yourself.
20 When I take the photograph, look .... the camera and smile.
21 Barry is looking .... a job. He wants to work in a hotel.

100.3 Complete the sentences. Use **It depends ...** + one of these:

> **what time I leave**   ~~**where you're going**~~   **how much it is**   **how I feel**

1	Do you want to come out with us?	*It depends where you're going.* ....
2	Are you going out this evening?	It depends ....
3	What time will you arrive?	It ....
4	Are you going to buy the book?	....

201

UNIT 101 go in fall off run away etc.
(phrasal verbs 1)

A *phrasal verb* is a verb (**go/look/be** etc.) + **in/out/on** etc. ▶ Appendix 5 for other *phrasal verbs*

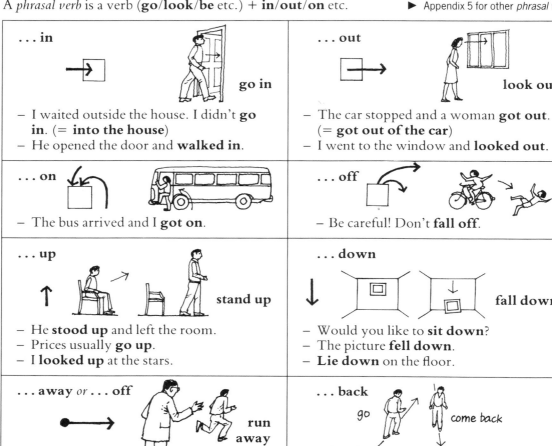

. . . in

go in

- I waited outside the house. I didn't **go in**. (= **into the house**)
- He opened the door and **walked in**.

. . . out

look out

- The car stopped and a woman **got out**. (= **got out of the car**)
- I went to the window and **looked out**.

. . . on

- The bus arrived and I **got on**.

. . . off

- Be careful! Don't **fall off**.

. . . up

stand up

- He **stood up** and left the room.
- Prices usually **go up**.
- I **looked up** at the stars.

. . . down

fall down

- Would you like to **sit down**?
- The picture **fell down**.
- **Lie down** on the floor.

. . . away *or* **. . . off**

run away

- The thief ran out of the shop and **ran away**. (*or* . . . **ran off**.)
- The woman got into the car and **drove away**. (*or* . . . **drove off**.)

go away = go to another place:
- Ann has **gone away**. She's **coming back** next week.

. . . back

go   come back

- After dinner at a restaurant, we **went back** to our hotel.
- **Go away** and don't **come back**!

. . . over

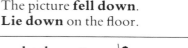

- The wall wasn't high, so we **climbed over**.
- When you come to the end of a page, **turn over**.
- I **fell over** because my shoes were too big for me.

fall over

. . . round

look round

- Somebody shouted, so I **looked round**.
- We went for a long walk. After four miles we **turned round** and **went back**.

UNIT 101 Exercises

101.1 Look at the pictures and complete the sentences with **in/out/up** etc.

1 I went to the window and looked ..**out**..
2 The door was open, so we went ....
3 He heard a plane, so he looked ....
4 She got on her bike and rode ....

5 I said hello and he turned ....
6 The bus stopped and she got ....
7 There was a free seat, so I sat ....
8 A car stopped and two men got ....

101.2 Complete the sentences. Use **out/away/back** etc.

1 'Why is that picture on the floor?' 'It fell **down**.'
2 Please don't go .... ! Stay here with me.
3 She heard a noise behind her, so she looked ....
4 I'm going .... now to do some shopping. I'll be .... at 5 o'clock.
5 I'm tired. I'm going to lie .... on the sofa.
6 Ann is going on holiday next month. She's going .... on 5th and coming .... on 24th.
7 When babies try to walk, they often fall ....
8 Jim is from Canada. He lived in Europe for ten years, but last year he went .... to Canada.

101.3 Complete the sentences. Use one of the verbs in the box + **on/up/off** etc. (These verbs are all in Appendix 5.)

breaks	carried	gave	got	hold	+	up	down
~~hurry~~	slowed	speak	takes	wash		on	off

1 **Hurry up**................! We haven't got much time.
2 I was very tired this morning. I .... very late.
3 This car isn't very good. It .... a lot.
4 It's difficult to hear you. Can you ...., please?
5 'It's time to go.' '................ a minute. I'm not ready yet.'
6 That was a lovely meal. Now we must ....
7 The train .... and finally stopped.
8 I like flying but I'm always nervous when the plane ....
9 I told him to stop but he .... Perhaps he didn't hear me.
10 I tried to find a job but I .... It was impossible.

UNIT 102   put on your shoes   put your shoes on
(*phrasal verbs 2*)

Sometimes a phrasal verb (**turn off** / **put on** etc.) has an *object*. For example:

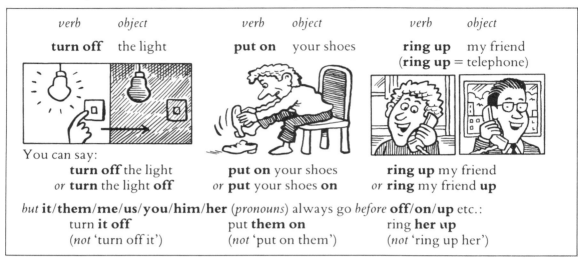

verb	*object*	*verb*	*object*	*verb*	*object*
turn off	the light	**put on**	your shoes	**ring up**	my friend
					(**ring up** = telephone)

You can say:
> **turn off** the light
> *or* **turn** the light **off**

> **put on** your shoes
> *or* **put** your shoes **on**

> **ring up** my friend
> *or* **ring** my friend **up**

but **it/them/me/us/you/him/her** (*pronouns*) always go *before* **off/on/up** etc.:
> turn **it** off
> (*not* 'turn off it')

> put **them** on
> (*not* 'put on them')

> ring **her** up
> (*not* 'ring up her')

---

put on / take off
- It was cold, so I **put my coat on**.
  (*or* . . . I **put on my coat**.)
- Here's your coat. **Put it on**.
- **Take off that hat**! It looks stupid.
  (*or* **Take that hat off**!)

turn on / turn off
- It was dark, so I **turned on the light**.
  (*or* . . . I **turned the light on**.)
- I don't want to watch this programme.
  You can **turn it off**.

pick up / put down
- That's my key on the floor. Can you **pick
  it up** for me, please?
- She stopped reading and **put her book
  down**. (*or* . . . **put down her book**.)

bring back / take back / give back / put back
- You can take my umbrella but please
  bring it back.
- I **took my new pullover back** to the
  shop. It was too small for me.
- John gave me his keys but I **gave them back** to him.
- I read the letter and then **put it back** in the envelope.

▶ Appendix 6 for other *phrasal verbs + object*

UNIT 102   Exercises

102.1 You can write the same sentence in three different ways. Complete the table.

1	I turned off the light.	I turned the light off...	I turned it off...
2	He put on his shirt.	He	He ....
3	She put on her glasses.	She	He ....
4	Can you .... ?	Can you turn the TV on?	.... them ....
5	She rang up her brother.	She	Can .... ?
6	....	We took our shoes off.	....
7	They gave back the money.	....	....
8	She put down her bags.	....	....
9	....	I switched the engine on.	....
10	....	She filled the form in.	....
11	We put out the fire.	....	

102.2 Complete the sentences. Use one of the objects in the box + on/off/up etc.

object	**my book** **the light**	**my gloves** **the radio**	**my jacket** **the photograph**	**it** ~~it~~	**it** **them**	**them** **them**	+	**on** **up**	**off** **down**	**back**

1 Don't forget to turn ....*the light off*..................................... before you go to bed.
2 That hat looks stupid! Take ...*it off*.....................................
3 I wanted to hear the news, so I turned ....
4 Thanks for lending me your cassettes. I'll give .... to you tomorrow.
5 I was reading when the phone rang. So I put .... and went to answer it.
6 There was some money on the floor, so I picked ....
7 My hands were cold, so I put ....
8 It was warm, so I took ....
9 She borrowed my keys and she hasn't brought .... yet.
10 I picked ...., looked at it, and put .... on the table.

The verbs in 11–20 are in Appendix 6.

object	**your cigarette a glass it it** **some shoes me us them it it**	+	**on** **down**	**out** **over**	**away** **round**	**up**

11 I knocked .... and broke it.
12 If you don't understand the word, look .... in a dictionary.
13 I want those magazines. Don't throw ....
14 He hit me so hard, he knocked ....
15 Please put .... You're not allowed to smoke here.
16 That music is very loud. Can you turn .... a little?
17 I tried .... in the shop but they were too big.
18 We visited the school. One of the teachers showed ....
19 I wrote the wrong name on the form, so I crossed ....
20 'Do you smoke?' 'No, I gave .... two years ago.'

UNIT 103 and but or so because

| and | but | or | so | because |

We use these words (*conjunctions*) to put two sentences together. They make one longer sentence from two shorter sentences:

sentence A | The car stopped. |——| The driver got out. | *sentence B*

longer sentence | The car stopped **and** the driver got out. |

■ **and/but/or ...**

sentence A	**and/but/or**	*sentence B*
We stayed at home	**and**	(we)* watched television.
My sister is married	**and**	(she)* lives in London.
He doesn't like her	**and**	she doesn't like him.
I bought a newspaper	**but**	I didn't read it.
It's a nice house	**but**	it hasn't got a garden.
Do you want to play tennis	**or**	are you too tired?

* The subjects in sentences A and B are the same. It is not necessary to say 'we' and 'she' after 'and' in sentence B.

■ **so ...** (*the result of something*):

sentence A	**so**	*sentence B*
It was too hot,	**so**	I opened the window.
The water wasn't clean,	**so**	we didn't go swimming.
They like films,	**so**	they often go to the cinema.

■ **because ...** (*the reason for something*):

sentence A	**because**	*sentence B*
I opened the window	**because**	it was too hot.
We didn't go swimming	**because**	the water wasn't clean.
She's hungry	**because**	she didn't have breakfast.

Because + *sentence B* is also possible at the beginning:
  – **Because the water wasn't clean**, we didn't go swimming.

■ You can use *more than one* conjunction to make a longer sentence:
  – It was late **and** I was tired, **so** I went to bed.
  – I always enjoy visiting London, **but** I wouldn't like to live there **because** it's too big.

UNIT 103 Exercises

103.1 Make longer sentences. Use **and/but/or** + the sentences in the box.

He didn't see me.	Did you stay at home?	They don't use it very often.
Don't come back!	~~We watched television.~~	I can't remember his name.
She looked out.	~~I didn't read it.~~	She swam to the other side.
Do you want to get a taxi?		They took some photographs.

1 We stayed at home ..*and watched television.*..................
2 I bought a newspaper ...*but I didn't read it.*................
3 She went to the window ....
4 I saw Jack ....
5 The girl jumped into the river ....
6 Did you go out last night ....?
7 They walked round the town ....
8 They've got a car ....
9 I can remember his face ....
10 Go away ....
11 Shall we walk to the hotel ....?

103.2 Make longer sentences. Use **so/because** + the sentences in the box.

She was ill.	We didn't play tennis.	~~It was very hot in the room.~~
Don't phone me.	~~We didn't go swimming.~~	She's friendly and interesting.
I walked in.	They haven't got a key.	I couldn't sleep.
We walked home.	She does the same thing all the time.	

1 I opened the window ..*because it was very hot in the room.*...............
2 The water wasn't very clean, *so we didn't go swimming.*...........
3 The door was open ....
4 Ann didn't go to work ....
5 I like Carol ....
6 It was raining ....
7 There were no buses ....
8 I got up in the middle of the night ....
9 I won't be at home this evening ....
10 They can't get into the house ....
11 She doesn't like her job ....

103.3 Write sentences about what *you* did yesterday.

1 (and) *In the evening, I stayed at home and studied.*................
2 (because) *I went to bed very early because I was tired.*...........
3 (and) ....
4 (but) ....
5 (so) ....
6 (because) ....

UNIT 104 When...

■ **When I went out, it was raining.**

This sentence has two parts:

part A when I went out	+	*part B* it was raining

You can begin with part A *or* part B:

- **When I went out**, it was raining.
- **It was raining** when I went out.

We write a comma (**,**) if part A (**When . . .**) is before part B:

- **When you're tired**, don't drive.
- Don't drive **when you're tired**.
- Ann was very happy **when she passed the examination**.
- **When Ann passed the examination**, she was very happy.

We do the same in sentences with **before/while/after** (▶ Unit 93):

- Always look both ways **before you cross the road**.
- **Before you cross the road**, always look both ways.
- **While I was waiting for the bus**, it began to rain.
- It began to rain **while I was waiting for the bus**.
- He never played tennis again **after he broke his leg**.
- **After he broke his leg**, he never played tennis again.

■ **When I am . . . / When I go . . .** etc. for the *future*:

> I will be in London **next week**.
> **When I'm** in London, I'm going to visit the British Museum.

The time is *future* (**next week**) but we say:
When **I'm** in London, . . . (*not* 'When I **will be** in London . . .')

We use the *present* (I **am** / I **go** etc.) with a *future meaning* after **when**:
- **When** I **get** home this evening, I'm going to have a shower. (*not* 'When I will get home')
- I can't talk to you now. I'll talk to you later **when** I **have** more time.

We do the same after **before/while/after/until**:
- Please close the window **before** you **go** out.
  (*not* 'before you will go')
- Julia is going to live in our house **while** we **are** away on holiday. (*not* 'while we will be')
- I'll wait here **until** you **come** back. (**until** ▶ Unit 92)

UNIT 104   Exercises

104.1 Write sentences. Use **when** + a sentence from box A + a sentence from box B.

	A
when +	~~I went out~~
	I'm tired
	I phoned them
	she first met him
	she goes to London
	the programme ended
	they arrived at the hotel

	B
+	I switched off the TV
	she always stays at the same hotel
	she didn't like him very much
	there were no rooms free
	~~it was raining~~
	there was no answer
	I like watching TV

1 ..When I went out, it was raining...
2 ....
3 ....
4 ....
5 ....
6 ....
7 ....

104.2 Complete the sentences. Choose an ending from the box.

while I was reading	when you heard the news	before I go to sleep
when I explained it to her	~~before you cross the road~~	while I was out
before he answered the question	after they got married	

1 Always look both ways ..before you cross the road..............................
2 Were you surprised .... ?
3 He thought carefully ....
4 She understood the problem ....
5 They went to live in New Zealand ....
6 Did anybody telephone .... ?
7 I fell asleep ....
8 I usually read in bed ....

104.3 Which is right? Choose the correct form.

1 I ~~wait~~ / I'll wait here until <u>you come</u> / <del>you'll come</del> back. (<u>I'll wait</u> and <u>you come</u> are *right*)
2 I'm going to bed when <u>I finish</u> / <u>I'll finish</u> my work.
3 <u>We come</u> / <u>We'll come</u> and see you when <u>we're</u> / <u>we'll be</u> in England again.
4 When <u>I see</u> / <u>I'll see</u> you tomorrow, <u>I show</u> / <u>I'll show</u> you the photographs.
5 Would you like something to drink before <u>you go</u> / <u>you'll go</u> to bed?
6 Don't go out yet. Wait until the rain <u>stops</u> / <u>will stop</u>.
7 She's going away soon. <u>I'm</u> / <u>I'll be</u> very sad when <u>she leaves</u> / <u>she'll leave</u>.
8 I'm going to New York next month. While <u>I'm</u> / <u>I'll be</u> there, I hope to see lots of old friends.
9 A: Don't forget to give me your address.
   B: Okay, <u>I give</u> / <u>I'll give</u> it to you before <u>I go</u> / <u>I'll go</u>.

UNIT 105   If...

You want to travel from Paris to Geneva. You are not sure which train you will travel on – the 7.35 or the 10.34.

> **If** you leave at 7.35, you will arrive at 11.08.
> **If** you leave at 10.34, you will arrive at 14.03.

```
┌─────────────────────────────────┐
│  PARIS ᴛᴏ GENEVA                 │
├─────────────────────────────────┤
│  DEPART            ARRIVE        │
│  07.35 _____ 11.08          │
│  10.34 _____ 14.03           │
│  12.00 _____ 15.35           │
│  15.30 _____ 19.00           │
└─────────────────────────────────┘
```

■ **If** can be *at the beginning* of the sentence or *in the middle*:
> **If ..., ...**   (**if** *at the beginning*)

If you speak slowly,	I can understand you.
If we don't hurry,	we'll be late.
If you're hungry,	have something to eat.
If the phone rings,	can you answer it, please?

> **... if ...**   (**if** *in the middle*)

I can understand you	**if** you speak slowly.
We'll be late	**if** we don't hurry.
I'm going to the concert	**if** I can get a ticket.
Do you mind	**if** I smoke? (= Is it okay if I smoke?)

In conversation, we often use the **if**-part of the sentence alone:
> – 'Are you going to the concert?'   'Yes, **if I can get a ticket**.'

■ **if** you **see** ... / **if** I **am** ... etc. for the *future*. For example:

> – **If** you **see** Ann this evening, can you ask her to phone me?

We say: **if** you **see** (*not* 'if you will see'), **if** I **am** (*not* 'if I will be'). Use the present (*not* 'will') after **if**:

> – **If** I'**m** late this evening, don't wait for me. (*not* 'If I will be late')
> – What shall we do **if** it **rains**? (*not* 'if it will rain')
> – **If** I **don't feel** well tomorrow, I'll stay at home.

■ **if** and **when**

if I go out = it is possible that I will go out, but I'm not sure:
> – A: Are you going out later?
> – B: Perhaps. **If I go out**, I'll close the window.

when I go out = I'm going out (for sure):
> – A: Are you going out later?
> – B: Yes, I am. **When I go out**, I'll close the window.

> – **When** I get home this evening, I'm going to have a shower.
> – **If** I'm late this evening, don't wait for me. (*not* 'When I'm late')
> – We're going to play tennis **if** it doesn't rain. (*not* 'when it doesn't')

UNIT 105   Exercises

105.1 Make sentences beginning with **If ...**   Choose from the boxes.

if +
~~we don't hurry~~
I can get a flight
you come home late tonight
I don't feel well tomorrow
you have any problems

+
please come in quietly
I'm not going to work
~~we'll be late~~
I'll try to help you
I'll fly home on Sunday

1 If we don't hurry, we'll be late. ....
2 If I can ....
3 If ....
4 ....
5 ....

105.2 Make sentences with **if** in the middle (... **if** ...).

~~I can understand you~~
It will be nice
You'll be cold
What are you going to do
I'm sure they'll understand

+ if +
you don't wear a coat
you don't pass your examinations
you explain the problem to them
~~you speak slowly~~
you can come to the party

1 I can understand you if you speak slowly. ....
2 It ....
3 ....
4 ....
5 ....

105.3 Choose the correct form of the verb.

1 If I don't feel / ~~won't feel~~ well tomorrow, ~~I stay~~ / I'll stay at home. (don't feel and I'll stay
   are *right*)
2 If the weather is / will be nice tomorrow, we can go to the beach.
3 It will be difficult to find a hotel if we arrive / we'll arrive late.
4 The alarm will ring if there is / will be a fire.
5 I'm / I'll be surprised if they get / they'll get married.
6 Do you go / Will you go to the party if they invite / they'll invite you?

105.4 Put in **if** or **when**.

1 ..If.. I'm late this evening, don't wait for me.
2 .... I don't see you tomorrow, I'll phone you.
3 Do you mind .... I close the window?
4 .... I get up in the morning, I usually drink a cup of coffee.
5 Have something to eat. .... you don't eat now, you'll be hungry later.
6 John is still at school. .... he leaves school, he wants to go to university.
7 Be careful! .... you aren't careful, you'll fall.

UNIT 106 a person who...   a thing that/which...
(relative clauses 1)

| I met a woman.   **She** can speak six languages. |
| *2 sentences* |

she → who

| *1 sentence* |
| I met **a woman who** can speak six languages. |

| Jim was wearing a hat.   **It** was too big for him. |
| *2 sentences* |

it → that *or* **which**

| *1 sentence* |
| Jim was wearing **a hat that** was too big for him. |
| *or* |
| Jim was wearing **a hat which** was too big for him. |

■ **who** ... is for *people* (*not things*):

> A thief is **a person who** steals things. (*not* 'a person which . . .')
> Do you know **anybody who** can play the piano?
> I know **somebody who** knows you.
> **The people who** work in the office are very friendly.

■ **that** ... is for *things* (and *sometimes people*):

> An aeroplane is **a machine that** flies.
> Jack lives in **a house that** is 500 years old.

That is also possible for people ('Do you know **anybody that** can play the piano?'), but it is usually better to say **who**.

■ **which** ... is only for *things*:

> An aeroplane is **a machine which** flies. (*not* 'a machine who . . .')
> Jack lives in **a house which** is 500 years old.

Do *not* use **which** for people:
> – Do you know **the man who** was playing the piano at the party?
> (*not* 'the man which . . .')

212

UNIT 106   Exercises

106.1 Write sentences about the people in box A: **A ... is a person who ...** Choose an ending from box B to complete your sentence. Use a dictionary if necessary.

	A
~~a thief~~	
a butcher	a dentist
a musician	a fool
a patient	a genius
a photographer	a liar

	B
takes photographs	
sells meat	is very intelligent
is ill in hospital	plays a musical instrument
~~steals things~~	doesn't tell the truth
is very stupid	looks after your teeth

1 A thief is a person who steals things. ....
2 A butcher is a person who ....
3 A musician is a person ....
4 A patient is ....
5 ....
6 ....
7 ....
8 ....
9 ....

106.2 Make one sentence from two sentences. Use **who**.

1 A man phoned. He didn't say his name.
The man who phoned didn't say his name. ....
2 A woman opened the door. She was wearing a yellow dress.
The woman .... a yellow dress.
3 Some people live next door to us. They are very nice.
The people ....
4 A policeman stopped our car. He wasn't very friendly.
The policeman ....
5 A boy broke the window. He ran away.
The boy ....

106.3 Put in **who/that/which**.

1 I met a woman ...who........ can speak six languages.
2 What's the name of the man .... lives next door?
3 What's the name of the river .... goes through the town?
4 Everybody .... went to the party enjoyed it very much.
5 Do you know anybody .... wants to buy a car?
6 Where is the picture .... was on the wall?
7 She always asks me questions .... are difficult to answer.
8 I have a friend .... is very good at repairing cars.
9 A coffee-maker is a machine .... makes coffee.
10 I don't like people .... never stop talking.
11 Have you seen the money .... was on the table?
12 Why does he always wear clothes .... are too small for him?

UNIT 107

the people we met   the hotel you stayed at
(*relative clauses 2*)

<table>
<tr><td>The man is carrying a box.
It's very heavy.   } 2 sentences</td></tr>
</table>

The box (that) he is carrying is very heavy.
└─────── *1 sentence* ───────┘

<table>
<tr><td>Ann took some photographs.
Have you seen them?   } 2 sentences</td></tr>
</table>

Have you seen **the photographs (that) Ann took**?
└─────── *1 sentence* ───────┘

■ In these sentences, you do not need '**that**'. You do not need **that/who/which** when it is the *object*:

subject	verb	object	
The man	was carrying	a box.	→ **the box** (that) **the man was carrying**
Ann	took	some photographs.	→ **the photographs** (that) **Ann took**
You	wanted	the book.	→ **the book** (that) **you wanted**
We	met	some people.	→ **the people** (who) **we met**

   – Did you find **the book (that) you wanted**?
   – **The people (who) we met** were very nice.
   – **Everything (that) I told you** was true.

■ Sometimes there is a *preposition* (**to/in/at** etc.) after the verb:

Jill is **talking to** a man.   →   Do you know **the man Jill is talking to**?
   I **slept in** a bed.   →   **The bed I slept in** was very hard.
You **stayed at** a hotel.   →   What's the name of **the hotel you stayed at**?

You can also say (*a place*) **where . . .** :
   – What's the name of **the hotel where we stayed**? (= the hotel we stayed at)

Note that we say:
   – Do you know the man Jill is **talking to h̶i̶m̶**? (*not* **. . . talking to him**?')
   – The film **we saw ̶i̶t̶** was very good. (*not* 'The film **we saw it** . . .')

■ Remember that you need **who/that/which** when it is the *subject*   (▶ Unit 106):

	subject	verb	
I met a woman	**who**	can speak	six languages.
Jim was wearing a hat	**that**	was	too big for him.

214

UNIT 107   Exercises

107.1 Make one sentence from two.

1 (Ann took some photographs. Have you seen them?)
   Have you seen the photographs Ann took. ?
2 (You lost a key. Did you find it?)   Did you find the .... ?
3 (Jill is wearing a jacket. I like it.)   I like the ....
4 (I gave you some money. Where is it?)   Where is the .... ?
5 (She told us a story. I didn't believe it.)
   I .... the ....
6 (You bought some oranges. How much were they?)
   How .... ?

107.2 Complete the sentences. Use the information in brackets (   ).

1 (we met some people)   The ...*people we met*... were very nice.
2 (I'm wearing shoes)   The shoes .... are not very comfortable.
3 (you're reading a book)   What's the name of the .... ?
4 (I wrote a letter to her)   She didn't get the .... I ....
5 (you gave me an umbrella)   I've lost ....
6 (they invited some people to dinner)
   The people .... didn't come.

107.3 Complete the sentences. Use this information:

you went to a party	Linda is dancing with a man	you stayed at a hotel
we looked at a map	you were looking for a book	I was sitting on a chair
they live in a house	you spoke to a woman	

1 What's the name of the hotel *you stayed at* .... ?
2 What's the name of the woman you .... ?
3 The house .... is too small for them.
4 Did you enjoy the party .... ?
5 The chair .... wasn't very comfortable.
6 The map .... wasn't very clear.
7 Did you find the book .... ?
8 Who is the man .... ?

107.4 Complete the sentences with **where ...**   Use this information:

| we had dinner in a restaurant | John works in a factory |
| we stayed at a hotel | they live in a village |

1 What's the name of the hotel *where we stayed* .... ?
2 What's the name of the restaurant .... ?
3 Have you ever been to the village .... ?
4 The factory .... is the biggest in the town.

215

APPENDIX 1   List of irregular verbs (▶ Unit 36)

infinitive	past simple	past participle
be(am/is/are)	**was/were**	**been**
beat	**beat**	**beaten**
become	**became**	**become**
begin	**began**	**begun**
bite	**bit**	**bitten**
blow	**blew**	**blown**
break	**broke**	**broken**
bring	**brought**	**brought**
build	**built**	**built**
buy	**bought**	**bought**
catch	**caught**	**caught**
choose	**chose**	**chosen**
come	**came**	**come**
cost	**cost**	**cost**
cut	**cut**	**cut**
do	**did**	**done**
draw	**drew**	**drawn**
drink	**drank**	**drunk**
drive	**drove**	**driven**
eat	**ate**	**eaten**
fall	**fell**	**fallen**
feel	**felt**	**felt**
fight	**fought**	**fought**
find	**found**	**found**
fly	**flew**	**flown**
forget	**forgot**	**forgotten**
get	**got**	**got**
give	**gave**	**given**
go	**went**	**gone**
grow	**grew**	**grown**
hang	**hung**	**hung**
have	**had**	**had**
hear	**heard**	**heard**
hide	**hid**	**hidden**
hit	**hit**	**hit**
hold	**held**	**held**
hurt	**hurt**	**hurt**
keep	**kept**	**kept**
know	**knew**	**known**
leave	**left**	**left**
lend	**lent**	**lent**

infinitive	past simple	past participle
let	**let**	**let**
lie	**lay**	**lain**
light	**lit**	**lit**
lose	**lost**	**lost**
make	**made**	**made**
mean	**meant**	**meant**
meet	**met**	**met**
pay	**paid**	**paid**
put	**put**	**put**
read /riːd/	**read** /red/	**read** /red/
ride	**rode**	**ridden**
ring	**rang**	**rung**
rise	**rose**	**risen**
run	**ran**	**run**
say	**said**	**said**
see	**saw**	**seen**
sell	**sold**	**sold**
send	**sent**	**sent**
shine	**shone**	**shone**
shoot	**shot**	**shot**
show	**showed**	**shown**
shut	**shut**	**shut**
sing	**sang**	**sung**
sit	**sat**	**sat**
sleep	**slept**	**slept**
speak	**spoke**	**spoken**
spend	**spent**	**spent**
stand	**stood**	**stood**
steal	**stole**	**stolen**
swim	**swam**	**swum**
take	**took**	**taken**
teach	**taught**	**taught**
tear	**tore**	**torn**
tell	**told**	**told**
think	**thought**	**thought**
throw	**threw**	**thrown**
understand	**understood**	**understood**
wake	**woke**	**woken**
wear	**wore**	**worn**
win	**won**	**won**
write	**wrote**	**written**

These verbs can be regular (**-ed**) or irregular (**-t**):

infinitive	past simple/past participle	infinitive	past simple/past participle
burn	**burned** or **burnt**	dream	**dreamed** or **dreamt**
learn	**learned** or **learnt**	smell	**smelled** or **smelt**

APPENDIX 2 Irregular verbs in groups

past simple / past participle the same		
1	cost → **cost** cut → **cut** hit → **hit** hurt → **hurt**	let → **let** put → **put** shut → **shut**

2	lend → **lent** send → **sent** spend → **spent** build → **built**	lose → **lost** shoot → **shot** get → **got** light → **lit** sit → **sat**
	burn → **burnt** learn → **learnt** smell → **smelt**	keep → **kept** sleep → **slept**
	feel → **felt** leave → **left** meet → **met** dream → **dreamt** /dremt/ mean → **meant** /ment/	

3 | bring → **brought** /brɔːt/
buy → **bought** /bɔːt/
fight → **fought** /fɔːt/
think → **thought** /θɔːt/
catch → **caught** /kɔːt/
teach → **taught** /tɔːt/ |

4 | sell → **sold**
tell → **told** |
find → **found**
have → **had**
hear → **heard**
hold → **held**
read → **read** /red/
say → **said** /sed/ |
pay → **paid**
make → **made** |
stand → **stood**
understand → **understood** |

past simple / past participle different			
1	break → **broke**	broken
	choose → **chose**	chosen
	speak → **spoke**	spoken
	steal → **stole**	stolen
	wake → **woke**	woken
2	drive → **drove**	driven
	ride → **rode**	ridden
	rise → **rose**	risen
	write → **wrote**	written
	beat → **beat**	beaten
	bite → **bit**	bitten
	hide → **hid**	hidden
3	eat → **ate**	eaten
	fall → **fell**	fallen
	forget → **forgot**	forgotten
	give → **gave**	given
	see → **saw**	seen
	take → **took**	taken
4	blow → **blew**	blown
	grow → **grew**	grown
	know → **knew**	known
	throw → **threw**	thrown
	fly → **flew**	flown
	draw → **drew**	drawn
	show → **showed**	shown
	wear → **wore**	worn
	tear → **tore**	torn
5	begin → **began**	begun
	drink → **drank**	drunk
	swim → **swam**	swum
	ring → **rang**	rung
	sing → **sang**	sung
	run → **ran**	run
6	come → **came**	come
	become → **became**	become

APPENDIX 3   Short forms (he's/I'd/don't etc.)

3.1   In spoken English, we usually pronounce '**I am**' as one word. The short form (**I'm**) is a way of writing this:

I am → **I'm**	– **I'm** feeling tired this morning.
it is → **it's**	– 'Do you like this jacket?' 'Yes, it**'s** very nice.'
they have → **they've**	– 'Where are your friends?' 'They**'ve** gone home.'
	etc.

When we write short forms, we use **'** (*an apostrophe*):

I ~~a~~m → I'm   he ~~i~~s → he's   you h~~a~~ve → you've   she w~~i~~ll → she'll

3.2   We use these short forms with **I/he/she** etc.:

	I'm						
am → **'m**							
is → **'s**		he's	she's	it's			
are → **'re**					we're	you're	they're
have → **'ve**	**I've**				we've	you've	they've
has → **'s**		he's	she's	it's			
had → **'d**	**I'd**	he'd	she'd		we'd	you'd	they'd
will → **'ll**	**I'll**	he'll	she'll	it'll	we'll	you'll	they'll
would → **'d**	**I'd**	he'd	she'd		we'd	you'd	they'd

- I**'ve** got blue eyes.
- We**'ll** probably go out this evening.
- It**'s** 10 o'clock. You**'re** late again.

's = **is** *or* **has**:
- She**'s** going out this evening. (she**'s** going = she **is** going)
- She**'s** gone out. (she**'s** gone = she **has** gone)

'd = **would** *or* **had**:
- A: What would you like to eat?
  B: I**'d** like a salad, please. (I**'d** like = I **would** like)
- I told the police that I**'d** lost my passport. (I**'d** lost = I **had** lost)

Do *not* use short forms if the verb is at the end of the sentence (▶ Unit 37):
- 'Are you tired?'   'Yes, I **am**.' (*not* 'Yes, I'm'.)

3.3   We use short forms with **I/you/he/she/it** etc. But we use short forms (especially **'s**) with other words too:

- **Who's** your favourite singer? (= who is)
- **What's** the time? (= what is)
- **There's** a big tree in the garden. (= there is)
- **My sister's** working in London. (= my sister is working)
- **Jack's** gone out. (= Jack has gone out.)
- **What colour's** your car? (= What colour is your car?)

3.4   Negative short forms   (▶ Unit 40)

not → n't:

isn't (= is not)	**don't** (= do not)	**can't** (= cannot)
aren't (= are not)	**doesn't** (= does not)	**couldn't** (= could not)
wasn't (= was not)	**didn't** (= did not)	**won't** (= will not)
weren't (= were not)		**wouldn't** (= would not)
hasn't (= has not)		**shouldn't** (= should not)
haven't (= have not)		**mustn't** (= must not)
hadn't (= had not)		**needn't** (= need not)

- We went to her house but she **wasn't** at home.
- 'Where's John?' 'I **don't** know. I **haven't** seen him.'
- You work all the time. You **shouldn't** work so hard.
- I **won't** be here tomorrow. (= I will not)

3.5   **'s** (*apostrophe* + **s**)

's can mean different things:

a) **'s** = **is** *or* **has** (see section 2 of this appendix)

b) **let's** = **let us**   (▶ Unit 48)
    - The weather is nice. **Let's** go out. (= **Let us** go out.)

c) Mary**'s** camera (= her camera) / my brother**'s** car (= his car) / the manager**'s** office (= his/her office)
    etc.   (▶ Unit 58)

Compare:
    - **Mary's** camera was very expensive. (**Mary's** camera = **her** camera)
    - **Mary's** a very good photographer. (Mary**'s** = Mary **is**)
    - **Mary's** got a new camera. (Mary**'s** got = Mary **has** got)

APPENDIX 4 Spelling

4.1 **-s** and **-es** (bird**s**/watch**es** etc.)

---

noun + **s** (*plural*) (▶ Unit 60):
 bird → bird**s**   place → place**s**   question → question**s**

verb + **s** (**he**/**she**/**it -s**) (▶ Unit 5):
 think → think**s**   live → live**s**   remember → remember**s**

---

but

+ **es** after **-s**, **-sh**, **-ch** *or* **-x**:
  bus →   bus**es**   pass →   pass**es**   address →   address**es**
  dish →   dish**es**   wash →   wash**es**   finish →   finish**es**
  wat**ch** →   wat**ch**es   tea**ch** →   tea**ch**es   sandwi**ch** →   sandwi**ch**es
  bo**x** →   bo**x**es
also
  potato →   potato**es**   do →   do**es**
  tomato →   tomato**es**   go →   go**es**

-f/**-fe** → **-ves**:
shel**f** → shel**ves**   kni**fe** → kni**ves**   *but* roo**f** → roo**fs**

4.2 **-y** → **-i-** (bab**y** → bab**ies** / stud**y** → stud**ied** etc.)

-y → **-ies**:
stud**y** → stud**ies** (*not* 'studys')   famil**y** → famil**ies** (*not* 'familys')
stor**y** → stor**ies**   cit**y** →   cit**ies**   bab**y** →   bab**ies**
  tr**y** →   tr**ies**   marr**y** →   marr**ies**   fl**y** →   fl**ies**

-y → **-ied** (▶ Unit 9):
stud**y** → stud**ied** (*not* 'studyed')
  tr**y** →   tr**ied**   marr**y** → marr**ied**   cop**y** → cop**ied**

-y → **-ier**/**iest** (▶ Units 81 and 84):
 eas**y** →   eas**ier** / eas**iest**   (*not* 'easyer/easyest')
happ**y** → happ**ier**/happ**iest**   luck**y** → luck**ier**/luck**iest**
heav**y** → heav**ier**/heav**iest**   funn**y** → funn**ier**/funn**iest**

-y → **-ily** (▶ Unit 80):
 eas**y** → eas**ily** (*not* 'easyly')
happ**y** → happ**ily**   luck**y** → luck**ily**   heav**y** → heav**ily**

---

y does *not* change to **i** if the ending is **-ay**/**-ey**/**-oy**/**-uy**:
holida**y** → holida**ys** (*not* 'holidaies')
 enj**oy** → enj**oys**/enj**oyed**   sta**y** → sta**ys**/sta**yed**   bu**y** → bu**ys**   ke**y** → ke**ys**
but
 sa**y** → **said**   pa**y** → **paid**   (*irregular verbs*)

4.3 -ing

> Verbs that end in **-e** (mak**e**/writ**e**/driv**e** etc.):
> **-e → ~~e~~ing**:
> mak**e** → mak**ing** writ**e** → writ**ing** com**e** → com**ing** danc**e** → danc**ing**

> Verbs that end in **-ie** (d**ie**/l**ie**/t**ie**):
> **-ie → -ying**:
> l**ie** → l**ying** d**ie** → d**ying**

4.4 stop → stopped (p → pp) / big → bigger (g → gg) etc.

vowel letters (*V*): a e i o u
consonant letters (*C*): b c d f g k l m n p r s t

Sometimes a word ends in *a vowel + a consonant* (*V + C*) – for example, st**op**, b**ig**.
Before **-ing/-ed/-er/-est**, the consonant at the end (**-p/-g/-t** etc.) is 'doubled' (→ **-pp-/-gg-/-tt-** etc.).
For example:

	V+C			
stop	S T **O** **P**	**p → pp**	sto**pp**ing	sto**pp**ed
run	R **U** **N**	**n → nn**	ru**nn**ing	
get	G **E** **T**	**t → tt**	ge**tt**ing	
swim	S W **I** **M**	**m → mm**	swi**mm**ing	
big	B **I** **G**	**g → gg**	bi**gg**er	bi**gg**est
hot	H **O** **T**	**t → tt**	ho**tt**er	ho**tt**est
thin	T H **I** **N**	**n → nn**	thi**nn**er	thi**nn**est

This does *not* happen
a) if the word ends in *two consonant letters* (*C + C*):

	C+C		
help	H E **L** **P**	he**lp**ing	he**lp**ed
work	W O **R** **K**	wo**rk**ing	wo**rk**ed
fast	F A **S** **T**	fa**st**er	fa**st**est

b) if the word ends in *two vowel letters + a consonant letter* (*V + V + C*):

	V+V+C		
need	N **E** **E** **D**	ne**ed**ing	ne**ed**ed
wait	W **A** **I** **T**	wa**it**ing	wa**it**ed
cheap	C H **E** **A** **P**	che**ap**er	che**ap**est

c) in longer words (two syllables or more) if the last part of the word is not stressed:

	stress		
happen =	**HAP**-pen	→ happening/happened (*not* 'happenned')
visit =	**VIS**-it	→ visiting/visited
remember =	re-**MEM**-ber	→ remembering/remembered
but prefer =	pre-**FER** (*stress at the end*)	→ prefe**rr**ing/prefe**rr**ed
begin =	be-**GIN** (*stress at the end*)	→ begi**nn**ing

d) if the word ends in **-y** or **-w**. (At the end of words, **y** and **w** are not consonants.)
   enjo**y** → enjo**y**ing/enjo**y**ed sno**w**/sno**w**ing/sno**w**ed fe**w**/fe**w**er/fe**w**est

221

APPENDIX 5   Phrasal verbs (**look out / take off** etc.)

This is a list of some important phrasal verbs   (▶ Unit 101):

out	**look out** /**watch out** = be careful:	
	– **Look out**! There's a car coming.	

on **come on** = be quick / hurry:
– **Come on**! Everybody is waiting for you.
hold on = wait
– Can you **hold on** a moment, please?
(= can you wait?)
carry on = continue
– Don't stop working. **Carry on**. (= Continue working.)
– A: Excuse me, where is the station please?
    B: **Carry on** along this road and turn right at the traffic lights.
       (= Continue along this road)
also **go on** / **walk on** / **drive on** = continue going etc.:
– Don't stop here. **Drive on**. (= Continue driving.)

off **take off** = leave the ground (*for planes*).
– The plane **took off** 20 minutes late.

up **wake up** = stop sleeping:
– I often **wake up** in the middle of the night.
get up = get out of bed:
– What time do you usually **get up** in the morning?
grow up = become an adult:
– What does your son want to do when he **grows up**?
speak up = speak more loudly:
– I can't hear you. Can you **speak up** a bit?
wash up = wash the dishes, plates etc. after a meal:
– After we finished eating, we **washed up**.
hurry up = go more quickly:
– **Hurry up**! We haven't got much time.
give up = stop trying:
– I know it's difficult but don't **give up**. Keep trying.

down **slow down** = go more slowly:
– You're driving too fast. **Slow down**.
break down = stop working (*for cars/machines* etc.):
– I'm sorry I'm late. The car **broke down**.

APPENDIX 6   Phrasal verbs + object
(ring up my friend / put out a fire etc.)

This is a list of some important phrasal verbs + object   (▶ Unit 102):

in	**fill in** (a form) (= complete a form): – Can you **fill in this form**, please?

out	**put out** (a fire / a cigarette): – The fireman arrived and quickly **put the fire out**. **cross out** (a mistake / a word etc.): – If you make a mistake, **cross it out**. **knock out** = make unconscious – A stone fell on my head and **knocked me out**.

CROSS OUT

KNOCK OUT

on/off | **switch on/off** (a light, TV etc.) = turn on/off:
– Don't forget to **switch off the light** when you leave.

on | **try on** (clothes) = put on clothes to see if they fit you:
– (in a shop) I like that jacket. I'm going to **try it on**.

up | **ring up** = telephone (also **ring** – without 'up'):
– Can you **ring me up** tomorrow? (or . . . **ring me** tomorrow?)
give up = stop something that you do:
– Tom **gave up smoking** three years ago. (= he stopped smoking)
– I started learning Italian but I **gave it up**.
look up (a word) (in a dictionary):
– I didn't know the meaning of the word, so I **looked it up** in a dictionary.
turn up = make louder (TV, radio, music etc.):
– Can you **turn the radio up**? I can't hear it.

down | **knock down** (a building) = demolish
– They are going to build a new school and **knock down the old one**.
turn down = make more quiet (TV, radio, music etc.):
– The radio is too loud. Can you **turn it down**, please?

KNOCK DOWN

over | **knock over** (a cup / a glass / a person etc.):
– Be careful with your cup. Don't **knock it over**.
also (be) **knocked down / knocked over** (by a car etc.):
– There was an accident at the end of the road. A man was **knocked over** (or **knocked down**) by a car.
(be) **run over** (by a car etc.):
– A lot of animals are **run over** on busy roads.
(These sentences are *passive* ▶ Unit 20.)

KNOCK OVER

KNOCK DOWN/OVER

round | **show** (somebody) **round** = take somebody on a tour of a place:
– We visited a factory last week. The manager **showed us round**.

away | **throw away** (rubbish etc., things you don't want):
– These apples are bad. **Throw them away**.
– Don't **throw away that picture**. I want it.

RUBBISH

THROW AWAY

Key

In many of these answers you can use the full form of the verb ('I am, it is, she will, he has' etc. or the short form of the verb ('I'm, it's, she'll, he's' etc.). See Appendix 3 for short forms.

Unit 1

1.1

2 they're
3 she's not / she isn't
4 it's
5 I'm not
6 you're not / you aren't
8 I am
9 you are
10 they are not
11 it is not
12 she is

1.2

2 am/'m
3 is
4 are
5 is
6 is/'s
7 am/'m
8 is
9 are
10 is . . . are
11 am/'m . . . is

1.3

2 My bed **is** very comfortable.
3 Your cigarettes **are** in your bag.
4 **I am not / I'm not** very happy today.
5 This restaurant **is** very expensive.
6 The shops **are not / aren't** open today.
7 Mr Kelly's daughter **is** six years old.
8 The houses in this street **are** very old.
9 The examination **is not / isn't** difficult.
10 Those flowers **are** very beautiful.

1.4

3 **I'm / I am** hungry. *or* **I'm not / I am not** hungry.
4 **It's / It is** warm today. *or* **It isn't / It's not** warm today.
5 Rome **isn't / is not** in Spain.
6 **I'm / I am** afraid of dogs. *or* **I'm not/I am not** afraid of dogs.
7 My hands **are** cold. *or* My hands **aren't / are not** cold.
8 Canada **is** a very big country.
9 The Amazon **isn't / is not** in Africa.
10 Diamonds **aren't / are not** cheap.
11 Motor-racing **is** a dangerous sport.
12 Cats **aren't / are not** big animals.

Unit 2

2.1

2 Are your parents at home?
3 Is this hotel expensive?
4 Are you interested in art?
5 Are the shops open today?
6 Is the park open today?

2.2

2 Where is / Where's my key?
3 Where are my socks?
4 How old is your father?
5 What colour are his eyes?
6 Why is John angry with me?
7 How much are these shoes?
8 Who is / Who's your favourite actor?
9 Why are you always late?

2.3

3 Are you British?
4 Where are you from?
5 How old are you?
6 Are you a student?
7 Is your wife a teacher?
8 Where is / Where's she from?
9 What is / What's her name?
10 How old is she?

2.4

3 Yes, it is. *or* No, it isn't / No, it's not.
4 Yes, I am. *or* No, I'm not.
5 Yes, I am. *or* No, I'm not.
6 Yes, it is. *or* No, it isn't. / No, it's not.
7 Yes, they are. *or* No, they aren't. / No, they're not.
8 Yes, I am. *or* No, I'm not.
9 Yes, he is. *or* No, he isn't. / No, he's not.
10 Yes, it is. *or* No, it isn't. / No, it's not.

Unit 3

3.1

2 are building
3 is swimming
4 are standing
5 is coming
6 am cooking
7 is having

3.2

3 **I'm / I am** sitting on a chair. *or* **I'm not / I am not** sitting on a chair.
4 **I'm / I am** eating. *or* **I'm not / I am not** eating.
5 **It's / It is** raining. *or* **It's not / It is not** raining.
6 **I'm / I am** learning English.
7 **I'm / I am** listening to the radio. *or* **I'm not / I am not** listening to the radio.

8 The sun **is** shining.   *or* The sun **isn't / is not** shining.
9 **I'm / I am** wearing shoes.   *or* **I'm not / I am not** wearing shoes.
10 **I'm / I am** smoking a cigarette.   *or* **I'm not / I am not** smoking a cigarette.
11 **I'm not / I am not** reading a newspaper.

3.3

2 In A the man is lying on the floor. In B he is standing on the chair.
3 In A it's raining. In B the sun is shining.
4 In A the woman is writing (a letter). In B she is reading a book.
5 In A the man is running. In B he is riding a bicycle. / In B he is cycling.
6 In A the woman is driving (the car). In B the man is driving (the car).

Unit 4

4.1

2 Where is / Where's   he going?
3 Why are they laughing?
4 What is / What's   he eating?
5 **What are they looking at?**
6 **Why is she crying?**

4.2

2 What are they doing?
3 What am I doing?
4 What is your wife doing?
6 Where are those children going?
7 Where is the girl with long hair going?
8 Where is the man on the bicycle going?

4.3

2 Are the children playing?
3 What are you doing?
4 What is / What's   Tom doing?

5 Is it raining?
6 Is that clock working?
7 Are you writing a letter?
8 Why are you running?

4.4

2 Yes, I am.   *or* No, I'm not.
3 Yes, I am.   *or* No, I'm not.
4 Yes, it is.   *or* No, it isn't. / No, it's not.
5 Yes, I am.   *or* No, I'm not.
6 Yes, I am.   *or* No, I'm not.
7 Yes, it is.   *or* No, it isn't. / No, it's not.
8 Yes, she is.   *or* No, she isn't. / No, she's not.

Unit 5

5.1

2 repairs	8 does
3 watches	9 thinks
4 listens	10 kisses
5 loves	11 buys
6 has	12 goes
7 pushes	

5.2

2 smokes	8 costs
3 have	9 cost
4 like . . . go	10 teaches
5 boils	11 meet
6 open	12 washes
7 closes	

5.3

1 George usually drinks coffee in the morning.
   (*example answer*) I sometimes drink coffee in the morning.
2 Bob and Ann often read newspapers.
   George never reads newspapers.
   (*example answer*) I often read newspapers.
3 Bob and Ann sometimes get up before 7 o'clock.
   George always gets up before 7 o'clock.
   (*example answer*) I never get up before 7 o'clock.

Unit 6

6.1

2 Jack doesn't play the piano very well.
3 You don't know the answer.
4 She doesn't work very hard.
5 They don't do the same thing every day.

6.2

3 They don't know.
4 She doesn't love him.
5 They don't speak English.
6 I want it.
7 She wants them.
8 He doesn't live in Rome.

6.3

1 Carol doesn't like classical music.
   I like / I don't like   classical music.
2 Bill and Rose don't like boxing.
   Carol likes boxing.
   I like / I don't like   boxing.
3 Bill and Rose don't like horror films.
   Carol likes horror films.
   I like / I don't like   horror films.
4 Bill and Rose like dogs.
   Carol doesn't like dogs.
   I like / I don't like   dogs.

6.4

2 don't sell
3 doesn't drive
4 don't go
5 doesn't wash
6 doesn't cost
7 doesn't play
8 don't know
9 doesn't wear
10 don't see

Unit 7

7.1

2 Do you play tennis?
3 Does Ann play tennis?
4 Do you know the answer?
5 Do you like hot weather?
6 Does your father smoke?
7 Do you do exercises every morning?
8 Do your friends speak English?
9 Do you want to be famous?
11 Where do you live?
12 How often do you watch TV?
13 Where do you have lunch?
14 What time do you get up?
15 How often do you go to the cinema?
16 How do you go to work?

7.2

2 do you speak
3 do you do
4 does your sister do
5 Does she smoke
6 does it rain
7 Do you like
8 do they (usually) go
9 do you (usually) have
10 does it cost

7.3

2 Yes, I do. *or* No, I don't.
3 Yes, I do. *or* No, I don't.
4 Yes, she does. *or* No, she doesn't.
5 Yes, I do. *or* No, I don't.
6 Yes, it does. *or* No, it doesn't.

Unit 8

8.1

2 Yes, she does. No, she isn't. She's / She is   playing the piano.
3 Yes, he does. Yes, he is. He's / He is   cleaning a window.

4 Yes, they do. No, they aren't. / No, they're not. They're / They are watching   television.

8.2

2 don't
3 are
4 does
5 don't . . . is/'s
6 do
7 does
8 am/'m
9 doesn't

8.3

4 is singing
5 wants
6 do you read
7 're sitting / are sitting
8 don't understand / do not understand
9 'm reading / am reading
10 does she finish
11 'm not listening / am not listening
12 doesn't usually drive / does not usually drive . . . walks

Unit 9

9.1

2 cleaned
3 smoked
4 started . . . finished
5 happened
6 wanted
7 lived
8 enjoyed . . . stayed
9 rained
10 opened
11 played
12 died

9.2

2 ate
3 paid
4 made
5 gave
6 left
7 saw
8 went
9 heard
10 found
11 bought
12 knew
13 stood
14 took
15 did
16 put
17 told
18 lost
19 thought
20 spoke

9.3

2 got up early.
3 lost his keys
4 I wrote a letter to Jane.
5 met her friends
6 I read two newspapers
7 they came to my house.
8 We went to the cinema
9 Tom had a shower
10 they bought a new car.
11 I ate an orange.
12 We did our shopping
13 Ann took (some) photographs.
14 We left home at 8.30

9.4

If possible, check your sentences with someone who speaks English.

Unit 10

10.1

2 didn't work
3 didn't go
4 didn't have
5 didn't do

10.2

2 Did you enjoy the party?
3 Did you have a good holiday?
4 Did you get up early this morning?
5 Did you sleep well last night?

10.3

2 I got up before 7.30. *or* I didn't get up before 7.30.
3 I had a shower. *or* I didn't have a shower.
4 I bought a magazine. *or* I didn't buy a magazine.
5 I spoke English. *or* I didn't speak English.
6 I did an examination. *or* I didn't do an examination.
7 I ate meat. *or* I didn't eat meat.
8 I went to bed before 10.30. *or* I didn't go to bed before 10.30.

10.4

2 What time did Harry arrive?
3 Who did you see?
4 What did they want?
5 What time did   the meeting
/ it   finish?
6 Why did   Pat/she   go home early?
7 What did you have for dinner?
8 How much did it cost?

10.5

2 waited . . . didn't come.
3 did you buy
4 saw . . . didn't speak
5 Did it rain
6 did you do

Unit 11

11.1

2 Carol and Jack were   at the cinema / in the cinema.
3 Sue was at the station.
4 Mr and Mrs Baker were   in a restaurant / at a restaurant.
5 Ben was   on the beach / on a beach / at the seaside / by the sea.
6 (*example answer*) I was at home.

11.2

2 is . . . was	8 is/'s
3 am/'m	9 was
4 was	10 were
5 were	11 was
6 are/'re	12 are . . .
7 were	were

11.3

2 was
3 weren't . . . were
4 wasn't . . . was
5 weren't . . . was
6 Were . . . wasn't . . . was

11.4

2 Were they friendly?
3 Was it difficult?
4 Were they expensive?
5 Was it interesting?

Unit 12

12.1

2 Carol and Jack were at the cinema. They were watching a film.
3 Tom was in his car. He was driving.
4 Catherine was at the station. She was waiting for a train.
5 Mr and Mrs Mason were in the park. They were walking.
6 (*example answer*) I was in the park. I was playing tennis.

12.2

2 she was swimming.
3 she was reading a newspaper.
4 she was cooking.
5 she was having breakfast.
6 she was listening to music.

12.3

2 What were you doing at 11 o'clock?
3 What was she wearing yesterday?
4 Was it raining when you went out?
5 Where were you living in 1981?

12.4

2 He was smoking a pipe.
3 He was carrying a bag.
4 He wasn't carrying an umbrella.
5 He wasn't going to the dentist.
6 He was wearing a hat.

Unit 13

13.1

1 Tom was walking down the street.
He saw Jack.
He said hello.
2 They were sitting in the garden.
It started to rain.
They went into the house.
3 Carol was painting the room.
She fell off the ladder.
She broke her arm.

13.2

4 was working
5 got . . . washed . . . dressed . . . had
6 came . . . was having
7 met . . . was wearing
8 broke . . . were playing
9 were waiting . . . arrived
10 got . . . was shining . . . went
11 wasn't driving / was not driving . . . happened
12 didn't go
13 did you do
14 were you doing . . . was watching

Unit 14

14.1

2 he's got
3 they've got
4 she hasn't got
5 it's got
6 I haven't got

14.2*

2 Have you got a passport?
3 Has your father got a car?
4 Has Carol got many friends?
5 Have Mr and Mrs Lewis got any children?
6 How much money have you got?
7 What kind of car has John got?

14.3*

3 Ann hasn't got a camera.
4 I've got a camera.   *or* I haven't got a camera.

5 I've got a bicycle *or* I haven't got a bicycle.
6 Jim hasn't got a bicycle.
7 Ann hasn't got black hair.
8 Ann has got two brothers.
9 Jim hasn't got black hair.
10 Ann has got a bicycle.
11 Jim has got a sister.
12 (*example answers*) I've got two sisters. / I haven't got any brothers or sisters.
★ In these exercises you can also use 'do/does . . . have' ('**Do** you **have** a passport?' 'Ann **doesn't have** a camera.' etc') ▶ Units 6–7

14.4

3 has got / 's got
4 have got
5 has got
6 haven't got
7 haven't got
8 have got / 've got
9 hasn't got
10 has got / 's got
11 has got / 's got
12 haven't got
13 hasn't got
14 have got / 've got

Unit 15

15.1

2 She has closed the door.
3 They have gone to bed.
4 It has stopped raining.
5 He has had a bath.
6 The picture has fallen down.

15.2

2 have bought
3 has gone
4 Have you done
5 have lost
6 has broken
7 Have you painted
8 has taken
9 has she gone
10 have read

Unit 16

16.1

3 Have you ever been to Australia?
4 Have you ever lost your passport?
5 Have you ever slept in a park?
6 Have you ever eaten Chinese food?
7 Have you ever been to New York?
8 Have you ever won a lot of money?
9 Have you ever broken your leg?

16.2

3 She has never been to Australia. (*example answer*) I have never been to Australia.
4 She has lost her passport once. (*example answer*) I have lost my passport twice.
5 She has never slept in a park. (*example answer*) I have never slept in a park.
6 She has eaten Chinese food a few times. (*example answer*) I have eaten Chinese food many times.
7 She has been to New York twice. (*example answer*) I have been to New York three times.
8 She has never won a lot of money. (*example answer*) I have never won a lot of money.
9 She has broken her leg once. (*example answer*) I have broken my leg twice.

16.3

2 She has travelled to many places.
3 She has done a lot of interesting things.
4 She has written ten books.
5 She has met a lot of interesting people.
6 She has been married five times.

16.4

2 gone
3 been . . . been
4 been
5 gone
6 been
7 been
8 gone

Unit 17

17.1

3 have been
4 has been
5 have lived / have been living
6 have known
7 have been
8 has worked / has been working
9 have been
10 has had

17.2

3 How long have they been in Brazil?
4 How long has she been learning Italian?
5 How long has he lived in Germany? *or* How long has he been living . . . ?
6 How long has it been raining?
7 How long has he been a teacher?
8 How long have you known her?
9 How long have you had a motor-bike?
10 How long have they been married?
11 How long has he worked in London? *or* How long has he been working . . . ?

17.3

2 He has been in hospital since Sunday.
3 They have been watching television for two hours.
4 It has been raining all day.
5 She has lived in Wales all her life.
6 He has had a beard for five years.

Unit 18

18.1

3 for . . . since   6 since
4 for   7 since
5 for   8 for

18.2

If possible, check your answers with someone who speaks English.

18.3

3 for 20 years
4 20 years ago
5 ten minutes ago
6 two months ago
7 for two months
8 for a long time
9 an hour ago

18.4

2 He has been here since Thursday.
3 It's been raining for an hour.
4 I've known her for two years.
5 I've had my camera since 1985.
6 They've been married for six months.
7 She has been studying medicine for three years.

18.5

If possible, check your sentences with someone who speaks English.

Unit 19

19.1

2 Yes, I saw him ten minutes ago.
3 Yes, we painted it last week.
4 Yes, she went (to France) on Friday.
5 Yes, they had dinner at 7 o'clock.
6 Yes, he started (it) yesterday.

19.2

2 What time did he go out?
3 When did you see her?
4 When did she leave her job?

19.3

3 *right*
4 *wrong* – I **finished** my work **at 2 o'clock**.
5 *wrong* – **When did** you **finish** your work?
6 *wrong* – George **left** school **three years ago**.
7 *right*
8 *wrong* – Napoleon Bonaparte **died in 1821**.
9 *right*
10 *wrong* – I **didn't see** you **at the party on Saturday**.
11 *wrong* – The weather **was** very bad **last week**.

19.4

4 played
5 did you go
6 Have you ever been
7 have washed
8 washed
9 didn't like
10 has visited
11 has worked
12 went . . . stayed

Unit 20

20.1

3 Glass is made from sand.
4 Stamps are sold in a post office.
5 Football is played in most countries.
6 This machine is not used very often. / This machine isn't used very often.
7 What language is spoken in Ethiopia?
8 What is this machine used for?

20.2

3 This room was painted last month.

4 These houses were built about 50 years ago.
5 Ann's bicycle was stolen last week.
6 Three people were injured in the accident.
7 When was this church built?
8 When was television invented?
9 How was the window broken?
10 Was anybody injured in the accident?
11 Why was the letter sent to the wrong address?

20.3

3 is made
4 were damaged
5 are spoken
6 were built
7 are shown
8 was made
9 was stolen . . . was found
10 was invented
11 is paid

20.4

2 Sally was born in Birmingham.
3 Her parents were born in Ireland.
4 I was born in . . .
5 My mother was born in . . .

Unit 21

21.1

2 Dick is going to the cinema.
3 Tom and Sue are going to a party.
4 Barbara is meeting Dave.
5 George is going on holiday.

21.2

If possible, check your sentences with someone who speaks English. Here are some example answers:

3–6 I'm having a party on Friday.

I'm going away at the
weekend.
I'm staying at home this
evening.
I'm playing tennis
tomorrow.

21.3

2 Are you working next
week?
3 What are you doing
tomorrow evening?
4 What time are Bob and Sue
coming?
5 When is Liz going on
holiday?

21.4

3 I'm meeting my friends this
evening.
4 Tom isn't coming to the
party on Thursday.
5 The English course finishes
on 10 May.
6 My sister is getting married
next December.
7 My train leaves at 8.45.
8 I'm not going to London
tomorrow.
9 What time does the train
leave?
10 What time are you leaving
tomorrow?
11 When are they getting
married?
12 When does the next English
course begin?

Unit 22

22.1

2 He's going to   have/take   a
bath.
3 They're going to buy a (new)
car.
4 He's going to   have/drink
a cup of coffee.
5 They're going to paint/
decorate   the room.
6 She's going to play the piano.

22.2

2 I'm (not) going to get up
before 6.30.
3 I'm (not) going to have
breakfast.
4 I'm (not) going to watch TV
in the morning.
5 I'm (not) going to cook a meal.
6 I'm (not) going to ride a bicycle.

22.3

2 When are you going to visit
me again?
3 What time is Tom going to
phone you tonight?
4 How long are your friends
going to stay here?
5 What time are you going to
get up tomorrow?

22.4

2 I'm going to walk.
3 He's going to study
4 It's going to rain.
5 I'm going to eat
6 We're going to give
7 I'm going to lie

Unit 23

23.1

2 she'll be in Munich.
3 she'll be in Athens.
4 she'll be in Vienna.
5 she'll be in Rome.

23.2

If possible, check your answers
with someone who speaks
English. Here are some
example answers:

2 I'll be at home.
3 I'll be in bed.
4 I'll probably be in the town
centre.
5 I don't know where I'll be.

23.3

2 I won't forget.
3 It won't happen.

4 You won't find it.

23.4

2 I think Jack will win the
game.
3 I think Sue will like her
present.
4 I think the weather will be
nice tomorrow.
5 I don't think they'll get
married.
6 I don't think I'll be at home
this evening.

23.5

2 are you doing
3 I'm going
4 he'll lend
5 I'm going out
6 will phone
7 She's working

Unit 24

24.1

2 I'll send   5 I'll do
3 I'll eat   6 I'll sit
4 I'll stay   7 I'll show

24.2

2 I think I'll have   *or* I think
I'll buy
3 I don't think I'll play
4 I don't think I'll buy

24.3

3 *wrong* – **I'll do** it later.
4 *wrong* – Okay, **I'll drive**.
5 *right*
6 *wrong* – **I'll lend** you some.

24.4

2 Shall I turn off the television?
3 Shall I make some
sandwiches?
4 Shall I turn on the light?

24.5

2 where shall we go
3 what shall we buy
4 who shall we invite

Unit 25

25.1

2 Can you ski?
3 Can you play chess?
4 Can you drive?
5 Can you run ten kilometres?
6 Can you ride a horse?
8 I can ski. *or* I can't ski.
9 I can play chess. *or* I can't play chess.
10 I can drive. *or* I can't drive.
11 I can run ten kilometres. *or* I can't run ten kilometres.
12 I can ride a horse. *or* I can't ride a horse.

25.2

2 can speak
3 can't hear
4 can't find
5 can see

25.3

2 couldn't understand
3 can't see
4 couldn't eat
5 can't go
6 couldn't go

25.4

2 Can you pass (me) the salt, please? *or* Could you pass ...?
3 Can you turn off the radio, please? *or* Could you turn ...?
4 Can I borrow your pen? *or* Could I borrow ...? *or* Can you lend me your pen? *or* Could you lend me ...?
5 Can I use your phone, please? *or* Could I use ...?
6 Can you give me your address (please)? *or* Could you give me ...? *or* Can I have your address (please)? *or* Could I have ...?

Unit 26

26.1

2 I may/might see Tom tomorrow.
3 Kay may/might be late.
4 It may/might snow today.
5 I may/might wear my new jeans.
6 They may/might not come.
7 I may/might not go out tonight.

26.2

2 I may/might go to a restaurant.
3 I may/might see her tomorrow / this evening.
4 I may/might buy some shoes.
5 I may/might go away.
6 I may/might phone him this evening / tomorrow.
7 I may/might have fish.

26.3

If possible, check your answers with someone who speaks English. Here are some example answers:

3 I might get up early.
4 I may go to the cinema.
5 I'm not going to have a shower.
6 I'm going to buy a newspaper.
7 I'm not going to play tennis.
8 I might make a telephone call.

Unit 27

27.1

2 must hurry
3 must meet
4 must phone
5 must learn
6 must read
7 must buy
8 must wash
9 must go
10 must help
11 must win
12 must be

27.2

2 must
3 had to
4 must
5 must
6 had to
7 must
8 had to
9 had to
10 had to

27.3

3 mustn't lose
4 needn't hurry
5 needn't take
6 mustn't tell
7 needn't buy
8 needn't wait
9 mustn't stick

Unit 28

28.1

2 should go
3 should clean
4 should visit
5 should wear
6 should read

28.2

2 You shouldn't work so hard.
3 He shouldn't eat so much.
4 She shouldn't watch TV so often.
5 You shouldn't talk so much.

28.3

2 Do you think I should buy a new camera?
3 Do you think I should get a new job?
4 Do you think I should do an English course?
5 Do you think I should learn to drive?

28.4

2 I think you should sell it.
3 I think they should have a holiday.
4 I think he should go to the doctor.
5 I think she should go to university.
7 I don't think they should get married.
8 I don't think we should stay there.
9 I don't think you should go to work today.

28.5

If possible, check your sentences with someone who speaks English. Here are some example answers:

1 I think everybody should learn a foreign language.
2 I think I should learn to drive.
3 I don't think the police should carry guns.

Unit 29

29.1

2 have to do
3 has to read
4 have to speak
5 has to travel

29.2

2 have to get
3 have to go
4 had to buy
5 have to change
6 had to answer

29.3

2 Why did they have to leave early?
3 How much (money) did you have to pay?
4 Why do you have to go (home) now?
5 How long did he have to wait?

6 Why does she have to work this evening?

29.4

2 (doesn't) have to wait.
3 didn't have to get up so early.
4 don't have to decide now.
5 doesn't have to work so hard.

29.5

3 has to
4 had to
5 have to
6 must   *or* have to
7 have to

Unit 30

30.1

2 Would you like an apple?
3 Would you like a biscuit?
4 Would you like some cheese?
5 Would you like a sandwich?
6 Would you like some cake?

30.2

2 Would you like to go to a concert on Sunday?
3 Would you like to play tennis tomorrow?
4 Would you like to dance?

30.3

2 Would you like
3 Do you like
4 would you like
5 Would you like
6 I like
7 I'd like
8 Would you like

Unit 31

31.1

2 Are there any books in the box?
3 Is there a man in the box?
4 Is there any money in the box?

5 Are there any clothes in the box?
6 Is there a key in the box?

31.2

2 There isn't a swimming-pool in Dunford. / There is no swimming-pool . . .
3 There is a hospital in Dunford.
4 There are two cinemas in Dunford.
5 There isn't a university in Dunford. / There is no university . . .
6 There aren't any big hotels in Dunford. / There are no big hotels . . .
7 There is a cathedral in Dunford. / There's a cathedral . . .

31.3

2 There is / There's
3 is there
4 There are
5 There isn't
6 are there
7 There aren't
8 Is there

31.4

2 There are 50 states in the USA.
3 There are 15 players in a rugby team.
4 There are nine planets in the solar system.
5 There are 26 letters in the English alphabet.
6 There are 30 days in September.

31.5

2 It
3 There
4 There . . . it
5 there . . . there
6 There . . . it

Unit 32

32.1

2 There was a carpet
3 There were some pictures
4 There was a small table
5 There were some flowers
6 There were some books
7 There was an armchair
8 There was a sofa

32.2

3 There was
4 Was there
5 There weren't
6 there wasn't
7 Were there
8 There wasn't
9 There was
10 there weren't

32.3

3 There are
4 There was
5 There is
6 There has been
7 there was
8 There will be
9 there were . . . there are

Unit 33

33.1

3 It's / It is   8 Is it
4 Is it   9 is it
5 Is it   10 It's / It is
6 is it . . . Is it   11 It's / It is
7 It's / It is   12 It's / It is

33.2

2 How far is it from New York to Washington?
3 How far is it from your house to the station?
4 How far is it from the hotel to the beach?

33.3

3 It   7 There . . . It
4 There   8 There
5 it . . . it   9 It
6 It

33.4

2 It's nice to see you again
3 It's impossible/difficult to sleep
4 It's dangerous/stupid to go out alone
5 It's difficult/impossible to save
6 It's stupid to wear
7 It's easy to meet people.

Unit 34

34.1

3 phone Jack
4 phone Jack
5 to phone Jack
6 to phone Jack
7 phone Jack
8 to phone Jack
9 phone Jack
10 phone Jack

34.2

3 get
4 going
5 watch
6 raining
7 driving
8 listening
9 eat
10 doing . . . staying
11 wear
12 waiting

34.3

4 to go   11 studying
5 going . . . go   12 hear
6 help   13 lie
7 see   14 to lie
8 to leave   15 to go
9 rain   16 go
10 to have

Unit 35

35.1

3 are   7 do
4 Does   8 Are
5 Do   9 Does
6 Is   10 does

11 are   13 Is
12 do   14 Are

35.2

3 don't
4 am not / 'm not
5 isn't
6 don't
7 aren't
8 doesn't
9 don't
10 am not / 'm not

35.3

3 were   9 was
4 did   10 was
5 was   11 did
6 were   12 have
7 Has   13 Did
8 did   14 Have

35.4

3 is   8 has
4 have   9 were
5 was   10 have
6 are   11 was
7 Have   12 is

Unit 36

36.1

3 got   10 bought
4 thought   11 heard
5 paid   12 cost
6 sat   13 caught
7 left   14 lost
8 built   15 understood
9 put

36.2

2 began   begun
3 ate   eaten
4 drank   drunk
5 gave   given
6 ran   run
7 spoke   spoken
8 wrote   written
9 came   come
10 drove   driven
11 took   taken
12 went   gone
13 knew   known

14 threw   thrown
15 forgot   forgotten

36.3

3 slept
4 saw
5 rained
6 lost . . . seen
7 stolen
8 went
9 finished
10 built
11 learnt/learned
12 ridden
13 fell . . . hurt
14 known

36.4

2 met	7 driven
3 woken	8 sold
4 swam	9 told
5 spoken	10 flew
6 cost	

Unit 37

37.1

2 do	5 do
3 did	6 does
4 does	

37.2

2 doesn't	5 doesn't
3 didn't	6 didn't
4 don't	

37.3

2 have	7 were
3 can	8 will
4 are	9 does
5 is	10 has
6 was	

37.4

2 isn't
3 won't
4 hasn't
5 wasn't
6 didn't
7 am not / 'm not
8 don't

37.5

2 Yes, I have. *or* No, I
  haven't.
3 Yes, it is. *or* No, it isn't.
4 Yes, I do. *or* No, I don't.
5 Yes, I am. *or* No, I'm not.
6 Yes, I do. *or* No, I don't.
7 Yes, I will. *or* No, I
  won't.
8 Yes, I have. *or* No, I
  haven't
9 Yes, I did. *or* No, I didn't.
10 Yes, I was. *or* No, I
  wasn't.

Unit 38

38.1

2 Do you	5 Didn't you
3 Did he	6 Do I
4 Doesn't she	

38.2

3 Have you
4 Was she
5 Can't you
6 Didn't you
7 Is it
8 Aren't you
9 Did you
10 Does she
11 Won't you
12 Isn't it

38.3

2 aren't they	5 don't you
3 wasn't she	6 doesn't he
4 haven't you	7 won't you

38.4

2 are you	5 do you
3 isn't she	6 didn't she
4 can't you	7 was it

Unit 39

39.1

2 either	5 either
3 too	6 either
4 too	7 too

39.2

2 So am I.
3 So have I.
4 So do I.
5 So will I.
6 So was I.
7 Neither can I.
8 Neither did I.
9 Neither have I.
10 Neither am I.
11 Neither do I.

39.3

1 So am I.
2 So can I. *or* I can't (ride a
  bicycle).
3 Neither am I. *or* I am
  (tired).
4 So do I. *or* I don't (like
  dancing).
5 Neither do I. *or* I do. *or* I
  like cold weather.
6 So did I. *or* I didn't (sleep
  well last night).
7 Neither have I. *or* I have
  (been to India).
8 Neither do I. *or* I do. *or* I
  often go to the cinema.
9 So am I. *or* I'm not (going
  out tomorrow evening).
10 Neither have I. *or* I have (a
  headache). *or* I've got a
  headache.
11 Neither did I. *or* I did. *or*
  I watched TV last night.
12 So do I. *or* I don't (need a
  holiday).

Unit 40

40.1

3 They aren't married. /
  They're not married.
4 I haven't had dinner.
5 It isn't cold today. / It's not
  cold today.
6 I can't see you.
7 We weren't late.
8 I'm not going out.
9 She hasn't gone out.
10 I won't be late tonight.
11 It wasn't expensive.
12 You shouldn't go.

40.2

3 I don't like fish.
4 She doesn't smoke.
5 Don't look at me!
6 I didn't get up early.
7 They didn't understand.
8 Don't phone me tonight.
9 I didn't do the shopping.
10 He doesn't live near here.
11 It didn't rain yesterday.
12 They didn't do the work.

40.3

3 She can't swim.
4 They aren't on holiday. / They're not on holiday.
5 He doesn't speak German.
6 I didn't enjoy the film.
7 It isn't important. / It's not important.
8 We didn't watch TV.
9 They weren't angry.
10 He won't be pleased.
11 I didn't go to the bank.
12 She hasn't got a camera.
13 Don't open the door.
14 I couldn't hear them.

40.4

3 am not / 'm not
4 can't
5 doesn't
6 isn't / 's not
7 don't ... haven't
8 didn't/couldn't ... wasn't
9 Don't
10 didn't
11 haven't
12 didn't
13 won't/can't
14 didn't
15 couldn't
16 weren't

Unit 41

41.1

3 Were you late this morning?
4 Has Ann got a key?
5 Will you be here tomorrow?
6 Is Tom going out this evening?

7 Have you finished your work?
8 Do you like your job?
9 Does Pam live near the city centre?
10 Did you enjoy your holiday?
11 Did you have a shower this morning?

41.2

2 Can/Do you play the piano?
3 Are you married?
4 Do you live in a city?
5 Have you (ever) been to India?
6 Did you go out last night?
7 Do you like chocolate?
8 Did you watch TV yesterday?
9 Did you sleep well last night?

41.3

3 Why is it important?
4 What are you reading?
5 What time did she go home?
6 When are they going away?
7 What kind of music do you like?
8 Where did you meet him?
9 How long is he going to stay here?
10 Where have they gone?
11 Why can't you come (to the party)?
12 How did you break the window?
13 How much money do you need?
14 When did she do her driving test?
15 Why don't you like her?
16 How often does it rain?

Unit 42

42.1

3 Who is / Who's coming?
4 Who took your umbrella?
5 What made you angry?
6 Who wants to see me?

7 Who told you about the accident?
8 What went wrong?

42.2

3 What are you reading?
4 Who did you see?
5 What do you want?
6 Who did you phone?
7 What are you going to cook?
8 What did you buy?

42.3

3 What have they lost?
4 Who cleaned the kitchen?
5 Who did you ask for money?
6 Who asked you for money?
7 What happened last night?
8 What did Jack buy?
9 Who telephoned you yesterday?
10 Who did you telephone yesterday?
11 Who knows the answer?
12 What woke you up this morning?
13 Who has / Who's got your pen?
14 What did they see?
15 Who saw the accident?
16 Who did the washing-up?
17 What did she do?
18 What does it mean? / What does this word mean?

Unit 43

43.1

3 Who are you waiting for?
4 Who did she dance with?
5 What is he interested in?
6 Who did you have dinner with?
7 What are they looking for?
8 Who was George with?
9 Who did you give the money to?
10 What are you looking at?
11 What were they talking about?
12 Who did you dream about?
13 What was he afraid of?

Key

14 Which restaurant are they
   going to?
15 Who did she speak to?
16 Which hotel did you stay at?

43.2

2 What is the food like?
3 What is the weather like?
4 What are the people like?
5 What is your city like?
6 What are the shops like?
7 What are the schools like?
8 What are the TV
  programmes like?

43.3

2 What was the film like?
3 What was the flight like?
4 What was the concert like?
5 What were the lessons like?
6 What was the hotel like?

Unit 44

44.1

2 Which restaurant are you
  going to?
3 Which newspaper does she
  read?
4 Which language are you
  going to learn?
5 Which places did they visit?
6 Which bus are you waiting
  for?

44.2

3 Which	8 Who
4 What	9 What
5 What	10 What
6 Which	11 Which
7 Which	12 What

44.3

2 What time did you get up?
3 How old are you?
4 What colour is the door?
5 How often do you watch
  TV?
6 What size are these shoes?
7 How far is it from Paris to
  Moscow? / How many
  miles is it from Paris to
  Moscow?

8 How big is your room?
9 What kind of music do you
  like? / What sort of music
  do you like?
10 How far can you run? /
   How many kilometres can
   you run?
11 What size is your pullover?
12 How tall are you?
13 What day is it (today)?
14 How heavy is this box?
15 How fast can this plane fly?
16 What kind of films do you
   like? / What sort of films do
   you like?

Unit 45

45.1

2 How long does it take by car
  from Rome to Milan?
3 How long does it take by bus
  from the city centre to the
  airport?
4 How long does it take by
  plane from Cairo to London?
5 How long does it take by taxi
  from the station to the hotel?
6 How long does it take by
  train from Paris to Geneva?
7 How long does it take by
  boat from Dover to Ostend?
8 How long does it take by
  bicycle from your house to
  your work?

45.2

2 It takes 50 minutes.
3 It takes an hour/one hour.
4 It takes an hour and a
  quarter / an hour and 15
  minutes / one and a quarter
  hours.
5 It takes an hour and 25
  minutes.
6 It takes an hour and ten
  minutes.

45.3

2 How long did it take you to
  walk to the station?
3 How long did it take them to
  clean the house?

4 How long did it take you to
  learn to swim?
5 How long did it take him to
  find an apartment?

45.4

2 It took us an hour to walk
  home.
3 It took me a long time to
  learn to drive.
4 It took them all day to repair
  the car.
5 If possible, check this
  sentence with someone who
  speaks English.

45.5

If possible, check your
sentences with someone who
speaks English. Here are some
example answers:

2 It takes me about five
  minutes to have a shower.
3 It takes two hours to fly to
  London from Italy.
4 It takes six years to study to
  be a doctor in Britain.
5 It takes (me) about ten
  minutes to walk from my
  house to the nearest shop.

Unit 46

46.1

2 Excuse me, can you tell me
  where the museum is?
3 Excuse me, can you tell me
  where the information centre
  is?
4 Excuse me, can you tell me
  where the nearest bank is?

46.2

1 I don't know where he is.
2 I don't know when they're /
  they are leaving.
3 I don't know why he was
  angry.
4 I don't know where they're /
  they are from.
5 I don't know how old the
  house is.

6 I don't know when he'll / he will be here.

46.3

2 I don't know where she works.
3 Do you know where they live?
4 Do you remember what he said?
5 Do you know what time the concert begins?
6 I don't know why they left early.
7 I don't remember how the accident happened.

46.4

2 Do you know if/whether they are married?
3 Do you know if/whether she likes her job?
4 Do you know if/whether George will be here tomorrow?
5 Do you know if/whether he passed his examination?

46.5

2 Do you know where Ann is?
3 Do you know if/whether Pat is working today?
4 Do you know what time they start work?
5 Do you know if/whether they work on Sundays?
6 Do you know why they were so nervous?
7 Do you know where Stella went?
8 Do you know if/whether the shops are open tomorrow?

Unit 47

47.1

3 to do
4 to swim
5 to work ... talking

6 cleaning
7 to go
8 going
9 to send
10 to be
11 reading
12 travelling ... flying / to fly
13 to come
14 to see
15 working
16 to speak
17 to talk
18 crying / to cry
19 visiting

47.2

2 Do you like writing letters?
3 Do you like travelling by train?
4 Do you like visiting museums?
5 Do you like eating in restaurants?
'Do you like **to write** / **to travel**' etc. is possible in these sentences, especially in American English.

7–10. If possible, check your sentences with someone who speaks English. Here are some example answers:

7 I don't like writing letters.
8 I like travelling by train.
9 I don't mind visiting museums.
10 I like eating in restaurants.

47.3

3 living
4 to do
5 to help
6 travelling ('**to travel**' is possible, especially in American English)
7 teaching ('**to teach**' is possible, especially in American English)
8 to lose
9 to leave ('**leaving**' is *not* possible after '**would prefer**')
10 losing ('**to lose**' is possible, especially in American English)

Unit 48

48.1

3 I want you to listen carefully.
4 I don't want you to be angry.
5 Do you want me to wait for you?
6 I don't want you to phone me tonight.
7 I want you to meet Sarah.
8 Do you want me to make some coffee?

48.2

2 The doctor advised me to stay in bed.
3 I asked her to phone me.
4 Tom persuaded me to go to the party.
5 They let me use their phone. (*not* 'to use')
6 Ann's mother taught her to play the piano.

48.3

3 The man told me to get into the car.
4 I told the children to be quiet.
5 She told me not to lose the key.
6 Tom told me to phone him later.
7 I told Tom not to say anything.

48.4

2 to get
3 to explain
4 sleep
5 to hear
6 walk
7 to arrive
8 cry
9 to know
10 clean / to clean
11 wait
12 to do

Unit 49

49.1

2 Yes, he told me that he was married.
3 Yes, she said that she could play tennis.
4 Yes, they told me that they were from Italy.
5 Yes, she told me that she had (got) a job.
6 Yes, they said that they would help us.
7 Yes, he said that he was going to India.
8 Yes, she told me that she worked in a bank.
9 Yes, they told me that they lived in London.
10 Yes, she said that she was studying art.

49.2

2 She said that she would phone later.
3 He said that he didn't want to study.
4 He said that he hadn't been to London.
5 She said that she had lost her key.
6 She said that she was learning German.
7 He said that he couldn't drive a car.
8 She said that she knew the answer.
9 She said that she wasn't going out.
10 He said that he had (got) a lot of problems.
You can say all these sentences without '**that**'. For example (sentence 3):
He said (that) he didn't want to study. (with *or* without '**that**')

49.3

3 told	7 tell
4 told	8 told
5 said	9 said
6 say	10 tell

Unit 50

50.1

2 I went to the bank to get some money.
3 I went to the supermarket to buy some food.
4 I went to the post office to get some stamps.
5 I went to the chemist to get some medicine.
6 I went to the café to meet a friend.

50.2

2 to read the newspaper.
3 to open this door?
4 to clean it.
5 to let some fresh air into the room.
6 to wake them up.
7 to get some petrol.
8 to see the Pyramids.
9 to tell him about the party.
10 to see who it was.

50.3

2 for	7 to
3 for	8 to
4 to	9 to
5 to	10 for
6 for	

50.4

2 for the rain to stop
3 for them to come
4 for the film to begin

Unit 51

51.1

2 get some petrol.
3 get a doctor.
4 get your shoes?
5 get a ticket.
6 get the job.
7 get some milk?
8 gets a very good salary.

51.2

2 getting late.
3 getting married

4 getting ready
5 getting dark.

51.3

2 get tired.
3 get wet.
4 got married
5 got lost.
6 get old.
7 got better.

51.4

2 I left London at 10.15 and got to Bristol at 11.45.
3 I left home at 8.30 and got to the airport at 9.30.
4 I left the party at 11.15 and got home at midnight.

51.5

2 got off
3 got out of
4 got on

Unit 52

52.1

3 to
4 to
5 (*no preposition*)
6 for
7 to . . . to
8 on (holiday) to (Italy)
9 for
10 to
11 (*no preposition*)
12 to
13 on
14 to

52.2

2 Diane went fishing.
3 Peter went shopping.
4 Harry went swimming.
5 Linda went skiing.
6 Sheila went climbing.

52.3

2 fishing
3 to sleep
4 to the bank
5 riding

6 for a walk
7 shopping
8 home
9 on holiday . . . to Portugal

Unit 53

53.1

2 him	6 her
3 them	7 him
4 her	8 them
5 them	

53.2

2 he . . . me
3 I . . . them
4 they . . . us
5 he . . . her
6 she . . . them
7 they . . . me
8 we . . . him
9 she . . . you

53.3

2 him	7 us
3 me	8 them
4 them	9 her
5 it	10 them
6 them	

53.4

2 it (to) him
3 them (to) her
4 it (to) me
5 it (to) them
6 them (to) us

Unit 54

54.1

2 They live with their parents.
3 We live with our parents.
4 Ann lives with her parents.
5 I live with my parents.
6 John lives with his parents.
7 Do you live with your parents?
8 Most children live with their parents.

54.2

2 She's going to wash her hands.
3 We're going to wash our hands.
4 He's going to wash his hands.
5 They're going to wash their hands.
6 Are you going to wash your hands?

54.3

2 their	6 their
3 his	7 her
4 his	8 their
5 her	

54.4

2 your	11 your
3 his	12 our
4 Her	13 his
5 his	14 their
6 your	15 her
7 My	16 his
8 her	17 their
9 Our/My	18 its
10 their	

Unit 55

55.1

2 mine	6 They're yours
3 ours	7 They're mine
4 hers	8 It's his
5 It's theirs	

55.2

3 your
4 yours
5 my . . . Mine
6 our . . . theirs
7 their
8 My . . . hers . . . hers

55.3

3 (a) friend of hers
4 (some) friends of ours
5 (a) friend of mine
6 (a) friend of his
7 (a) friend of yours

55.4

2 Whose books are these?
3 Whose umbrella is this?
4 Whose jacket is this?
5 Whose glasses are these?
6 Whose cigarettes are these?
7 Whose hat is this?
8 Whose keys are these?
9 Whose camera is this?
10 Whose gloves are these?
11 Whose car is this?
12 Whose watch is this?

Unit 56

56.1

2 Yes, I know her but I can't remember her name.
3 Yes, I know them but I can't remember their names.
4 Yes, I know you but I can't remember your name.

56.2

2 He invited us to stay with him at his house.
3 They invited me to stay with them at their house.
4 I invited her to stay with me at my house.
5 We invited them to stay with us at our house.
6 You invited him to stay with you at your house.
7 She invited me to stay with her at her house.

56.3

3 Give it to him.
4 Give them to her.
5 Give it to us.
6 Give it to them.
7 Give them to him.
8 Give it to me.

56.4

2 I gave her my address and she gave me hers.
3 He gave me his address and I gave him mine.
4 We gave her our address and she gave us hers.

5 I gave them my address and they gave me theirs.
6 She gave us her address and we gave her ours.
7 You gave him your address and he gave you his.
8 We gave them our address and they gave us theirs.
9 They gave you their address and you gave them yours.
10 She gave him her address and he gave her his.

Unit 57

57.1

2 myself
3 herself
4 ourselves
5 yourself
6 ourselves
7 themselves
8 himself

57.2

2 yourself
3 myself
4 themselves
5 myself
6 themselves
7 herself
8 myself
9 himself
10 yourself
11 yourselves

57.3

2 John lives by himself.
3 Do you live by yourself?
4 She went to the cinema by herself.
5 When I saw him, he was by himself.
6 Don't go out by yourself.
7 I had dinner by myself.

57.4

2 We know each other.
3 They like each other.
4 We can help each other.
5 They understand each other.
6 They give each other presents. / They give presents to each other.
7 Tom and Jill didn't see each other.
8 We didn't speak to each other.
9 They often write letters to each other.

Unit 58

58.1

2 Philip's
3 Ann's
4 Robert's
5 Ted's
6 Robert's
7 Charles's
8 Ann's
9 Robert's
10 Charles's

58.2

2 Alice's
3 Jane's
4 Jane's
5 Alice's
6 Alice's
7 Alice's
8 Jane's
9 Jane's
10 Alice's

58.3

3 your sister's birthday
4 the colour of this coat
5 the top of the page.
6 Jill's address
7 the cause of the accident
8 My parents' house.
9 Maria's spoken English
10 the best part of the day.
11 My brother's job
12 the end of the street.
13 Pat's favourite colour
14 The walls of this house

Unit 59

59.1

3 a window
4 a horse
5 an airport
6 a university
7 an organisation
8 a restaurant
9 a Chinese restaurant
10 an Indian restaurant
11 an accident
12 a bad accident
13 a question
14 an important question
15 a hamburger
16 an hour
17 an economic problem
18 a nice evening

59.2

2 It's a river.
3 It's an animal.
4 It's a game.
5 It's a flower.
6 It's a tool.
7 It's a vegetable.
8 It's a planet.
9 It's a musical instrument.
10 It's a fruit.

59.3

2 He's a shop assistant.
3 He's a photographer.
4 She's a taxi-driver.
5 She's a nurse.
6 He's a private detective.
7 She's a road-sweeper.
8 I'm a/an . . .

59.4

2 We went to **a party** last night.
3 My brother is **an artist**.
4 It's **a beautiful day** today.
5 I ate **a sandwich** and **an apple**.
6 Britain is **an industrial country**.
7 I had **a bath** this morning.
8 Barbara works in **an office**.
9 It's **a very difficult question**.
10 We stayed at **an expensive hotel**.

Unit 60

60.1

3 boats
4 languages
5 watches
6 countries
7 knives
8 women
9 addresses
10 sheep
11 teeth
12 leaves
13 children
14 feet
15 umbrellas
16 people
17 families
18 holidays
19 sandwiches
20 cities
21 mice

60.2

3 are	8 are	13 are
4 is	9 is	14 are
5 are	10 are	15 are
6 is	11 are	
7 are	12 is	

60.3

3 . . . two brothers and four sisters.

4 . . . with a lot of beautiful trees.

5 *okay*

6 Do you make many mistakes . . .

7 . . . and she has three children.

8 Most of my friends are students.

9 He put on his pyjamas . . .

10 *okay*

11 . . . three **people** in the car . . .

12 I like your trousers. Where did you get **them**?

13 . . . full of tourists.

14 These scissors aren't very sharp.

60.4

2 are	7 Do	
3 don't	8 are	
4 watch	9 them	
5 were	10 some	
6 live		

Unit 61

61.1

3 a hat	9 soap
4 tea	10 a bucket
5 toothpaste	11 sand
6 a toothbrush	12 a credit
7 a cup	card
8 money	

61.2

3 . . . **a** hat

4 . . . for **a** job

5 *okay*

6 . . . to **a** party

7 *okay*

8 . . . **a** cup of coffee

9 *okay*

10 . . . **an** island

11 . . . **a** very bad mistake

12 *okay*

13 . . . **a** car

14 . . . **a** very good idea

61.3

2 a piece of wood

3 a glass of water

4 a bar of chocolate

5 a cup of tea

6 a piece of paper

7 a bowl of soup

8 a loaf of bread

9 a jar of honey

Unit 62

62.1

2 I bought some cigarettes, a lighter and a newspaper.

3 I bought some bread, some postcards and some stamps.

4 I bought some toothpaste, some batteries and a pen.

62.2

2 Would you like some coffee?

3 Would you like a cigarette?

4 Would you like some bread? / a piece of bread?

5 Would you like a chocolate?

6 Would you like some chocolate? / a piece of chocolate?

62.3

2 **some** money . . . **some** food

3 **some** interesting people

4 **a** window . . . **some** fresh air

5 **an** apple . . . **some** bread

6 **a** big house . . . **a** nice garden . . . **some** beautiful trees

7 **a** table . . . **some** wood

8 **some** very good advice

9 **a** letter . . . **a** pen . . . **some** paper

10 **some** nice weather *or* '**We had nice weather**' *without* '**some**'

62.4

2 chairs

3 furniture

4 eyes

5 hair

6 information

Unit 63

63.1

3 the

4 a

5 a

6 the

7 a

8 an

9 a

10 the

11 a . . . a

12 the

13 **the** bathroom
   a bath

14 the . . . the

15 **an** old house
   the station
   the centre

63.2

2 . . . can I ask **a** question . . .

3 Alan is **the** best player . . .

4 . . . from here to **the** airport?

5 . . . don't forget to send me **a** postcard!

6 Have you got **a** ticket for **the** concert tomorrow night?

7 What is **the** name of **the** director of **the** film we saw last night?

8 Yesterday I bought **a** jacket and **a** shirt. **The** jacket was cheap but **the** shirt was expensive.

9 Peter and Mary have two children, **a** boy and **a** girl. **The** boy is seven years old and **the** girl is three.

63.3

3 a bicycle
4 the roof
5 the play
6 a difficult language
7 a cigarette
8 the kitchen
9 the next train
10 a nice day

Unit 64

64.1

3 **the** third floor.
4 **the** fire brigade.
5 **the** first man . . . **the** moon?
6 **the** capital
7 **the** largest city . . . **the** world?
8 **the** army?
9 **the** sea?
10 *okay*
11 **the** top shelf . . . **the** right.
12 **the** country . . . **the** nearest village.
13 **the** end of May . . . **the** beginning of April.
14 **the** same price.
15 **The** Prime Minister . . . **the** most important person . . . **the** British government.
16 **the** man . . . **the** left?
17 **the** name.
18 **the** first time
19 *okay*
20 **the** fridge

64.2

2 the same time.
3 the same problem.
4 the same age.
5 the same colour.
6 the same day.

64.3

3 **The** sun
4 television
5 (any) breakfast.
6 **The** police
7 **the** guitar
8 lunch
9 **the** radio.
10 **The** sky

Unit 65

65.1

2 They're at **the** cinema.
3 She's in **hospital**.
4 She's at **the** airport.
5 They're at **home**.
6 He's in **prison**.

65.2

3 **the** dentist
4 bed
5 university
6 **the** cinema
7 **the** airport
8 school
9 home
10 **the** station

65.3

3 **the** doctor
4 *okay*
5 *okay*
6 **the** bank
7 *okay*
8 **the** city centre
9 *okay*
10 **the** theatre
11 *okay*
12 **the** toilet
13 *okay*
14 *okay*
15 *okay*
16 **the** post office
17 *okay*
18 *okay*

Unit 66

66.1

If possible, check your sentences with someone who speaks English. Here are some example answers:

2 I don't like dogs.
3 I hate hard work.
4 I love Italian food.
5 I hate loud music.
6 I don't mind small children.
7 I like hot weather.
8 I don't like staying in hotels.
9 I love opera.
10 I don't mind big cities.

66.2

If possible, check your sentences with someone who speaks English. Here are some example answers:

2 I'm not interested in politics.
3 I'm very interested in sport.
4 I don't know much about art.
5 I don't know anything about astronomy.
6 I'm interested in economics.

66.3

3 friends
4 coffee
5 **the** coffee
6 parties
7 Tennis
8 **The** water
9 cold water
10 **The** paintings
11 Money . . . happiness
12 English
13 Children . . . things
14 **the** salt
15 restaurants
16 capitalism
17 photographs
18 **the** photographs

Unit 67

67.1

3 Switzerland
4 **The** Amazon
5 Asia
6 **The** Pacific
7 **The** Rhine
8 **The** United States
9 Kenya
10 **The** Andes
11 Tokyo
12 Malta
13 **The** Alps
14 **The** Red Sea
15 **The** Bahamas

67.2

3 At **the** Intercontinental Hotel.
4 Milan is a large city in **the** north of Italy.
5 *okay*
6 Manila is the capital of **the** Philippines.
7 **The** National Gallery is in Trafalgar Square in London.
8 *okay*
9 **The** Rocky Mountains are in North America.
10 In London, **the** Houses of Parliament are beside **the** River Thames.
11 Have you ever been to **the** British Museum?
12 *okay*
13 Last night we saw a play at **the** Royal Theatre.
14 You must visit **the** Museum of Modern Art.
15 *okay*
16 When I finish my studies, I'm going to **the** United States for a year.
17 **The** Panama Canal joins **the** Atlantic Ocean and **the** Pacific Ocean.
18 There are two cinemas in our town – **the** Regal and **the** Plaza.
19 If you sail from Britain to Denmark, you cross **the** North Sea.
20 Mary comes from a small village in **the** west of Ireland.
21 *okay*
22 Have you ever been to **the** USA?

Unit 68

68.1

3 this sandwich
4 these things
5 these children
6 this place
7 these houses
8 these trousers
9 that picture
10 those socks
11 those men
12 that tree
13 those eggs
14 that woman
15 that room
16 those plates

68.2

2 Is that your umbrella?
3 Are those your books?
4 Is this your hat?
5 Are these your cigarettes?
6 Are those your keys?
7 Is that your bicycle?
8 Are those your glasses?
9 Is this your watch?
10 Are these your gloves?

68.3

2 Who lives in **that house**?
3 Look at **those birds**!
4 How much are **these postcards**?
5 Excuse me, is **this seat** free?
6 **These plates** are dirty.

Unit 69

69.1

2 No, I don't need one.
3 No, I can't ride one.
4 I'm sorry, I haven't got one.
5 Yes, there's one in Mill Road.
6 No thank you, I've just had one.

69.2

2 a new one.
3 a better one.
4 a big one.
5 an old one.
6 a different one.

69.3

2 B: Which ones?
   A: The green ones.
3 B: Which one?
   A: The one with the red door.
4 B: Which one?
   A: The black one.
5 B: Which ones?
   A: The ones on the wall.
6 B: Which ones?
   A: The ones on the top shelf.
7 B: Which one?
   A: The tall one with long hair.
8 B: Which ones?
   A: The yellow ones.
9 B: Which one?
   A: The one with a moustache and glasses.
10 B: Which ones?
   A: The ones I took on the beach last week.

Unit 70

70.1

3 some
4 any
5 any
6 any
7 some
8 any
9 any . . . some
10 any
11 some
12 any . . . any.
13 any . . . some.
14 some
15 some . . . any
16 some

70.2

2 any shampoo
3 some stamps.
4 any foreign languages
5 any photographs.
6 some problems
7 any chairs
8 some fresh air.
9 any batteries
10 some milk
11 some friends
12 some cheese

70.3

2 something

3 anything
4 anything
5 Somebody/Someone
6 anything
7 anybody/anyone
8 something
9 anything
10 anybody/anyone

Unit 71

71.1

2 There are no pictures on the walls.
3 Carol has got no free time.
4 There is no restaurant in this hotel.
6 There isn't any oil in the tank.
7 I haven't got any stamps.
8 Tom hasn't got any brothers or sisters.

71.2

3 any
4 no
5 any
6 any . . . any
7 no
8 no
9 any
10 any

71.3

2 any cigarettes
3 no money.
4 no swimming-pool.
5 any questions.
6 no friends.
7 no difference
8 any photographs . . . no film
9 any furniture

71.4

If possible, check your answers with someone who speaks English. Here are some example answers:

2 Three.
3 Two cups.
4 None.
5 None.

Unit 72

72.1

2 There's nobody in the office.
3 I've got nothing to do.
4 There's nothing on TV tonight.
5 Jack has got no-one to help him.
6 We found nothing.

72.2

2 I haven't got anything to read.
3 There isn't anybody in the bathroom.
4 We haven't got anything to eat.
5 There wasn't anyone on the bus.
6 She didn't hear anything.

72.3

3 Nothing
4 Nobody/No-one
5 Nobody/No-one
6 Nothing
7 Nothing
8 Nobody/No-one

3a I don't want anything.
4a I didn't meet anybody/anyone.
5a Nobody/No-one   knows the answer.
6a I didn't buy anything. I bought nothing.
7a Nothing happened.
8a Nobody/No-one   was late.

72.4

3 anything.
4 Nobody/No-one
5 Nothing
6 anything.
7 Nobody/No-one knows . . . didn't tell anybody/anyone
8 Nothing
9 anything
10 Nothing
11 anybody/anyone.
12 nobody/no-one

Unit 73

73.1

2 something.
3 somewhere.
4 somebody/someone.
6 Nowhere.
7 Nothing.
8 Nobody/No-one.

6a I'm not going anywhere.
7a I don't want anything.
8a I'm not looking for anybody/anyone.

73.2

3 anything
4 anything   *or*   anybody/anyone.
5 somebody/someone.
6 something
7 'Did **anybody/anyone** see you?' 'No, **nobody/no-one**.'
8 anything.
9 Nobody/No-one
10 anybody/anyone
11 Nothing
12 anywhere.

73.3

2 anything to eat.
3 nothing to do / nothing to read / nowhere to go / nowhere to play.
4 anywhere to sit.
5 something to drink
6 somewhere to play / somewhere to go / something to do.
7 something to read / something to do
8 nowhere to stay.

Unit 74

74.1

2 Every day
3 Every room
4 every time.
5 every word.

74.2

3 every	8 all
4 all	9 every
5 every	10 every
6 Every	11 all
7 all	12 every

74.3

2 everything
3 Everybody/Everyone
4 everything
5 everywhere
6 Everybody/Everyone
7 everywhere.
8 Everything

74.4

2 everybody is tired today.
3 everybody likes Mary.
4 everybody is going to the party.
5 everybody has seen the film.
6 everybody was surprised.

In all these sentences you can use '**everyone**'. For example (sentence 2):
'Yes, **everyone** is tired today.'

Unit 75

75.1

3 **Some** people
4 **Most of** the shops
5 **most** banks
6 **any of** the pictures
7 **all** (of) his money
8 **None of** my friends
9 **any of** the people
10 **Most** birds
11 **most of** the film
12 **Some** sports
13 **All** (of) the hotels
14 **some of** this cheese
15 **most of** the time

75.2

2 All of them.
3 Some of them.
4 None of them.
5 Most of them.
6 Some of them.

75.3

2 Most of them.
3 All of them.
4 All of it.
5 Most of them.
6 Some of them.
7 None of them.
8 Most of it.
9 Some of them.

Unit 76

76.1

3 Both
4 Neither
5 Neither
6 both
7 Either
8 neither
9 Neither
10 either
11 Both
12 neither

76.2

2 Both windows are open.
3 Neither man is wearing a hat.
4 Both men have (got) cameras. *or* ... are carrying cameras.
5 Both buses go to the airport. *or* .. are going to the airport.
6 Neither answer is right.

76.3

3 Both of them are students.
4 Neither of them has (got) a car.
5 Both of them live in London.
6 Both of them like fish.
7 Neither of them is interested in politics.
8 Neither of them can play the piano.
9 Both of them smoke.

Unit 77

77.1

2 I've got some but not **much**.
3 I've got some but not **many**.
4 I've got some but not **many**.
5 I've got some but not **much**.
6 I've got some but not **many**.

77.2

2 How many stamps did you buy?
3 How much money did you lose?
4 How much water did you drink?
5 How many mistakes did you make?
6 How many letters did you write?
7 How much food did you buy?
8 How many people did you invite?

77.3

3 much
4 a lot of
5 much
6 many
7 many
8 a lot of ... much.
9 a lot of
10 a lot
11 much.
12 much.
13 many
14 much

77.4

3 A: Do you go swimming much?
B: No, not much.
4 A: Do you play tennis much?
B: Yes, a lot.
5 A: Do you travel much?
B: Yes a lot.
6 A: Do you use the phone much?
B: No, not much.

Unit 78

78.1

2 A few. 6 A little.
3 A little. 7 A few.
4 A few. 8 A little.
5 A little.

78.2

2 a little milk
3 A few days
4 a little Russian.
5 a few friends.
6 A few times.
7 a few houses
8 a little fresh air.
9 a few chairs.

78.3

2 very little coffee.
3 very little rain.
4 very few hotels.
5 very little time.
6 very few tables.

78.4

2 A few 6 few
3 little 7 a little
4 a little 8 little
5 a few 9 Few

Unit 79

79.1

2 black clouds
3 long holiday.
4 interesting person.
5 dangerous job.
6 fresh air.
7 old photograph *or*
  interesting photograph
8 serious problem
9 sharp knife
10 expensive hotels.

79.2

2 It looks new.
3 I feel ill.
4 You look surprised.
5 They smell nice.
6 It tastes awful.

79.3

2 He doesn't sound American.
3 She doesn't look rich.
4 I don't feel cold.
5 You don't sound English.
6 They don't look friendly.
7 It doesn't taste good.

Unit 80

80.1

2 badly
3 quietly
4 angrily
5 dangerously *or* fast
6 fast

80.2

2 Come quickly
3 know . . . well.
4 work hard.
5 sleep well
6 win easily.
7 Think carefully
8 explain . . . clearly.

80.3

2 angry
3 careful . . . carefully
4 slowly
5 slow
6 good
7 well
8 hard
9 suddenly
10 well
11 well (= not ill – *adjective*)
12 quickly
13 nice
14 badly
15 quiet

Unit 81

81.1

2 bigger
3 slower
4 more expensive
5 higher
6 more dangerous

81.2

2 stronger
3 happier
4 more careful
5 more important
6 worse
7 more difficult
8 larger
9 further
10 more serious
11 more crowded
12 prettier

81.3

2 hotter/warmer
3 dearer / more expensive
4 worse
5 further
6 more difficult

81.4

3 taller.
4 harder.
5 more comfortable.
6 better.
7 nicer.
8 heavier.
9 more interested
10 warmer
11 better.
12 bigger.
13 more beautiful.
14 sharper
15 more polite.

Unit 82

82.1

3 Liz is taller than Ben.
4 Liz starts work earlier than Ben.
5 Ben works harder than Liz.
6 Ben has got more money than Liz.
7 Liz is a better driver than Ben.
8 Ben is friendlier than Liz. / Ben is more friendly than Liz.
9 Ben is a better dancer than Liz.
10 Liz is more intelligent than Ben.

11 Liz speaks French better than Ben. / Liz speaks better French than Ben. / Liz's French is better than Ben's.

12 Ben goes to the cinema more than Liz (does). / Ben goes to the cinema more often than Liz (does).

82.2

2 You're older than her. / . . . than she is.

3 You work harder than me. / . . . than I do. / . . . than I work.

4 You smoke more than him. / . . . than he does. / . . .than he smokes.

5 You're a better cook than me. / . . . than I am.

6 You know more people than us. / . . . than we do. / . . . than we know.

7 You've got more money than them. / . . . than they have.

8 You can run faster than me. / . . . than I can.

9 You've been here longer than her. / . . . than she has.

10 You got up earlier than me. / . . . than I did. / . . . than I got up.

11 You're more interesting than him. / . . . than he is.

82.3

2 Jack's mother is much younger than his father.

3 My camera cost a bit more than yours. / . . . than your camera. *or* My camera was a bit more expensive than yours. / . . . than your camera.

4 I feel much better today than yesterday. / I feel much better today than I did yesterday. / I feel much better today than I felt yesterday.

5 It's a bit warmer today than yesterday. / It's a bit warmer today than it was yesterday.

6 Ann is a much better tennis player than me. / . . . than I am. *or* Ann is much better at tennis than me. / . . . than I am. *or* Ann plays tennis much better than me. / . . . than I do.

Unit 83

83.1

2 A is longer than B but not as long as C.

3 C is heavier than A but not as heavy as B.

4 A is older than C but not as old as B.

5 B has got more money than C but not as much (money) as A. *or* . . . but less (money) than A.

6 C works harder than A but not as hard as B.

83.2

2 Your room isn't as big as mine. / . . . as big as my room.

3 I didn't get up as early as you (did). / . . . as early as you got up.

4 They didn't play as well as us. / . . . as well as we did. / . . . as well as we played.

5 You haven't been here as long as me. / . . . as long as I have (been here).

83.3

2 as	6 than
3 than	7 as
4 than	8 than
5 as	

83.4

2 Julia lives in the same street as Caroline.

3 Julia got up at the same time as Andrew.

4 Andrew's car is the same colour as Caroline's (car).

Unit 84

84.1

2 C is longer than A.
 D is the longest.
 B is the shortest.

3 D is younger than C.
 B is the youngest.
 C is the oldest.

4 D is more expensive than A.
 C is the most expensive.
 A is the cheapest.

5 A is better than C.
 A is the best.
 D is the worst.

84.2

2 Everest is the highest mountain in the world.

3–6 Alaska is the largest state in the USA.
 Brazil is the largest country in South America.
 Jupiter is the largest planet in the solar system.
 The Nile is the longest river in Africa.

84.3

2 the happiest day

3 the best film

4 the most popular singer

5 the worst mistake

6 the prettiest village

7 the coldest day

8 the most interesting person

Unit 85

85.1

3 enough paint.

4 big enough.

5 long enough.

6 enough chairs.

7 enough wind.

8 strong enough.

85.2

3 old enough.

4 enough time

5 big enough
6 eat enough.
7 enough fruit
8 tired enough.
9 enough clothes
10 practise enough.

85.3

2 old enough to get married.
3 warm enough to sit in the garden.
4 enough bread to make sandwiches.
5 enough money to go on holiday.
6 well enough to go to work (today).

Unit 86

86.1

2 too high.   5 too big.
3 too hot.   6 too crowded.
4 too fast.

86.2

3 enough   6 enough
4 enough   7 too many
5 too much

86.3

3 It's too far.
4 It's too expensive.
5 It isn't big enough.
6 It wasn't warm enough.
7 I'm too busy.
8 It isn't sharp enough.

86.4

2 It's too early to go to bed.
3 It's too warm to wear a coat.
4 They're too young to get married.
5 It's too dangerous to go out at night.
6 It's too late to phone Ann (now).
7 They were too surprised to say anything.

Unit 87

87.1

2 I don't like football very much.
3 I lost my watch last week.
4 Tom read the letter slowly.
5 Do you know London very well?
6 We ate our dinner very quickly.
7 Did you buy that jacket in England?
8 I don't speak French very well.
9 They crossed the street carefully.
10 I borrowed £50 from my brother.
11 We enjoyed the party very much.
12 Ann passed the examination easily.
13 We do the same thing every day.
14 I don't like this picture very much.
15 The woman put the money in her bag.
16 Did you watch the news on television?
17 I explained my plan carefully.
18 She smokes ten cigarettes every day.
19 I did a lot of housework yesterday.
20 We met some friends at the concert.
21 You wear the same clothes every day.
22 I want to speak English fluently.

87.2

2 We arrived at the party early.
3 I didn't go to work yesterday.
4 Are you going to work tomorrow?
5 They have lived here since 1984.
6 Will you be at home this evening?
7 They are going to London next week.
8 Did you go to the cinema last night?
9 Will they be here on Monday?
10 Jill goes to Italy every year.
11 Alice was born in London in 1951.
12 I had my breakfast in bed this morning.
13 Barbara is going to university in October.
14 My parents have been to the United States many times.
15 I saw a beautiful bird in the garden this morning.
16 I think I left my umbrella in the restaurant last night.

Unit 88

88.1

2 He sometimes smokes.
3 He is often ill.
4 He never eats fish.
5 He is always late for work.
6 He very rarely writes letters.   *or* He seldom writes letters.

88.2

2 Susan is always polite.
3 I usually finish work at half past five.
4 Jill has just started a new job.
5 I rarely go to bed before midnight.
6 The bus isn't usually late.
7 I don't often eat meat.
8 I will never forget what you said.
9 Have you ever broken your leg?
10 Do you still work in the same place?
11 They always stay in the same hotel.
12 Diane doesn't usually work on Saturdays.
13 I can never remember his name.
14 What do you usually have for breakfast?

15 When I arrived, Jan was
   already there.

88.3

2 Yes, and I also speak French.
3 Yes, and I'm also hungry.
4 Yes, and I've also been to
   Ireland.
5 Yes, and I also bought some
   books.

88.4

2 They both like football.
3 They are both students.
4 They have both got cars. /
   They both have cars.
5 They are all married.
6 They were all born in
   England.
7 They all live in New York.

Unit 89

89.1

2 Do you still smoke?
3 Are you still a student?
4 Do you still go to the cinema
   a lot?
5 Have you still got a
   motor-bike? / Do you still
   have a motor-bike?
6 Do you still play tennis?

89.2

2 Is Ann here yet? / Has Ann
   arrived yet? / Has Ann come
   yet?
3 Have you finished (reading
   the newspaper) yet? / Have
   you finished with the
   newspaper yet?
4 Are you ready (to go out)
   yet?
5 Have you decided (where
   you're going) yet? / Do you
   know where you're going
   yet?

89.3

2 They were waiting for the
  bus.

They're still waiting for the
bus.
The bus hasn't come yet.
3 He was looking for a job.
   He's still looking for a job.
   He hasn't found a job yet.
4 She was asleep. / She was in
   bed.
   She's still asleep. / She's still
   in bed.
   She hasn't woken up yet. /
   She isn't awake yet. / She
   hasn't got up yet. / She isn't
   up yet.
5 They were having dinner. /
   They were eating.
   They're still having dinner. /
   They're still eating.
   They haven't finished (their)
   dinner yet. / They haven't
   finished eating yet.

Unit 90

90.1

2 He gave the TV set to Jack.
3 He gave the books to his
   sister.
4 He gave the cassettes to a
   friend.
5 He gave the radio to his
   cousin.
6 He gave the lamp to Sarah.

90.2

2 I gave Alice   a box of
   chocolates / some chocolates.
3 I gave Mark   a pair of gloves
   / some gloves.
4 I gave Diane a watch.
5 I gave Kevin a pen.
6 I gave Mary some flowers.

90.3

2 Can you lend me   an
   umbrella? / your umbrella?
3 Can you give me my coat?
4 Can you lend Mary   a
   bicycle? / your bicycle?
5 Can you send Tom some
   information?

6 Can you show me the letter?
7 Can you lend them £100?

90.4

2 Yes, can you give it to me,
   please?
3 Yes, can you give them to
   me, please?
4 Yes, can you give it to me,
   please?
5 Yes, can you give it to me,
   please?
6 Yes, can you give them to
   me, please?

Unit 91

91.1

3 on	9 in	16 on
4 at	10 at	17 at
5 in	11 on	18 at
6 in	12 in	19 at
7 on	14 in	20 on
8 on	15 on	21 at

91.2

2 on	9 in	16 at
3 at	10 at	17 In
4 in	11 on	18 in
5 in	12 in	19 at
6 in	13 at	20 at
7 on	14 in	
8 on	15 on	

91.3

2 I'll phone you in three days.
3 My exam is in two weeks.
4 Tom will be here in half an
   hour. / . . . in 30 minutes.

91.4

3 in
4 (no preposition)
5 (no preposition)
6 at
7 (no preposition)
8 (no preposition)
9 on
10 (no preposition)
11 at
12 in

Unit 92

92.1

2 Alex lived in Canada **until** 1985.
3 Alex has lived in England **since** 1985.
4 Alice lived in France **until** 1986.
5 Alice has lived in Switzerland **since** 1986.
6 Carol worked in a hotel **from** 1985 **to** 1988. / ... **from** 1985 **until** 1988.
7 Carol has worked in a restaurant **since** 1988.
8 Gerry was a teacher **from** 1978 **to** 1984. / ... **from** 1978 **until** 1984.
9 Gerry has been a salesman **since** 1984.
11 Alex has lived in England for ... years.
12 Alice has lived in Switzerland for ... years.
13 Carol worked in a hotel for three years.
14 Carol has worked in a restaurant for ... years.
15 Gerry was a teacher for six years.
16 Gerry has been a salesman for ... years.

92.2

2 until	9 since
3 for	10 until
4 Since	11 for
5 Until	12 until
6 for	13 Since
7 for	14 for
8 until	

Unit 93

93.1

2 after lunch
3 before the end.
4 during the course.
5 before they went to Australia.
6 during the night
7 after the concert
8 before you cross the road.

93.2

3 while	6 while
4 while	7 during
5 during	8 while

93.3

2 Think carefully before answering the question.
3 Mary put on her glasses before reading the letter.
4 Before getting into the car, the man took off his coat.
5 We were very tired after walking for three hours.
6 I felt sick after eating too much chocolate.
7 After reading the book a second time, I understood it better. *or* I understood the book better after reading it a second time.
8 After leaving school, John worked in a department store for two years. *or* John worked in a department store for two years after leaving school.

Unit 94

94.1

2 in a box.
3 at the airport.
4 in bed.
5 at the end of the street.
6 in the sky.
7 in hospital.
8 at a party.

94.2

2 in that field.
3 in the river
4 in my tea
5 in this book
6 in this photograph

94.3

2 at		10 at	
3 at ... at		11 in	
4 in		12 at	
5 in		13 at	
6 at		14 in	
7 at		15 at	
8 In		16 in	
9 in			

Unit 95

95.1

2 to bed.
3 to the bank
4 to a concert / to the cinema.
5 to France
6 to the cinema
7 to hospital

95.2

2 to		9 in	
3 to		10 to	
4 in		11 in	
5 to		12 in	
6 in		13 to	
7 in ... in		14 in	
8 to			

95.3

2 to
3 to
4 at
5 at
6 to
7 at *or* in a restaurant ... to the hotel
8 (*no preposition*)
9 at
10 to ... at
11 (*no preposition*)
12 to
13 at
14 (*no preposition*)
15 to

16 at
17 at
18 at

Unit 96

96.1

2 on the beach.
3 on this plant
4 on the door.
5 on his finger.
6 on a bicycle.

96.2

2 behind
3 above
4 in front of
5 on
6 opposite
7 below   *or* under
8 above
9 under
10 on

96.3

2 on
3 between
4 on . . . next to
5 above
6 above . . . below

96.4

2 on the right.
3 in the middle.
4 behind
5 in front of
6 next to / beside

Unit 97

97.1

2 Go under the bridge.
3 Go up the hill.
4 Go down the stairs.
5 Go along the street.
6 Go into the hotel.
7 Go past the hotel.
8 Go to the station.
9 Go round the corner.
10 Go across the road.
11 Go over the bridge.
12 Go through the park.

97.2

2 off
3 over
4 out of   *or* through
5 through
6 out of
7 into
8 round

97.3

2 in
3 on   *or* over
4 out of   *or* from
5 through . . . into
6 out of   *or* through
7 round
8 over
9 on

Unit 98

98.1

2 by
3 with
4 about . . . by
5 by
6 by
7 with
8 about
9 by
10 at

98.2

2 By . . . on	12 by
3 at	13 at
4 without	14 with
5 with	15 without
6 by	16 by
7 about	17 about
8 by	18 with
9 with	19 by
10 at	20 with
11 about	21 at
	22 by

Unit 99

99.1

2 in	5 on
3 to	6 with
4 of	

99.2

2 of	9 of
3 to	10 on
4 on	11 of
5 at	12 in
6 on	13 from
7 about	14 for
8 on	

99.3

2 at remembering
3 in going.
4 with wearing
5 for getting
7 without stopping.
8 without speaking.
9 without asking

Unit 100

100.1

2 to	5 at
3 for	6 for
4 to	

100.2

2 to	12 (*no preposition*)
3 to	13 to
4 for	14 on
5 to	15 about/of
6 about/of	16 at
7 for	17 after
8 on	18 for
9 to	19 after
10 for	20 at
11 to	21 for

100.3

2 It depends how I feel.   *or* It depends on how . . .
3 It depends what time I leave.   *or* It depends on what time . . .
4 It depends how much it is.   *or* It depends on how much . . .

Unit 101

101.1

2 in	6 off
3 up	7 down
4 away/off	8 out
5 round	

101.2

2 away/out
3 round.
4 out . . . back
5 down
6 away . . . back
7 over/down.
8 back

101.3

2 got up	6 wash up.
3 breaks down	7 slowed down
4 speak up	8 takes off.
5 Hold on	9 carried on
	10 gave up

Unit 102

102.1

2 He put on his shirt.
   He put his shirt on.
   He put it on.
3 She put on her glasses.
   She put her glasses on.
   She put them on.
4 **Can you turn on the TV?**
   Can you turn the TV on?
   Can you turn it on?
5 She rang up her brother.
   She rang her brother up.
   She rang him up.
6 **We took off our shoes.**
   We took our shoes off.
   We took them off.
7 They gave back the money.
   They gave the money back.
   They gave it back.
8 She put down her bags.
   She put her bags down.
   She put them down.

9 **I switched on the engine.**
   I switched the engine on.
   I switched it on.
10 **She filled in the form.**
   She filled the form in.
   She filled it in.
11 We put out the fire.
   We put the fire out.
   We put it out.

102.2

3 (turned) on the radio / (turned) the radio on.
4 (give) them back
5 (put) down my book / (put) my book down
6 (picked) it up
7 (put) on my gloves / (put) my gloves on.
8 (took) off my jacket / (took) my jacket off.
9 (brought) them back
10 (picked) up the photograph / (picked) the photograph up . . . (put) it back / (put) it down
11 (knocked) over a glass / (knocked) a glass over
12 (look) it up
13 (throw) them away.
14 (knocked) me out / (knocked) me down / (knocked) me over.
15 (put) out your cigarette / (put) your cigarette out
16 (turn) it down
17 (tried) on some shoes / (tried) some shoes on
18 (showed) us round.
19 (crossed) it out.
20 (gave) it up

Unit 103

103.1

3 and (she) looked out.
4 but he didn't see me.
5 and (she) swam to the other side.
6 or did you stay at home
7 and (they) took some photographs.
8 but they don't use it very often.

9 but I can't remember his name.
10 and don't come back!
11 or do you want to get a taxi

103.2

3 so I walked in.
4 because she was ill.
5 because she's friendly and interesting.
6 so we didn't play tennis.
7 so we walked home.
8 because I couldn't sleep.
9 so don't phone me.
10 because they haven't got a key.
11 because she does the same thing all the time.

103.3

If possible, check your answers with someone who speaks English! Here are some example answers:

3 *see example 1*
4 I wrote a letter but I didn't post it.
5 I was tired, so I went to bed early.
6 *see example 2*

Unit 104

104.1

2–7 When I'm tired, I like watching TV.
   When I phoned them, there was no answer.
   When she first met him, she didn't like him very much.
   When she goes to London, she always stays at the same hotel.
   When the programme ended, I switched off the TV.
   When they arrived at the hotel, there were no rooms free.

104.2

2 when you heard the news
3 before he answered the question.
4 when I explained it to her.
5 after they got married.
6 while I was out
7 while I was reading.
8 before I go to sleep.

104.3

2 I finish
3 We'll come . . . we're
4 I see . . . I'll show
5 you go
6 stops
7 I'll be . . . she leaves
8 I'm
9 I'll give . . . I go

Unit 105

105.1

2 If I can get a flight, I'll fly home on Sunday.
3–5 If you come home late tonight, please come in quietly.
If I don't feel well tomorrow, I'm not going to work.
If you have any problems, I'll try to help you.

105.2

2 It will be nice if you can come to the party.
3–5 You'll be cold if you don't wear a coat.
What are you going to do if you don't pass your examinations?
I'm sure they'll understand if you explain the problem to them.

105.3

2 is
3 we arrive
4 is
5 I'll be . . . they get
6 Will you go . . . they invite

105.4

2 If   5 If
3 if   6 When
4 When   7 If

Unit 106

106.1

2 A butcher is a person who sells meat.
3 A musician is a person who plays a musical instrument.
4 A patient is a person who is ill in hospital.
5–9 A photographer is a person who takes photographs.
A dentist is a person who looks after your teeth.
A fool is a person who is very stupid.
A genius is a person who is very intelligent.
A liar is a person who doesn't tell the truth.

106.2

2 The woman who opened the door was wearing a yellow dress.
3 The people who live next door to us are very nice.
4 The policeman who stopped our car wasn't very friendly.
5 The boy who broke the window ran away.

106.3

2 who   (or that)
3 that   (or which)
4 who   (or that)
5 who   (or that)
6 that   (or which)
7 that   (or which)
8 who   (or that)
9 that   (or which)
10 who   (or that)
11 that (or which)
12 that (or which)

Unit 107

107.1

2 Did you find the key you lost?
3 I like the jacket Jill is wearing.
4 Where is the money I gave you?
5 I didn't believe the story she told us.
6 How much were the oranges you bought?

107.2

2 The shoes **I'm wearing** are not very comfortable.
3 What's the name of the **book you're reading**?
4 She didn't get the **letter I wrote to her**.
5 I've lost **the umbrella you gave me**.
6 The people **they invited to dinner** didn't come.

107.3

2 What's the name of the woman you **spoke to**?
3 The house **they live in** is too small for them.
4 Did you enjoy the party **you went to**?
5 The chair **I was sitting on** wasn't very comfortable.
6 The map **we looked at** wasn't very clear.
7 Did you find the book **you were looking for**?
8 Who is the man **Linda is dancing with**?

107.4

2 What's the name of the restaurant **where we had dinner**?
3 Have you ever been to the village **where they live**?
4 The factory **where John works** is the biggest in the town.

INDEX